CLASSICAL TRINITARIAN THEOLOGY

CLASSICAL
TRINITARIAN THEOLOGY

A Textbook

TARMO TOOM

t&t clark

NEW YORK • LONDON

T&T Clark International, 80 Maiden Lane, New York, NY 10038

T&T Clark International, The Tower Building, 11 York Road, London SE1 7NX

T&T Clark International is a Continuum imprint.

Except as otherwise indicated, Scripture is quoted from the *New Revised Standard Version Bible*, copyright 1989, by the Division of Christian Education of the National Council of the Churches of Christ in the USA, and is used by permission.

Library of Congress Cataloging-in-Publication Data

Toom, Tarmo, 1961-
    Classical trinitarian theology : a textbook / Tarmo Toom.
        p. cm.
    Includes bibliographical references.
    ISBN-13: 978-0-567-02669-9 (hardcover : alk. paper)
    ISBN-10: 0-567-02669-8 (hardcover : alk. paper)
    ISBN-13: 978-0-567-02699-6 (pbk. : alk. paper)
    ISBN-10: 0-567-02699-X (pbk. : alk. paper)
    1. Trinity Textbooks. I. Title.

BT111.3.T66 2007
231'.044--dc22

                                        2007015400

To Merle

Magna res et amor

Contents

Books for Further Study   **187**

Preface

This book came to be while I was, so-to-speak, on the field. Unlike many other books, it was not written during sabbaticals or research leaves. Rather, it has ripened between lectures, during after-hours, and on weekends. Even so, there are many wonderful people who have made this project not only possible but at times also quite pleasurable. I am deeply indebted to Professor Phillip Cary, who took time to advise and correct me in many important matters—pedagogy, theology, and grammar. Various other scholars with kind hearts and sharp minds have read, commented, and made improvements on sections of my manuscript. Among them are Professor Rebecca Weaver, who has encouraged me since the project was largely a mere idea; and Professors Pauline Allen, Paul Gavrilyuk, Joseph Trigg, Philip Rousseau, Daniel Williams, and Jeffrey Willetts. Ruth Muhlbauer diligently proofread the whole manuscript and provided the most valuable feedback. I also express my gratitude to Cheryl Adams from the Library of Congress, Deborah Brown from Dumbarton Oaks, and Mitzi Budde from Virginia Theological Seminary Library for their gracious help with supplying all the books I needed. My sincerest thanks go to Henry Carrigan (now with Northwestern University Press), Katie Gallof, and Gabriella Page-Fort of Continuum / T&T Clark, who have patiently and generously guided this book through its production. Last but not least, my institution, The John Leland Center for Theological Studies, has proved to be a good working environment with encouraging colleagues—and for that I am truly grateful.

Introduction

My first serious study of Christology took place during my second year in a seminary. We read, chapter by chapter, Jürgen Moltmann's *The Way of Jesus Christ* (1990). The text was a challenge because, among other things, I was being asked to rethink something I'd never really explicitly considered. As a novice, I suddenly learned that metaphysical categories were no longer helpful in Christology. It was better to leave behind the metaphysics of substance and subject, and focus on relational ontology, pneumatology, and eschatology. It was rather confusing! But I was instinctively reluctant to debunk something about which I knew so little. Later I realized that negation has to come after affirmation. My curiosity to know exactly what I was about to negate only increased with time. Eventually it even decided the course of my education. I went on to study historical theology, especially the theology of the first millennium.

The postmodern hostility to metaphysics is the cultural context of my writing a textbook on classical Trinitarian theology. Perhaps an altogether doomed and despised move! But from the outset I should clarify that this book is neither an agitated apology for discredited theories nor an attempt to rescue a hastily buried onto-theology. Christians do *not* have to think in ancient metaphysical categories in order to be theologically astute. Yet, because until modern times metaphysics (i.e., philosophy that deals with the abstract first principles of things) and ontology (i.e., metaphysics that deals with the question of being) were the primary systems of thought, some familiarity with these systems is necessary. After the Council of Constantinople (AD 381), which affirmed the full divinity of the Father, Son, and Holy Spirit, theologians went on to engage in other fascinating discussions about God. However, most of the later debates presupposed what the title of this book calls the "classical doctrine of the Trinity." Thus, the goal is to understand classical/patristic Trinitarian theology and its formulations *before* we wander to new and equally exciting theological grounds.

To limit the scope of this textbook to a particular theme (i.e., classical Trinitarian theology), I have made a distinction between two interrelated issues discussed in the early church: the full divinity of the Son of God, and the coexistence of the divine and human natures in the one person of the incarnated Son. The first issue concerns the Trinitarian phase of Christological debates. The second issue concerns the Christological phase of Christological debates. These two phases had a significant temporal and conceptual overlap because the doctrine of the Trinity always had implications on Christology and vice versa. Nevertheless, the issue of the full divinity of the Son had to be addressed before the issue of coexistence of the fully divine and fully human natures could really be addressed. Hence, this book focuses only on the Trinitarian phase of the Christological debates. This means that our discussion basically ends with the establishment of the classical Trinitarian orthodoxy at the ecumenical Council of Constantinople (AD 381). It is not to say that no further deliberations about the Trinity occurred. Quite the contrary! But it is to say that the *establishing* of Trinitarian orthodoxy by the end of the fourth century is the subject matter of this textbook.

The next question is whether another textbook on the Trinity is really needed. I find that seminary teachers face a problem when assigning secondary readings in patristic Trinitarian theology. There are wonderful, gigantic, and comprehensive scholarly monographs (e.g., Hanson [1988] and Ayres [2004]) next to the myriad of the more specific monographs; and there are slim and rather shallow textbooks. In between, there are several first-rate studies, which consider classical Trinitarian theology as a significant part of the overall theology of the patristic church (e.g., Hall [1991], Studer [1993], Osborn [1993], Chadwick [2001], Wilken [2003], and Behr [2001, 2004]). In addition, one can find helpful textbooks on the doctrine of the Trinity, which include ancient, medieval, and modern authors. These are written for undergraduate college students and/or general readers (e.g., O'Collins [1999], Lorenzen [1999], Olson and Hall [2002], La Due [2003], and Hunt [2005]). What seems to be missing, however, is a textbook exclusively on classical/patristic Trinitarian theology, a textbook that can be assigned for master's students within the more general courses. Part 1, and in some instances also Part 2, should be suitable for classes in historical theology and systematic theology. For instance, Part 1 can be assigned as a reading for the doctrine of God in a rather traditional course "Christian Theology I." Alternatively, in a course on patristic theology, Part 2 or sections of it can be used as a secondary source for introducing primary texts. Perhaps the book as a whole can also serve as a handbook, providing brief descriptions of the most significant patristic Trinitarian theologies. In short, my primary purpose is to create a useful tool for the classroom by presenting the classical doctrine of the Trinity in accordance with recent patristic studies.

There seems to be a particular problem in the current situation of seminary education. At least in the United States, many MDiv, MA, and MTS students have never formally studied theology before enrolling in their master's program. This indeed presents a serious difficulty, because there is a huge gap in knowledge that needs to be quickly bridged. Therefore, this book begins with a rather basic overview (Part 1), which better-prepared readers might profitably use as a review. Introducing some elementary concepts, Part 1 takes a synchronic look at the Trinitarian issues discussed in the first millennium.

The largest section of the book (Part 2) deals with the main theologians, theological trajectories, and councils. I assess these in a more-or-less chronological order. Yet the primary purpose is not to provide chronology but to identify theological positions and present these in a form of three charts and a commentary. I do not try to include as many theologians, movements, trajectories, councils, and documents as possible. Quite the contrary, I keep the number of included entries to a bare minimum; naturally, selecting this minimum is always a matter of taste and convenience. I am all too aware of much that is missing, but the risk of overwhelming busy seminarians is also quite real. "For us who have undertaken the toil of abbreviating, it is no light matter but calls for sweat and loss of sleep" (2 Macc 2:26). Since we are dealing with a tremendously rich tradition, there are indeed many authors who deserve to be mentioned. I have omitted several, including two important Trinitarian theologians, Didymus the Blind and Asterius, whose respective theological traditions (i.e., the Alexandrian and the Eusebian tradition) are represented by other figures. This textbook is for English-speaking students and, at the moment, there are no English translations of the extant (Trinitarian) texts of Didymus and Asterius. Even though Eusebius of Caesarea's *Against Marcellus* and *Ecclesiastical Theology* and the fragments of the writings of Marcellus of Ancyra are also unavailable in English, I could not possibly bypass them altogether. (Dr. Kelley McCarthy Spoerl is working on a translation of Eusebius's *Against Marcellus* and *Ecclesiastical Theology*; Dr. Maurice James Dowling has translated a few fragments by Marcellus in the Appendix of his dissertation of 1987 [Queens University, Belfast]; and Dr. Sara Parvis is working on publishing her translation of the fragments by Marcellus.)

The included theologians are presented in a summary fashion. This means that the development of Trinitarian thought within the literary corpus of a given author—all the rethinking, modifying, and shifting of emphases—is not laid out in an exact chronological sequence. For instance, almost no textual space is reserved for discussing the "early" and "late" Athanasius. I have offered panoramic snapshots rather than exhaustive theological biographies of the thirty or so theologians.

Presenting the classical Trinitarian theology through the selected main representatives has its disadvantages. One of them is that the issues tend to become overshadowed by the persons discussing them. Theology yields to history. But J. Rist has reminded us, "The study of individual figures in sequence is not enough. . . . We must above all look at the types of problems they try to solve" (Evans 2004, 111). Accordingly, I invite readers of this book to focus on the questions the theologians ask and the theological problems they face. Ideas, including Trinitarian doctrines, do not float independently from temporal, cultural, and political circumstances, of course. A. Löhr rightly calls attention to the fact that "the fourth- and fifth-century sources describe the great doctrinal debates of the fourth century as a contest between warring factions, full of deceit and intrigue and more often than not with a powerful emperor as the final arbiter" (in Barnes and Williams 1993, 81). Yet in this book I offer no introductory biographies of theologians and almost no descriptions of their social, historical, and ideological contexts. I do *not* intend to provide a general and introductory narrative or survey of the patristic era. The deliberate omission of such factors as the politics of state and church, economics, and cultural "presupposition pools" (i.e., conventional values systems) does not mean that such matters are insignificant. It merely means that there are many other books that adequately deal with those contextual matters. My focus is on *theological* ideas, and I center on the arguments, concepts, and reasoning employed in the making of the case for the doctrine of the Trinity. This book is about historical *theology* rather than about the (social) history of the first four centuries.

I believe in revisiting theological issues over and over again—for the sake of gaining better understanding. In Estonia, where I come from, we have a not-so-original-saying: "Repetition is the mother of learning." To underline the needed element of repetition, I have called the parts "First Time Around," "Second Time Around," and "Third and Fourth Times Around."

1. Once more, Part 1 introduces classical Trinitarian theology with the help of short discussions, definitions, and comparisons. Few individual theologians are identified. It is designed for novices who have never formally studied theology, but who need to get a firm grasp of what Trinitarian orthodoxy is. Most incoming seminary students have probably heard something about Arianism, Athanasius, ecumenical councils, and the splitting of the Eastern and Western church over the issue of *filioque* (adding "and the Son" to the Nicene Creed, thus confessing that the Spirit proceeds from the Father and the Son). The learning process begins with the knowledge we bring to the subject matter. Initially, as we study Trinitarian orthodoxy, it makes sense to operate with general and conventional categories, such as Arians and Anomoeans, although many theological connoisseurs would consider these as inadequate categories that need further nuancing.

2. Part 2 is meant for more advanced seminarians completing their master's degree. It comments on the three charts, which can be found on pages [46–49] and which attempt to depict graphically the patristic search for an adequate doctrine of the Trinity. In other words, while Part 1 presents the classical Trinitarian orthodoxy, Part 2 provides a more nuanced presentation of the debates of how the classical Trinitarian orthodoxy was established. The charts and the commentary are meant for students who already have some familiarity with systematic theology, scriptural studies, and church history, but could use some guidance in reading primary texts on the doctrine of the Trinity.

3. Part 3 is a handy reference tool for students who enjoy tackling primary sources. It provides a list of some important Greek and Latin primary texts about the Trinity and the available translations in English. Primary texts remain the proper "nourishment" for theologians. Everyone who is seriously interested in theological matters will always return to the writings of Origen, Gregory, and Augustine. I have given titles of ancient and medieval works on first use and then in later citations abbreviated them as in the "Guide List" in

Part 3 and in general accord with *The SBL Handbook of Style* (Peabody, MA: Hendrickson, 1999). The point of the title "Third and Fourth Times Around" is precisely to indicate that the task of reading primary texts is endlessly rewarding. Yet textbooks, after they have helped budding theologians on their feet, are often forgotten, rethought, and even discredited—and they should be! Textbooks are meant to be left behind! They are like the solid rocket boosters, which carry the space shuttle to the orbit and then burn up. No book burning though, please!

4. The "Reference List: Books for Further Study" offers guidance in selecting scholarly monographs for further study and identifies modern works cited. In the text an author's name and year point to this reference list, which gives further publishing details.

The order of the chapters may seem mistaken, since primary texts should come *before* the discussion of what these texts say. However, there is an aspect in learning that needs to be taken seriously. Clement of Alexandria asserted that "every question is solved from preexisting knowledge" (*Stromata* 8.4). Augustine reiterated, "Our thought is formed from what we know" (*De Trinitate* 15.50). Much closer to our time, Heidegger insisted that "interpretation is never a presuppositionless grasping of something" (1996, 141). We tend to see in texts what we already know. Therefore, introductions, summaries, and simplifications launch the very possibility of more advanced understanding of the subject matter. Nothing is fundamentally wrong with their coming before the primary texts. Most of us come to a subject matter with certain preunderstandings. We have heard something about the topic. Otherwise we wouldn't know to ask about it. Yet these preunderstandings need to become explicit knowledge. Assumptions need to be tested, convictions examined, and categories refined. Ultimately, several terms, formulas, and groupings found in Part 1 will have to be abandoned. This procedure of fine-tuning is undertaken in Part 2 and continues in many specialized scholarly monographs.

The authors of textbooks want to be as clear as possible, but this proves to be an almost impossible task. What some theologians have asserted about the Trinity is often obscure, ambiguous, and quite unclear. Sometimes the relevant documents have not survived. Other times the documents are incomplete or have been altered over the years. At still other times the assertions are just inconsistent, or they change radically over time. Writing a readable textbook on the classical doctrine of the Trinity is much like preparing a popular translation of the Scriptures which tries to give a clear rendering of the completely puzzling and unclear idiomatic passages. Indeed, creating a relatively short textbook has its own dangers, such as a tendency toward rash generalizations, occasional reductionism, insufficient clarification, inadequate consideration of detail, and imposition of preconceived categories. "Brevity often misleads both learner and teacher, and a concentrated discourse either causes a subject not to be understood, or spoils the meaning of an argument where a thing is hinted at, and is not proved by a full demonstration" (Hilary of Poitiers, *De synodis* 62). Nevertheless, I think that neither "learner nor teacher" should be afraid of simple and clear statements. To paraphrase Augustine,

> What is the point, after all, of fancy sophistications which the hearers are unable to follow and understand, seeing that there is absolutely no point in speaking at all, if the people do not understand, whom we are speaking to precisely in order that they may understand? (*De doctrina Christiana* 4.10.24)

So, even though the doctrine of the Trinity can be complex beyond imagination, for the purposes of learning, this textbook strives for simplicity and clarity.

This textbook also pays much attention to the study of technical terms whose meanings have changed over time. A seminary student definitely has to learn the language in which the Trinitarian theology is discussed. Basil of Caesarea wrote, "Those who are idle in the pursuit of righteousness count theological terminology as secondary" (*De Spiritu Sancto* 1.2). True, there is an unfortunate downside to focusing extensively on terms. It may be difficult to see the forest (the larger issues of the Trinitarian theology) for the trees (technical terminology). If we try to have a more-or-less comprehensive picture of the patristic beliefs about God, we should also consider liturgical acts of worship, narration of the divine actions, and poetic praise in songs. In a sense, paying attention to the technical discourse is like reducing the study of the New Testament Christology to the titles employed (Son of God, Son of man, *Logos*, et al.). Such an approach bypasses much that is embedded in the narrative and in the letters of Paul. Yet, my pragmatic concerns prevent the launching of a more comprehensive study of "God-ology," to invent a term for distinguishing the technical Trinitarian theology from the holistic theology of the Christian God.

Finally, I cannot adequately acknowledge the contribution of those contemporary scholars and teachers from whom I have learned so much, especially Professor Robin Darling Young. My debt is only partially redeemed by the suggested reading list ("Books for Further Study"). Works mentioned in this list will guide seminarians to the topics that have suffered neglect in this textbook. The omission of scholarly apparatus is deliberate, as is appropriate for the genre of a textbook. Nevertheless, omitting the footnotes is not intended to be an excuse for making the achievements of others look as if they were my own. All direct quotes are acknowledged in parentheses.

Because the standard abbreviations of the titles of primary sources are either in Greek or Latin (see SBL, Appendix H), I have spelled out the titles at their first occurrence. For an English translation of these titles, please see Part 3: Guide List to Ancient Works on the Trinity.

PART ONE
First Time Around

"We for our part declare that human nature is not sufficient to seek out God in any way and to arrive at a pure apprehension of him unless it is assisted by the one whom it is seeking" (Origen, *Contra Celsum* 7.42).

In 1715, Alessandro Scarlatti composed his oratorio *The Most Holy Trinity* (*La Santissima Trinità*). It begins with a dialogue between Faith and Theology. Faith insists that it is impossible to understand such a mystery as the Trinity. Theology responds with a clever compliment, "Yes, with your help I can." However, both characters become upset with each other as Faith comes to be accused of blind fideism (the view that religious truth must be accepted by faith only) and Theology is blamed for overly optimistic rationalism (the view that religious truth must be accepted by reason only). Yet no great controversy develops because the initial position is reiterated by a wonderful duet of Faith and Theology. They repeat over and over again, "No, it is not possible. . . . Yes, with your help I can."

It has been said that those who deny the Trinity are in danger of losing their salvation, but those who try to understand the Trinity are in danger of losing their mind. The second danger haunts seminary students and, to a no lesser extent, their professors. There is indeed a particular wisdom in Martin Luther's warning against investigating mysteries that ought to be believed and worshipped rather than rationally dissected. In neglecting adoration and focusing exclusively on scrutinizing incomprehensible secrets, curious people tend to harm themselves. "To aim at perfect comprehension is dangerous work, wherein we stumble, fall and break our necks" (*Tabletalk* 118). Already an early Christian scholar Clement of Alexandria warned, "But human teachers, speaking about God, are not reliable" (*Strom.* 6.18).

However, we should distinguish between the Trinity and the *doctrine* of the Trinity. God the Trinity may well be incomprehensible and ineffable. Yet doctrines of God, which are human statements in human language, are meant to be understood. Doctrines—even the doctrine of the Trinity—are supposed to make sense. With God's help, we hope it will.

The classical doctrine of the Trinity is an attempt to describe the Triune God with the assistance of certain metaphysical concepts available from the discourse of the day. The issue is not whether we ultimately accept the early philosophical framework of the discussion. We may not and some do not. But before subscribing to any modern theories of the Trinity, we should make sure that we understand what several contemporary theologians have reevaluated and modified—the classical doctrine of the Trinity.

When we are asked to elaborate and explain our understanding of the Triune God, what usually happens is that we commit many blunders because of ignorance and end up asserting things that actually are far from Christian Trinitarian beliefs. Therefore, let's begin by setting up some parameters for comprehending the doctrine of the Trinity. We will proceed by making two initial claims: (1) "God Is One," and (2) "The One God Is the Trinity." Then we discuss the divinity of the Son and the Spirit and their relation to the Father. We conclude Part 1 with a three-point clarification titled "What Trinitarian Belief Is and Is Not."

God Is One

There is one God, one Ultimate Being. "God is one" (Deut 6:4; Isa 45:14b; Rom 3:30; 1 Cor 8:6; Eph 4:6). Christians assume a monotheistic starting point. "We believe in one God," says the Nicene Creed (AD 325). Although there are important differences, Christianity, together with Judaism, teaches one God, as do classical philosophy and Islam—to mention just a few.

A comparison between the Christian notion of the Triune God and the neoplatonic notion of the Ultimate Realty may prove helpful. (Neoplatonism was a religious interpretation of the philosophy of Plato that flourished from the third to the sixth century.) The comparison will show that God can be understood in different ways.

Christianity

◎ —God = Father, Son, and Holy Spirit—three overlapping circles.

Christians understand the oneness of God in a particular way. Our God is a Triune God, both one and many. As far as God's divine nature is concerned, the Father, Son, and Holy Spirit do not constitute a hierarchy of beings. The idea of three overlapping circles comes from a fourth-century church father, Gregory of Nazianzus, who compares the Trinity to "three suns that mutually interconnect" and constitute "one mixture of light" (*Oratio* 31.14).

Neoplatonism

◯—the One or the Good—beyond essence, no divisions, absolute simplicity
⇓
The divine Mind—One and many, existence of the eternal Forms in the divine Mind
⇓
The (World)-Soul
⇓
Bodies

Some neoplatonic thinkers perceived the evolving of multiplicity from the One as a unitary process; others considered it to be strictly hierarchical.

Similarities

1. Although the One is not related to the Mind in the way the Father is related to the Son, both Christianity and neoplatonism argue for the existence of the one ultimate principle.
2. The neoplatonic first level of being, the One, is beyond explanation and description. In Christianity, the apophatic tradition (those who prefer to say what God *is not* rather than what God *is*) emphasizes God's transcendence and incomprehensibility.
3. For Neoplatonists, the Mind is eternally emanating from the One (Plotinus, *Enneades* V.1.6). For Christians, the Son is eternally begotten from the Father.
4. In Neoplatonism, the Mind has to mediate the absolutely transcendent One in order that lesser beings might become aware of it. Christians, too, believe that "Jesus Christ, himself human" (1 Tim 2:5) revealed the Father (John 1:18).
5. Because of God's uniplurality, the Christian concept of God has also some similarity to the neoplatonic second level of being, to the Mind. The Mind, which has the Forms in itself (the archetypical ideas of certain kind of things), cannot be simple in the strict sense of the word. Likewise, Christians confess one God, yet the Trinity. God is both one and many. The Latin word *trinitas* was a neologism; it combined the notions of God's oneness and threeness. It can be rendered as "triunity."
6. The Christian concept of the Triune God has also certain affinities to the neoplatonic threefold reality of the One, the Mind, and the Soul. Already Middle Platonists (from the first century BC to the second century AD) called the Mind by the alternative name *logos* (word), and this well suited the Christian understanding of the Son as the Word of God.

The similarity between the Christian concept of the Trinity and the neoplatonic triad of One-Mind-Soul is a huge topic of its own, but pointing out some resemblances is all that we are concerned with at the moment.

Differences

Before we are carried away by the similarities between the Christian and neoplatonic perceptions of God, some important differences have to be pointed out. We need to keep in mind that similarities between concepts do not necessarily prove that one came from the other. Even completely unrelated things can look alike. The Trinity is not merely a "baptized" neoplatonic triad, for the following reasons:

1. The Christian version of monotheism does not perceive God in absolute solitude and/or sterile privacy. Our God is "social," as it is now fashionable to say. We believe in a relating God and God in relationships.
2. A distinction is sometimes drawn between monotheism (there is only one God) and henotheism (there is one supreme God among the other divinities). Christianity is a monotheistic religion; neoplatonism is a henotheistic philosophy.
3. Christianity perceives the Father, Son, and Holy Spirit as divine persons. neoplatonism speaks about the impersonal One (or about the One who is beyond the designation "person").
4. Christian theology insists that Christ is mediator in his human nature. The *incarnated* Son mediates the Father (John 1:14–18). Neoplatonism, however, says nothing about the incarnation of the divine Mind. "But that 'the word was made flesh and dwelt among us,' I did not read there [in the neoplatonic books]" (Augustine, *Confessiones* 7.9.13).
5. The Christian concept of the Holy Spirit does not fit at all into the neoplatonic scheme. A fourth-century church father Augustine of Hippo wrote, "Of the Holy Spirit, however, he [the Neoplatonist Porphyry] says nothing" (*De civitate Dei* 10.23).

Next, we compare the Jewish notion of God, which Christians inherited from the Scriptures; and the Neoplatonic notion of the divine, which was available to the fourth-century Christian theologians. Both thought systems assumed the oneness of God, although in different ways. Where Judaism and neoplatonism differed, Christians usually sided with their mother religion rather than with the "pagan" philosophy.

Judaism	Neoplatonism
God is …	
Invisible	
Incorporeal	
Immutable	
(Some question this as a common characteristic. Immutability may well have been understood differently in Judaism and Neoplatonism)	
Sovereign	

Omnipotent	
Omnipresent	
Does not originate in anything earlier	
Eternal	
Personal God (who)	Impersonal, or beyond personal divinity (what)
YHWH	No name
God is worshipped.	The divine has no (communal) festivals, hymns, sacrifices, or liturgies.
God is described through stories.	The divine has no descriptive stories.
God acts, wills, makes choices, feels.	The divine emanates, overflows automatically.
God is involved.	The divine is beyond involvement; nothing happens to the Immutable One.
God is transcendent, yet positively related to creation.	The divine is utterly transcendent.
God makes deliberate and purposeful decisions.	The divine is utterly purposeless, beyond goals.
God reveals himself in theophanies and through the Law and Prophets.	The divine offers no self-revelation.
God's self-revelation is a gratuitous gift to the creation.	The divine does not communicate grace.

This chart identifies some similarities and differences between the doctrines of God in the two most important ancient rivals of Christianity. In its conception of the one God, Christianity had a greater affinity to Judaism than to Neoplatonism. This takes us to the unique aspect of the Christian doctrine of God, which distinguishes Christianity from Judaism.

The One God Is the Trinity

Here is our next claim. The first was that "God is one." The second states that "God is the Trinity." Christians accepted Jesus Christ as God's unique self-revelation and recognized God in the Son and the Holy Spirit (as in Mark 1:9–11; 2 Cor 13:13), thus professing the one God as the Trinity. Jews, however, remained strict monotheists. In a form of a simple scheme, Christians asserted that

$$\text{Father} = \text{God}$$
$$\text{Son} = \text{God}$$
$$\text{Holy Spirit} = \text{God}$$

At the same time, Christians also clarified that although the Father, Son, and Holy Spirit are equally divine,

$$\text{Father} \neq \text{Son}$$
$$\text{Son} \neq \text{Holy Spirit}$$
$$\text{Holy Spirit} \neq \text{Father}$$

Augustine put it this way: "The Father is God, and the Son is God, and the Holy Spirit is God, but the Son is not the Father, and the Holy Spirit is neither the Father nor the Son" (*Contra sermonem Arianorum* 15).

Furthermore, Christians do not confess three Gods but one Triune God. This is the crux of the matter! Here is the assertion that distinguishes Christianity from other religions:

$$\text{God} = \text{Father, Son, and Holy Spirit}$$

To make the same claim in the form of an old diagram, see image of Holy Trinity on p. 14. (A little help with Latin for those who need it: "God" = *Deus*, "Father" = *pater*, "Son" = *filius*, "Holy Spirit" = *spiritus sanctus*, "is" = *est*, "is not" = *non est*.) This diagram says that the one God is Father, Son, and Holy Spirit. Yet the Father is neither the Son nor the Holy Spirit, the Son is neither the Father nor Holy Spirit, and the Holy Spirit is neither the Father nor the Son. However, Father is God (*Deus*), Son is God (*Deus*), and the Holy Spirit is God (*Deus*). Not three Gods but one Triune God.

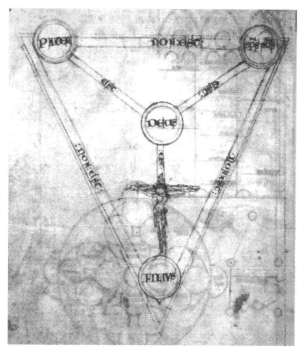

The Holy Trinity. Peter of Poitiers, 1208–1216,
Compendium historiae in genealogia Christi.
British Library, MS Cotton Faustina B. VII.

A caveat: diagrams are not theologically innocent (properly speaking, it is not diagrams but the people who draw them that have theologies). If misinterpreted, the diagram above can lead to heretical conclusions. Thus the word "God" (*Deus*) in the central circle does not designate some fourth thing behind Father, Son, and Spirit. There is no archetypical Godhead outside, above, in addition to, or apart from Father, Son, and Holy Spirit. Augustine warned, "Not that the Divinity, which they have in common, is a sort of fourth person, but that the Godhead is ineffably and inseparably a Trinity" (*Epistula* 120). Thus a triangle, the ancient symbol of the Trinity, with no extra circle within it, is indeed a better way to diagram God. However, Augustine also cautioned that any material or formal analogy to the Trinity, including a triangle, could be misleading. For instance, God the "triangle" has no angle, no spatial area, which is reserved exclusively for one of the divine persons and excludes the others. Nevertheless, diagrams are helpful for comprehension and thus Ambrose of Milan, among others, defended the process of learning about the unknown (the Trinity) with the help of the known (diagrams and triangles): "For it is often convenient to consider from our own words the things that are above us, and, since we cannot see them, we may draw inferences from those things which we can see" (*De Spiritu Sancto* 3.3.13).

The Divinity of the Son
and the Holy Spirit

It took centuries to figure out the implications of the scriptural witness for the doctrine of the Trinity. Though the search for an adequate doctrine of the Trinity was a long, messy, complicated, and sometimes rather hideous process, Trinitarian orthodoxy was established by the end of the fourth century. Chronologically speaking, the divinity of the Son was discussed before that of the Holy Spirit.

God the Son

Some fourth-century Christian theologians were attracted to the neoplatonic idea of the Mind emanating eternally from the One. It looked like a helpful philosophical analogy to articulate the Christian belief that the Son originated eternally from the Father. However, this borrowed analogy came with a considerable price tag—in the neoplatonic hierarchy, the Mind was considered inferior to the One. For the Neoplatonists, every effect was slightly inferior to its cause. Thus, using the concept of the Mind emanating from the One as an analogy for the Son begetting from the Father led inevitably to subordinationism, which assigns to the Son and Spirit a status inferior to the Father. Orthodox Christianity came to reject subordinationism.

Arius was a fourth-century theologian from the city of Alexandria, and his name has been associated with one of the great heresies about the Trinity. He tried to defend the simplicity of God (a doctrine that guards the uniqueness of God) by asserting that the Son was a lesser divine being than the Father. The Christian Scriptures (as in John 14:28), the Jewish notion of God's absolute oneness, and the philosophical necessity to affirm only one "first principle"—all suggested to Arius that to acknowledge the inferiority of the Son was the right thing to do. So, in defending the simplicity and uniqueness of God and by equating God with the Father, Arius contended that the Son was not fully God. Rather, the Son was the first among all created beings. At the same time, as a Christian, Arius did not hesitate to call the Son "divine." Yet by the divinity of the Son, Arius did not mean the ultimate divinity of the Father but the semidivinity of the first created being.

17

Now, Arius argued that since the Son was a created being unlike the Father, the Creator, the Son was *made*, not *begotten*. We make things that are of a different nature from ourselves, but we beget children who are of the same nature as ourselves. Being born from someone means sharing the same nature; being made by someone means a difference in nature.

Arius

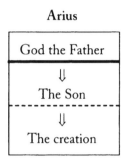

The solid horizontal line marks the essential difference between the Father and the Son. It also indicates the difference between the uncreated and created realm, which is the same as the difference between eternity and time. This diagram shows how Arius thought about God (or at least how his opponents said he thought about God). He numbered "the [uncreated] Creator among the creatures" (Athanasius, *Epistula ad Adelphium* 8). By providing these categories, Athanasius presented a "crude alternative: either a Son is fully equal to the Father, or a creature just like any other creature" (Stead, in *VC*, 1976, 129).

For Arius, however, the distinction between the Creator and the created seems not to have been the primary cognitive device. Instead, he operated with the notion of the hierarchical chain of being, with God the Father alone as the "first principle." Arius thought that the doctrine of the "monarchy of the Father" (a doctrine affirming that the Father is the source of all things [*monos* (only/single) + *archē* (principle)]) affirmed the superiority of the Father to the Son. In that scheme of things, the Son did not share in the Father's divine nature. Rather, the Son/Wisdom/Word was a preeminent "product" of the divine will and thus something between the Creator and the creation. Arius read from the Scriptures, "The LORD created me at the beginning of his work" (Prov 8:22) and "[Christ is] the firstborn of all creation" (Col 1:15). He believed that the only begotten Son was the first creation through whom everything else was created. Other theologians were not really happy with Arius's conjecture as it was presented by Athanasius. Christians were worshipping Christ. But they would not want to worship anything that is created, made, and less than the Creator! That would be idolatry! They also asked whether a created less-than-divine mediator could save. Not really! Athanasius, one of the main opponents of Arius, argued, "If being a creature, he [the Son] had become human, humanity would have remained just as it was, not joined to God" (*Orationes contra Arianos* 2.67). A less-than-divine Savior cannot redeem sinners!

For these and other reasons, a pro-Nicene theologian Athanasius explained that the doctrine of the "monarchy of the Father" could *not* mean that the Son was less in being than the Father. The Son was (and is) God, not in the pagan sense of an "immortal being," but in a Jewish sense of the "LORD" (YHWH). The Son was equally divine but not identical with the Father, having the same divine nature but being a different person (John 10:30). Because the Son was of the same nature or consubstantial with the Father, the Son was indeed *begotten* and not *made*; he was begotten from the Father's substance and not made from nothing.

The doctrine of the "monarchy of the Father" could also *not* mean that the Son came after the Father in time. If God the Father was indeed eternal and immutable, then God had to be eternally a Father. The names "Father" and "Son" are correlative terms: the first implies the second. It follows that the Son must be coeternal with the Father, without a beginning in time. Otherwise the Father would not always be a Father.

Consequently, Athanasius and other pro-Nicene theologians rejected Arian subordinationism and taught that the Son had to be perceived as being on the side of the Creator rather than the creation.

Athanasius

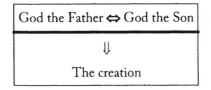

Here, too, the bold horizontal line marks the essential difference between the Creator and the creation. The Son is on the same level of divinity as the Father. "The Word was God" (John 1:1). The Council of Nicaea (AD 325) confessed this orthodox belief:

<blockquote>

In one Lord Jesus Christ, the Son of God,

the only-begotten Son of God,

begotten from the Father before all the ages, God from God,

light from light, true God from true God,

begotten not made,

consubstantial with the Father

</blockquote>

God the Holy Spirit

The Council of Nicaea affirmed the equal divinity of the Father and the Son. The next ecumenical council, the Council of Constantinople (AD 381), affirmed the equal divinity of the Holy Spirit. This council rejected two forms of subordinationism held by some fourth-century Christians:

Macedonians or "Spirit-Fighters"

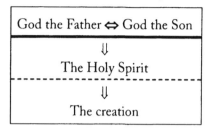

Aetius and Eunomius

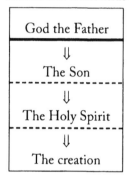

Again, the bold line marks the difference between the Creator and the creation.

At least some of the so-called Spirit-Fighters acknowledged the equal divinity of the Father and the Son but denied the equal divinity of the Holy Spirit. They did not believe that the Holy Spirit was of the same nature with the Father and the Son.

On the other hand, two fourth-century theologians, Aetius and Eunomius, taught that the Father was the only true God. They contended that the Son had an inferior status in the chain of being, and the Holy Spirit was more inferior yet. The Father alone was the uncreated Creator. Because Aetius and Eunomius denied the essential likeness to the Son and the Spirit, they were known as Anomoeans (dissimilar [essence]). One of their main opponents, Gregory of Nyssa, summarized, "The whole controversy, then, between the church and the Anomoeans turns to this: Are we to regard the Son and the Spirit as belonging to created or uncreated existence?" (*Contra Eunomium* 1.18).

Over against the Spirit-Fighters and Anomoeans, the Council of Constantinople acknowledged the divinity of the Holy Spirit. The Council maintained that since the Father, Son, and Holy Spirit were coworshipped (worshipped together), and since Christians were baptized in the name of the Father, Son, and Holy Spirit (Matt 28:19), the Spirit was equally divine and coeternal God. Ambrose of Milan, a Latin theologian contemporary with the council, summed up the orthodox position: "Every creature is below; the divinity of the Father and of the Son and of the Holy Spirit is above" (*Spir.* 1.3.46).

The Council of Constantinople

God the Father ⇔ God the Son ⇔ God the Holy Spirit
⇓
The creation

The Constantinopolitan Creed confessed:

We believe . . . in the Spirit . . .

coworshipped and coglorified

with Father and Son

So far so good! Christians believe in one God, and by one God they mean the Father, Son, and Holy Spirit. Yet why does the one God have three different names? How shall we understand this mathematical impossibility (but theological possibility) that there are three who are divine and yet there is one God? How shall we perceive the distinctions between the Father, Son, and Holy Spirit?

What Trinitarian Belief
Is and Is Not

Maximus the Confessor, a seventh-century theologian, said something important for all future students of theology: "To discourse on something without making the necessary distinctions is to spread confusion" (*Disputatio cum Pyrrho*). When we make distinctions, we show that this thing is not that thing. So, to avoid spreading confusion and to address the questions asked at the end of the last chapter, we make distinctions that result in *six negations*.

Six Negations

1. The three persons cannot be distinguished by *nature*. The Father, Son, and Holy Spirit have the same divine nature. To say they are consubstantial is to say they are of the same nature. The fact that the Father is "unbegotten," the Son "begotten," and the Holy Spirit "proceeds" (the Father's "unbegottenness" is deduced from John 1:18; 15:26) applies to the particular characteristics of the divine *persons* and not to their shared *nature*.

2. The three persons cannot be described as *parts* of God. All three divine persons have the fullness of Godhead, which by definition is absolutely one, simple, immaterial, and hence without parts. "The unity of Godhead is not divided into parts" (Augustine, *Contra Maximinum Arianum* 2.10.1). "The Divine is without parts and indivisible, not to be cut or divided" (Eusebius, *Demonstratio evangelica* 5.1). To call God "Father, Son, and Holy Spirit" is to introduce neither parts nor subdivisions into the one Godhead. Think of three overlapping circles rather than a circle divided into three parts. God cannot have parts because God is simple, that is, noncomposite being. Only in composite beings are parts before the whole. But nothing can be before God, and thus God is a "partless" simple being. What the second negation tries to clarify is that the three persons do not make up one God, as if the Father, Son, and Holy Spirit were incomplete parts of the Divinity. The three persons do not *become* God when they are added up as divine "parts." Each of them *is* God, not part of God.

22

3. The three persons are not just three *names* of the same thing. The names "Father," "Son," and "Holy Spirit" correspond to that which is individual in the Trinity. The names state the modes of origin (or the lack of it in the case of the Father, who is unoriginated) and the relations between the three divine persons (see below). Once again, the name "Father" designates the unbegotten first person of the Trinity; the name "Son," the begotten second person of the Trinity, and the name "Holy Spirit," the proceeding third person of the Trinity. At the same time, there is really no sequential "first," "second," or "third" in the Trinity, because the three divine persons are equally God and equally eternal. It is their causal or logical order (see point 6) and relation that the names "Father," "Son," and "Holy Spirit" indicate.

4. The three persons are not three successive *modes* of the same one God. The persons of the Trinity are coeternal. When someone teaches that the Father, Son, and the Holy Spirit are temporally consecutive "modes" of God, things are moving in a wrong direction. For instance, a popular comparison of the Trinity to water, ice, and steam (the three "modes" of H_2O) is inadequate precisely because H_2O cannot be all three at the same time. God, however, is the Father, Son, and Holy Spirit eternally and thus "simultaneously." The comparison also falls short because ice, water, and steam are material and dependent on external circumstances (such as temperature), but God is neither material nor dependent on anything external. The analogy of time consisting of past, present, and future is equally misleading. Since past becomes present and future, it may lead to thinking that the Father becomes the Son, and the Son becomes the Holy Spirit. But this is inadequate, because neither the Father nor the Son are "modes" that are left behind once the next "mode" arrives. Still, in other times the analogy of one person being a father, husband, and lawyer is used to explicate the Trinity. But the Father, Son, and Holy Spirit are not one person in different roles at different times but three persons with one power and common action. Hence the next point.

5. The three persons cannot be distinguished by *actions* (or acts), because the intercommunion of the divine persons guarantees the coinvolvement of the Father, Son, and Holy Spirit in everything that the Triune God does. The works of God are inseparable. "Whatever the Father does, the Son does likewise" (John 5:19). Basil of Caesarea explained that God did everything in a threefold unity: each act was originated by the Father, realized by the Son, and completed by the Spirit (*Spir.* 16.38). However, do not the Scriptures describe the particular actions of the Father, Son, and Holy Spirit? The Father did not become incarnate; the Son did. The Son did not come as the "Advocate"; the Holy Spirit did (John 14:26). Indeed! But the unique thing about the Trinity is precisely that in these particular actions all three divine persons are involved. The incarnation of the Son did not happen without the Father or the Spirit, and the coming of the Advocate did not take place without the Father and the Son. The actions of the Trinity are inseparable,

although they can be appropriated primarily to one of the divine persons. A recent ecumenical study of the Nicene Creed puts it this way, "Although the work of creation is attributed specifically to the Father, the work of redemption to the Son, and the work of sanctification to the Spirit, the work of each of the Trinitarian persons implies the presence and co-operation of all three. Thus God is one. None of the three persons of the Trinity has a life of his own apart from the others" (*Confessing the One Faith*, 1991, 22). On a popular level, the Trinity is sometimes "explained" through the analogy of a football team. In a football team on a field, many consubstantial persons (persons having the same human nature) are involved in the same action. This analogy is presented as if it illustrated the consubstantial Father, Son, and Spirit doing the same deed(s). But this analogy is not very close. There are other humans who do not play football, but there are no Gods outside the Trinity who are left out of the game. Furthermore, if player number 5 plays, it does not mean that player number 10 plays. Player number 10 can sit on a bench and never get a chance. But in the Trinity, there are no substitutes waiting for their turn to act. Unlike human beings, the Father, Son, and Holy Spirit are eternally coactive in all of their doings. It was not without a reason that Eusebius wrote, "The scope of the [Trinitarian] theology we are considering far transcends all illustrations" (*Dem. ev.* 4.3)

6. The three persons cannot be distinguished by *temporal priority*. All three persons of the Trinity are equally eternal, and therefore no one comes before the other in time. There is no "earlier and later God" (Hilary of Poitiers, *De Trinitate* 1.11). Human fathers exist before their sons in time. Things are different in the divine realm of eternity. We can say, however, that the Father has a *causal* priority over the Son and the Spirit. A cause has to be logically prior to its effect. But here's the tricky part: in the case of the coeternal divine persons, there cannot be any time between the cause (the Father) and the effects (the Son and the Holy Spirit). The Son is *eternally* begotten from the Father. The Holy Spirit proceeds *eternally* from the Father. In eternity, the cause can be logically prior, but it cannot be temporally prior to its effect(s). Being "unbegotten" implies being eternal, but being eternal does not necessarily imply being "unbegotten." The begotten Son and the proceeding Spirit are coeternal with the unbegotten Father.

Affirmations

If not three Gods, three divinities, three parts, three names, three modes, three activities, three sequences, then three *what?* Three *persons*!!! Notice that by now we have stated it six times(! cf. the opening phrase of the six points). In fact, many of us sing in the church about the proper distinction in the Trinity: "Holy,

Holy, Holy, Lord God Almighty, . . . God in three *persons*, blessed Trinity" (R. Heber).

The word "person," however, does not designate private individual consciousness. This is a modern definition of person. In Christian antiquity, "person" meant a unique collection of properties (attributes or characteristics) in a subject, which was defined through relations to other collections of properties in another subject. For instance, the Son is defined as a person with a unique collection of properties (the Son is coeternal, divine, caused, begotten, and incarnate). This set of personal properties, unique to the Son, is related to another unique collection of properties (eternal, divine, uncaused, and unbegotten), unique to the Father. The Trinitarian God is "three persons" in the ancient sense of the word. Hence the classical definition:

> The Triune God is *one nature* and *three persons*.

This said, all readers are begged to keep in mind that "to know you [meaning God] as you are in an absolute sense is for you alone" (Augustine, *Conf.* 13.16.19). Formulations do not capture God exhaustively. Formulations and doctrines are mere finite human attempts to discourse about the Infinite. "No matter what kind of language is used, it will be unable to speak of God as he is and what he is" (Hilary of Poitiers, *Trin.* 2.7).

Nevertheless, let us try to unpack the *doctrine* of God, the classical definition that employs the phrase "three persons." The three equally divine persons can be differentiated by their *modes of origination* (cf. point 3 above).

> The Son is *begotten* from the Father.
> The Holy Spirit *proceeds* from the Father.

This is the same as saying that

> The Father is *unbegottenness*.
> The Son is *begottenness*.
> The Holy Spirit is *procession*.

To be "unbegotten" is something particular to the Father, to be "begotten" is something particular to the Son, and to be "proceeding" is something particular to the Holy Spirit. The important thing here is not to repeat the fourth-century Anomoean teaching, which identified the Father's "unbegottenness" with *God's* nature. "Unbegottenness" is the attribute of the Father's *person* and not of the divine *nature*.

The three equally divine persons can also be distinguished by their *relational* names, which correspond to the distinct persons (cf. negation 3 above).

The *Father* is the begetter of the Son and the proper cause of the Holy Spirit.

The *Son* is the only-begotten Son of the Father.

The *Holy Spirit* is the Spirit of the Father (and the Son).

Personhood, defined by the mode of origination and relation, is what Father, Son, and Holy Spirit do *not* share.

The Procession of the Spirit

Now, if the Father is "unbegotten," the Son "begotten," and the Spirit "proceeds," then can we say "the Holy Spirit proceeds from the Father and the Son"?

In Latin, the phrase "and the Son" is *filioque*. In the eleventh–twelfth century, the addition of this phrase to the Nicene Creed became the main theological reason for the split between the Eastern and Western church. There was no complete agreement about a rather central question—the question about how to perceive the Christian Trinitarian God! This is not theological hairsplitting! It is a serious matter!

In a nutshell, the *Greek* logic, which asserts that "the Holy Spirit proceeds from the Father," goes as follows:

1. "The Son is begotten from the Father" means that the Son is begotten from the Father's person and not from the divine nature, which the Son also shares.
2. "The Holy Spirit proceeds from the Father" means that the Holy Spirit proceeds from the Father's person and not from the divine nature, which the Holy Spirit also shares.
3. Therefore the Father is the eternal *cause* of both the Son and the Holy Spirit, and the Son is *not* the proper cause of the Holy Spirit.

At the same time, Greek theologians did *not* teach that the proceeding of the Holy Spirit was unaffected by the relationship of the Son to the Father. Gregory of Nyssa clarified, "The Son ... declares the Spirit's proceeding from the Father through himself and with himself" (*Ad Petrum* 4].)

As we have mentioned, the doctrine that emphasizes the person of the Father as the sole cause within the Godhead is known as "the monarchy of the Father." The word "monarchy" means "one source, one rule, one principle." The notion of the monarchy of the Father retains the causal but not the *temporal* priority of the Father. The Father's priority cannot be temporal, because the Father, Son, and Holy Spirit are equally eternal (cf. negation 6 above).

To reiterate, the Holy Spirit cannot proceed from the Son, because it proceeds from what is particular to the Father (Father's person) and not from what is common to Father, Son, and Holy Spirit (the divine nature; cf. John 15:26)—although even such notional distinction between person and nature may be inadequate. At least the Holy Spirit cannot proceed eternally from the Son in the same sense as it proceeds from the Father, who is the only ultimate cause, the only "first principle." On Byzantine icons of the Trinity, the causal priority of the Father is affirmed by the turned faces of the Son and the Holy Spirit, who are looking toward the Father.

The *Latin* Trinitarian theology, which asserts that "the Holy Spirit proceeds from the Father *and the Son*," argues as follows:

1. The Holy Spirit proceeds principally or originally from the Father.
2. The Holy Spirit proceeds also from the Son, who himself is eternally begotten from the Father. The three persons are inseparable form the divine nature and action. Since they are inseparable, the Son is inevitably involved when the Father and Spirit do something.
3. Therefore, one can say that the Holy Spirit proceeds from the Father *and the Son*. In the New Testament, the Spirit is called the "Spirit of Christ" (Rom 8:9), "the Spirit of his Son" (Gal 4:6), and "the Spirit of Jesus" (Acts 16:7).

However, in explicating the *filioque* clause, Latin theologians preserved the notion of the monarchy of the Father. Augustine wrote, "We . . . call the Son God from God, but the Father we simply call God, not from God" (*Trin.* 2.1.2).

Augustine's analogy of lover (the Father), the loved (the Son), and love (the Holy Spirit) implicitly supported the so-called "double procession" of the Holy Spirit, as in the *filioque* doctrine. The obvious reason for the doctrine of the "double procession" is that love "proceeds" also from the loved (the Son) to the lover (the Father). Love is reciprocal. To assert that the Holy Spirit proceeds from the Father and the Son also avoids the unwanted implication that God the Father has two sons. In addition, it helps to distinguish the Son from the Holy Spirit.

In John 15:26, Jesus says, "When the Advocate comes, whom I *will send* to you from the Father, the Spirit of truth who *proceeds* from the Father. . . ." There is a sense in which we can truly say that the Holy Spirit, who is from the Father, is *sent* by the Father and the Son. Pay careful attention to the verbs used! The Scripture does not say that the Holy Spirit *proceeds* from the Father and the Son, but that the Holy Spirit is *sent* by Father and Son (cf. John 14:26, "the Holy Spirit, whom the Father will *send* in my name"). What is this distinction between "proceeding" and "sending" all about?

Both elements in John's text—the Holy Spirit proceeding from the Father, and the Father and Son sending the Holy Spirit—will make more sense when we distinguish between theological proceeding and economical sending (cf. Gregory of Nazianzus, *Or.* 38.8).

1. *Theological proceeding* of the Holy Spirit takes place eternally within the Godhead.

2. *Economical sending* of the Holy Spirit took place in time and history, at Pentecost (Acts 2; cf. Gal 4:4–5, "When the fullness of time had come, God *sent* his Son. . . . God has *sent* the Spirit of his Son"). Economical sending is also called "breathing" ("[Jesus] breathed on them and said to them, 'Receive the Holy Spirit'" [John 20:22]).

Theological proceeding concerns the metaphysical level of operation within the Godhead; the economical sending concerns the soteriological level of operation in human history. Maximus the Confessor, an Easterner who was active in the West, was among those who popularized an ancient alternative formula combining the theological and economical aspects. This formula, which retains both the monarchy of the Father and the mediating role of the Son, has become the basis of ecumenical discussions of the Trinity: "The Holy Spirit proceeds *from* the Father *through* [not *from*] the Son."

Theological

The Father

↓   ↓

The Son is *begotten.*   The Holy Spirit *proceeds.*

Economical

The Father and the Son

↓

The Holy Spirit is *sent* or *"breathed."*

One could say, roughly, that theological proceeding has been the primary focus of Eastern theologians, and economical sending the focus of Western theologians. The respective difference in emphasis can be partially explained by the difference in theological contexts:

1. When the Eastern church insisted that the Holy Spirit proceeded from the Father, it was an anti-Anomoean move, a defense of the divinity of the Holy Spirit. Eunomius had insisted that the Spirit was ontologically inferior not only to the Father but also to the Son, who was the "instrument" for the production of the Spirit. Thus, for the Orthodox to say that the Spirit proceeded from the Father's person secured at least the equality of the Son and the Spirit as caused yet eternal beings.
2. But when the Western church asserted that the Holy Spirit proceeded from the Father *and the Son,* it was an anti-Arian/anti-adoptionist move, which tried to secure the full divinity of the Son. The Spirit of God can proceed

only from God. To say that the Spirit proceeds from the Father *and the Son* implies that the Son is God.

What Trinitarian Belief Is Not

Most of the inadequate understandings of the Trinity can be reduced to either tritheism, subordinationism, or modalism. These "-isms" are not clear-cut theological positions represented by coherent and unified movements. Rather, they are theological tendencies present in various movements or trajectories.

Tritheism, which teaches three Gods, emphasizes the distinctions within the Godhead at the expense of the unity. Presumably, no Christian theologian has deliberately taught tritheism, but a number of them have been accused of it. For instance, a twelfth-century thinker Roscelinus speculated that the three persons within the Trinity were distinct "things," without a common substance. He argued that the three separate persons in the Trinity were linked only linguistically, that is, by the common name "God." If the three persons were identical in nature, then the Father and the Holy Spirit should have become incarnate together with the Son. In other words, since the Son indeed was incarnated, he could not have shared the same nature with the Father and the Holy Spirit.

It is crucial to understand what can be attributed to the shared divine *nature*, and what can be attributed to the distinct divine *persons*. Roscelinus failed to notice that it was not the divine *nature* that was incarnated. Rather, it was the divine Son as a *person* who became incarnate, although the incarnation was brought about by the common operation of the consubstantial Father, Son, and Spirit.

The next two inadequate solutions have tried to resolve the problem of three being one by eliminating one side of the paradox or the other: either the Father alone is God in a strict sense, or the three persons of the Trinity are not really distinct.

Subordinationism tries to retain the basic conviction that God is one. It tries to solve the difficulty by affirming that the Son and the Holy Spirit are inferior to the supremely divine Father. The Son and the Holy Spirit are not divine in the same sense or to a same degree as the Father is divine.

Against subordinationism, we need to emphasize that the Son was "begotten" and not "made." Whatever is begotten shares the nature of the one who begets.

Modalism, contrary to subordinationism, seeks to solve the problem by asserting that the Father, Son, and the Holy Spirit are successive "modes" of the same underlying divinity. God has manifested itself successively in the form of the Father, Son, and Holy Spirit. Modalism affirms the unity of God, but neglects the personal distinctions within this unity. For instance, the third- and fourth-century modalists taught that the Father, Son, and Holy Spirit were mere distinctions made by the human mind. We perceive the distinction between the

Father, Son, and Holy Spirit as we look at salvation history. Accordingly, the distinctions within the one God are temporary, and they designate certain phases in the economy of salvation. No distinguishable persons can be found in the single and eternal God.

Against modalism, we should emphasize that God is immutable. There is no sequential "becoming" or metamorphosis in the Godhead. The Triune God has eternally been the Father, Son, and Holy Spirit. Modalists confused the economical activities of the Father, Son, and Holy Spirit with the theological Trinity.

Trinitarian orthodoxy rejects tritheism, subordinationism, and modalism. Against these inadequate views the orthodox or classical "one nature three persons" formula affirms both unity and diversity in the Godhead. God the Trinity is "one nature and three persons." "This doctrine is enough for the believers. Beyond that the cherubim cover with their wings" (Athanasius, *Epistulae ad Serapionem* 1.17).

PART TWO
Second Time Around

Cast of Characters

Act I (Chart One)

Individuals

Dionysius of Alexandria (d. 264/265), bishop of Alexandria, was an anti-Monarchian theologian accused of teaching tritheism.

Dionysius of Rome (d. ca. 268), bishop of Rome, was an anti-Monarchian and anti-subordinationist theologian who condemned Alexander of Alexandria in 262.

Irenaeus (d. ca. 202), bishop of Lyons, refuted Gnostic understanding(s) of God in his principal work *Against Heresies* (*Adversus haereses*).

Justin Martyr (d. ca. 165), an early Christian apologist, was one of the first to articulate the Christian concept of God.

Novatian (mid-3rd century), bishop of Rome, was the author of the first Latin treatise on the Trinity.

Origen (d. 253) was one of the most significant biblical exegetes and theologians of the early centuries, a major shaper of Trinitarian theology.

Tertullian (d. ca. 220) was an anti-Monarchian Christian theologian who set direction for the Latin Trinitarian doctrine.

Theophilus of Antioch (2nd century) was bishop of Antioch, an early Christian apologist, one of the first to articulate the Christian concept of God.

Groups (No Uniformity Implied)

Gnostics—a common name for various second–third-century religious groups that dualistically severed the ultimate God from the lower beings and material world.

Monarchians—a common name for the second–third-century defenders of God's undiversified unity.

Dynamic Monarchians, represented by **Paul of Samosata**, taught that the Son was a divinely empowered human being.

Modalist Monarchians, represented by **Praxeas** and **Noetus**, taught that the Son was a "mode" of the Father.

Act II (Chart Two)

Individuals

Acacius of Caesarea (d. 365) succeeded Eusebius of Caesarea as a bishop of Caesarea and was a representative of the Homoeans.

Alexander of Alexandria (d. 328), bishop of Alexandria, condemned the Trinitarian views of his rebel-subordinate Arius at the Council of Nicaea.

Arius (d. 336) was an Alexandrian priest whose Trinitarian views were rejected by Alexander of Alexandria, Athanasius, and the Council of Nicaea.

Athanasius (d. 373) succeeded Alexander of Alexandria as a bishop of Alexandria, was the main opponent of Arius and Arians, and was one of the foremost architects of Trinitarian orthodoxy.

Basil of Ancyra (d. ca. 363) succeeded Marcellus of Ancyra as a bishop of Ancyra and was a representative of Homoeousians.

Cyril of Jerusalem (d. 386/387), bishop of Jerusalem, was a traditionalist who eventually sided with pro-Nicenes.

Eusebius of Caesarea (d. 339/340), bishop of Caesarea, was a leading anti-Marcellian (antimodalist) theologian.

Hilary of Poitiers (d. 367), bishop of Poitiers, was a leading Latin anti-Homoean theologian who learned about the Greek pro-Nicene Trinitarian theology in his exile.

Marcellus of Ancyra (d. 374), bishop of Ancyra, a leading antisubordinationist theologian who himself was condemned by Arians as a modalist.

Marius Victorinus (d. ca. 365) was a Latin rhetorician and a pro-Nicene theologian.

Groups (Often Polemical Constructs)

"**Arians**"—a common name for all those who argued for an essential difference between the Father, Son, and Spirit. (See "Excursus on Naming," in commentary "On Chart Two," below.)

"**Eusebians**"—a common name for the friends of Eusebius of Caesarea who promoted subordinationism and considered the pro-Nicene doctrine of the Trinity modalist. The most notable Eusebians were **Eusebius of Nicomedia** (after whom the group is named) and **Asterius**. The opponents of Eusebians considered them nothing but Arians. (See "Excursis on Naming," in commentary "On Chart Two," below.)

Homoeousians—a common name for the fourth-century theologians who taught that the Father and the Son were of like essence (*homoiousios*).

Homoeans—a common name for the fourth-century theologians who taught that the Father and the Son were alike (*homoios*).

Heteroousians—a common name for the fourth-century theologians who taught that the Father and the Son were of different essence (*heteroousios*) because the essence of God (the Father) was "unbegottenness." The most notable Heteroousians were **Aetius** and **Eunomius**.

Act III (Chart Three)

Individuals

Ambrose of Milan (d. 397), bishop of Milan, was a Latin anti-Homoean theologian who secured the dominance of the pro-Nicene Trinitarian doctrine in West.

Augustine of Hippo (d. 430), bishop of Hippo, was the main shaper of the Latin pro-Nicene Trinitarian theology.

Basil of Caesarea (d. 379), bishop of Caesarea, was one of the main architects of Trinitarian orthodoxy, which was accepted at the Council of Constantinople.

Gregory of Nazianzus (d. ca. 390) was bishop of Nazianzus and the first president of the Council of Constantinople, the main Greek theologian of the Trinity.

Gregory of Nyssa (d. ca. 395) was bishop of Nyssa and continued his brother Basil of Caesarea's literary battle with Heteroousians.

Groups

Latin Homoeans—a common name for the fourth-century Latin theologians who taught that the Father and the Son were alike (*homoios*).

Heteroousians—see Act II.

"Pneumatomachians"—a common name for the fourth-century theologians who denied the full divinity of the Holy Spirit. (See "Excursis on Naming," in commentary "On Chart Two," below.)

Trinitarian Terms

It is necessary to know the definition of things.

Evagrius Ponticus (*Kephalaia Gnostica* 17)

General Insights for the Meanings of Terms

- Like all words, the Trinitarian terms do not have a constant and fixed meaning. Meanings are constructed rather than inherited.
- Words are used long before they are identified as technical terms, and when words are identified as such, their meaning is often altered.
- Wittgenstein (1958) insists that meaning is use. Accordingly, the Trinitarian terms do not have some kind of "intrinsic" or "primary" meanings that can be deduced from their etymology. Rather, these terms receive their meaning from their actual contextual use.
- Barr (1961) warns against the "illegitimate totality transfer." This means that there is a misguided tendency to read into a word or term all the possible meanings from its wide semantic realm, and then to conclude that the given word signifies all those meanings at the same time and in a single passage.
- Theologians used the terms according to their discernment and preference. A unique usage of terms is always a possibility.
- One should not presume that one and the same theologian always employed the terms consistently and in the same sense.
- One should also not presume that the terms always meant the same thing in patristic theology and in the pagan philosophical discourse of the early centuries—although such presumption seems to provide a convenient clarity.
- The Trinitarian terms did not necessarily mean the same thing in the second, third, and fourth centuries.
- The technical terms caught on slowly, if at all, in preaching and worship.
- Language as a created finite reality always comes short of giving an exhaustive account of the infinite Creator. "There was no word prior to the Word" (Gregory of Nazianzus, *Or.* 38.3). Even the most refined technical terms (and the most trusted biblical expressions) cannot capture what God is. We speak about God analogically. Athanasius explained, "We receive the terms referring to God in one way, and we conceive of those that refer to human beings in another" (*De decretis* 11).

A Short List of Terms

This list provides a quick reference to what the terms came to mean in the fourth-century Trinitarian orthodoxy. In other words, it should *not* be assumed that these terms had their orthodox meaning before the end of the fourth century. For instance, the word *hypostasis* was a synonym of *ousia* for a "heretic" Marcellus and also for an orthodox Cyril of Jerusalem. If we assume that *hypostasis* means "person," we will misread both Marcellus and Cyril.

The selected terms appear in alphabetical order.

Essentia: Latin for "essence, being." The Father, Son, and Spirit have one divine *essentia*, and this is "to be."

Filioque: Latin for "and the Son" in the statement "Holy Spirit proceeds from the Father and the Son."

Genētos: Greek for "created." The Son was not *genētos*, because the Son was not part of the creation.

Gennētos: Greek for "begotten." The Son was *gennētos*, because the Son was born from the essence of the Father.

Homoousios: Greek for "consubstantial, coessential." The Father and Son are *homoousios*. The Father and Son are of the same (divine) nature.

Hypostasis: Greek for "person." The Father, Son, and Spirit are three distinct *hypostaseis* sharing the one divine *ousia*.

Natura: Latin for "nature." God's *natura* is nonmaterial. The Father, Son, and Spirit have one divine *natura*.

Ousia: Greek for "essence." The Father, Son, and Spirit have one divine *ousia*.

Persona: Latin for "person." The Father, Son, and Spirit are three distinct *personae* sharing the one divine *essentia/substantia/natura*.

Physis: Greek for "nature." God's *physis* is nonmaterial. The Father, Son, and Spirit have one divine *physis*.

Prosōpon: Greek for "person." The one God is revealed as three really subsisting *prosōpa* of the Father, Son, and Spirit.

Schesis: Greek for "relation." *Schesis* expresses how the equally divine Father, Son, and Spirit are distinct persons. The *unbegotten* Father is the Father of the *only-begotten* Son. The Spirit *proceeds* from the Father (and the Son).

Substantia: Latin for "essence, nature." The Father, Son, and Spirit have one divine *substantia*.

An Expanded List of Terms

The expanded list is not alphabetized. Rather, similar or related terms are grouped together for purposes of comparison.

All the following four words (i.e., *ousia, physis, hypostasis,* and *prosōpon*) plus two more form a spectrum in which meanings shade into one other:

Ousia (οὐσία): "being, reality, essence, substance, nature, property." *Ousia* designates the irreducible being of some kind of thing (e.g., human, tree). That is, *ousia* determines that something is this kind of thing and not that kind of thing. In Greek philosophy, it denoted an intelligible universal (*eidos*). Platonists considered the abstract universal to be prior to the particular manifestation of that universal. The abstract and intelligible universal, the "thisness" of something, was also considered to be more "real" than the particular and perceptible manifestation of it. God's *ousia*, the "godness" of God, has to remain without definition, however, because it is infinite, transcendent, and therefore beyond the descriptive capacity of finite human language. The word *ousia* does not occur in the Scriptures as a technical term.

Physis (φύσις): "nature, that which makes up a thing, a form." In Greek philosophy, it denoted a particular. In general usage, the semantic range of the word *physis* includes the meanings of "natural qualities," "condition," "disposition," or "outward appearance." For theology, *physis* is valuable in its connotation as something that constitutes the inner organizational principle from which the particular thing is formed. *Physis* is not necessarily material.

Hypostasis (ὑπόστασις): "subsistence, person, subject, the underlying essence (notice the prefix *hypo-*), actual reality as opposed to appearance." *Hypostasis* is less abstract than *ousia*. *Hypostasis* individualizes an abstract universal into a particular thing. *Hypostasis* can also mean "stuff," as in Stoic philosophy, where the actual existence of something presupposed matter. The wide semantic field of the word caused a lot of confusion in both Trinitarian and Christological controversies. Applied to the Trinity, it came to designate the distinctness of persons; applied to Christ, it designated the unity of person. The Cappadocians, rather than Athanasius, were responsible for turning *hypostasis* into a technical term in Trinitarian theology. "The Easterners . . . call the individualities of the subsistent persons '*hypostaseis*'" (Epiphanius, *Panarion* 72.16.1). But Augustine was famously confused: "The Greeks . . . make a distinction that is rather obscure to me between *ousia* and *hypostasis*" (*Trin.* 5.2.10).

Two other terms were, more or less, synonymous with *hypostasis*, but did not become technical terms in Christian discourse to the extent that *hypostasis* did:

Hypokeimenon (ὑποκείμενον): "subsistence, substratum, essence, that which persists through change."

Hyparxis (ὕπαρξις): "subsistence, reality, property, that which underlies exisence."

Prosōpon (πρόσωπον): "'face,' the observable appearance, external sensible aspect, manifestation of reality, source of action, concrete representation of the abstract *ousia* and underlying *hypostasis*." The semantic equivalents to *prosōpon* include "the particular body" (*sōma*), "the particular soul" (*psychē*), and "the particular human being" (*anthrōpos*). Since the Cappadocian fathers, the Greek equivalent to *prosōpon* was *hypostasis*; since Tertullian, its Latin equivalent was *persona*. However, because of the modalists' compromising use of the term *prosōpon*, Basil of Caesarea remained suspicious of it. When he used the term, he felt the need to affirm the true hypostatic subsistence of the three *prosōpa*. The term *prosōpon* received much attention in the Christological controversies.

- The first three terms (*ousia, hypostasis, physis*) were more or less synonymous during the first four centuries. Even the Council of Nicaea employed the phrase "from another hypostasis *or* substance" (*ex heteras hypostaseōs ē ousias*) to anathematize those who held that Christ was such.
- Tendencies: (*physis* ← [*ousia*] = (*hypostasis*] → *prosōpon*). *Ousia* and *hypostasis*, which are in square brackets, were synonyms, but *ousia* was increasingly identified with *physis*, and *hypostasis* with *prosōpon*.
- The Cappadocians distinguished *ousia* from *hypostasis* as that which characterized the species and the individual (that which is common and that which is particular). The Trinity has one *ousia* and three *hypostaseis*. They defined *hypostasis* in relational terms (see *schesis*).
- Although the next three points go beyond the scope of this textbook, it should be added that Cyril of Alexandria still used *hypostasis* and *physis* as synonyms in his Christological discourse.
- The Council of Chalcedon (AD 451) distinguished *hypostasis* from *physis*. Christ has one *hypostasis* and two *physeis*.
- Severus of Antioch, strictly following the Cyrillian use of terms, continued to employ the words *physis* and *hypostasis* as synonyms.

Essentia: "essence, substance, nature, being." A Latin equivalent to the Greek *ousia*. Since the word *essentia* is related to the verb "to be" (*esse*) and since *essentia* means "nature," it was concluded that the nature of God was "to be." "Essence is a reality which is" (Hilary of Poitiers, *Syn.* 12).

Substantia: "essential nature, makeup, something that stands under [notice the prefix *sub*-], the quality of being real or having actual existence." It is another Latin equivalent to *ousia*. However, *substantia* may have materialistic connotations (*substantia* as material of which a thing is made) which *ousia* does not necessarily have—unless it is understood in the Stoic sense. In earlier Christian usage, *substantia* was also a synonym of *hypostasis*, because *hypostasis* was not yet clearly distinguished from *ousia*. In the fourth century, Marius Victorinus still wrote, "The Greeks call 'to be' *ousian* or *hypostasin*; we call it in Latin by one term: substance [*substantia*]" (*De homousio recipi-*

endo). Ambrose agreed and used the phrase "substance or *ousia*" (*substantia vel ousia; De fide ad Gratianum* 1.18.120). Translating both *ousia* and *hypostasis* as *substantia* was bound to cause confusion and misunderstanding.

Subsistentia: another Latin equivalent to *hypostasis*. Some Latin authors avoided the ambiguity of translating both *ousia* and *hypostasis* with *substantia* by reserving *subsistentia* for translating *hypostasis*. That is, they used the word *subsistentia* for indicating the diversity of persons in the consubstantial Trinity.

Natura: "nature, substance, thing, particular characteristics, entity." A Latin equivalent to *physis*. It can refer to nature in general, to a specific nature, or to a specific thing. Being etymologically related to the verb "to be born" (*nascor*), *natura* has the sense of a thing sharing the nature of its origin.

Persona: a Latin equivalent to *prosōpon*. Its semantic equivalents include "the particular body" (*corpus*), "the particular soul" (*anima*), and "the particular human being" (*homo*). Boethius famously defined *persona* as "an individual substance of a rational nature" (*naturae rationabilis individua substantia; Opuscula sacra* 3.171–172), but the application of this anthropological definition to God was problematic, because the word *substantia* could be understood either as *ousia* or *hypostasis*. In modern Cartesian-Lockean usage, the term "person" means "center of consciousness," "power of self-determination," or "individuality," but these meanings should not be attributed to the word *persona* as it was used during the early centuries of the Trinitarian debates.

Dynamis (δύναμις): "power, potentiality." For pro-Nicenes, God's *dynamis* had a natural connotation (it belonged to God's nature); for anti-Nicenes, it had a volitional connotation (it belonged to God's [external] will as opposed to nature). With the Cappadocians, the pro-Nicene usage of the term *dynamis* prevailed. God's *dynamis* was understood as God's capacity for *ad extra* activities (creation, redemption). The causal sequence from nature to act was the following: *ousia* (nature) → *dynamis* (power) → *energeia* (activity) → *ergon* (act; M. Barnes 2001, 293, 303–4). The oneness of the divine power, which caused both the divine energies and acts, affirmed the consubstantiality and coeternity of the three divine persons. Latin equivalents of *dynamis* are *virtus* and *potentia*.

Energeia (ἐνεργεία): "activity, operation." Aristotle (*Physica* 1.191b) employed the word *energeia* as a correlate to the word *dynamis* (power). Both terms designated capacity and were associated with movement. In Christian discourse, God's *energeia* was understood as a characteristic activity of God's nature (*ousia*), which was produced by God's power (*dynamis*). That is, *energeia* was the activity of *dynamis*, which in turn belonged to *ousia*. Additionally, the distinction between God's nature (*ousia*) and God's energy (*energeia*) helped to clarify what could not be known and what could be known in God. God remained unknowable in God's essence, but God was known through God's energies, that is, through God's *ad extra* activities.

"His activities [*energeiai*] come down to us, but his nature [*ousia*] remains inaccessible" (Basil of Caesarea, *Epistula* 234.1). A Latin equivalent of *energeia* is *operatio*.

Ergon (ἔργον): "act, action, work, deed." A particular *ergon* is done by a person. An act is the actualization of an *energeia* and *dynamis* that the person has as a particular kind of being. In Trinitarian theology, this means that a particular *ergon* has to be attributed to one of the divine persons, yet so that all three consubstantial persons remain coactive in the same act. The fact that Father, Son, and Spirit act together through one of the divine *hypostaseis* testifies to the existence of one rather than three Gods. Confusingly, the Latin word *operatio* also translates the Greek *ergon*.

Idion (ἴδιον): "private, personal, characteristic property, that which is individual." The *Greek* term *idion* expressed the particular nonshared hypostatic properties of the Father, Son, and Holy Spirit (unbegottenness, begottenness, and procession). But since the word *idion* could also mean "one's own," it was also and somewhat confusingly employed for emphasizing the consubstantiality of the three divine *hypostaseis*—the Son and the Holy Spirit were the Father's "own" (they were not extrinsic to what the Father was).

Koinon (κοινόν): "common, public, that which is shared." The Greek term *koinon* designated the essential property, the divine nature (*ousia*), which the Father, Son, and Holy Spirit shared.

Schesis (σχέσις): "relation," synonym to the Aristotelian *ta pros ti* (things in relation to other things). *Schesis* designates the difference between the three divine *hypostaseis* and the mode of their origination. The Father is *unbegotten* (*agennētos*), the Son is *begotten* (*gennētos*) from the Father, and the Holy Spirit *proceeds* (*ekporeuetai*) from the Father (or from the Father and the Son [*filioque*]).

Perichōrēsis (περιχώρησις): "coinherence, interpenetration, rotation, 'going around something.'" It describes the dynamic intercommunion (*koinōnia*; as distinguished from "community") between the equally divine yet distinct persons of the Trinity. *Perichōrēsis* conveys the meaning of intimate closeness that never becomes identical. In Christian context, the word *perichōrēsis* was employed already by Gregory of Nazianzus, and by the time of John of Damascus, it had become a technical term.

Genētos-gennētos (γενητός-γεννητός): This pair of terms was originally more or less synonymous (as for Origen, Arius, Athanasius, and Eunomius). The Council of Antioch (AD 324/325) distinguished the "generation" of the Son from the "creation" of the world. Later the pro-Nicene theologians also distinguished *genētos* versus *agenētos*—"created" or "originated" versus "uncreated" or "unoriginated" on one hand; and *gennētos* versus *agennētos*— "begotten" versus "unbegotten" on the other hand. Father alone was *agennētos* (unbegotten); but Father, Son, and Holy Spirit were *agenētos* (uncreated).

Filioque: "and the Son." In the early Middle Ages, this Latin phrase was added to the Niceno-Constantinopolitan Creed, to the words "Holy Spirit proceeds from the Father." Since then, the Western church has confessed that the Holy Spirit proceeds "from the Father and the Son." The *filioque* clause became one of the main theological reasons for the mutual condemnation of Eastern and Western churches in 1054.

Homoousios (ὁμοούσιος): "the same essence, identity of substance, sharing of nature and essential properties, homogeneous." The Greek term *homoousios* was of pagan coinage (*Corpus hermeticum*). It could mean either the identity between two or more things, or that two or more distinct things have the same nature. There were several problems in adopting the word *homoousios* into orthodox Trinitarian discourse: it was unscriptural; common among the second-century Christian Gnostics; (mis)used by an adoptionist Paul of Samosata and condemned at the Council of Antioch (AD 268–269); rejected by Origenists; proposed by an unbaptized Emperor Constantine at the Council of Nicaea, arguably in consultation with his advisor bishop Hosius (Ossius) of Cordova; ignored by the Council of Sardica (or Serdica, AD 342/343) and by the very same bishop Hosius; and banned by the "Arian" Council of Sirmium (AD 357). However, Tertullian dropped a remark that is also valid for the term *homoousios*: "Truth must not therefore refrain from the use of such a term, and its reality and meaning, because heresy also employs it" (*Adversus Praxean* 8). Eventually, the word *homoousios* came to express the orthodox belief that the Father, Son, and Spirit were fully divine, for they and only they had the divine *ousia*. "The main point behind the use of this word [*homoousios*] was to exclude any idea that the Son was a different kind of reality from the Father, contingent and created" (*Confessing the One Faith*, 1991, 44). The Latin equivalent to the word *homoousios* is *consubstantialis*.

Homoiousios (ὁμοιούσιος): "the like essence." The term *homoiousios* was shorthand for the phrase *homoios kata tēn ousian* (like according to essence). Both designations were employed by Basil of Ancyra. He expected these to be suitable for both pro-Nicenes and Homoeans. Allegedly, the term *homoiousios* expressed a more clear distinction between the divine persons than the "modalist" *homoousios*. After AD 362, some Homoeousians joined the Athanasian pro-Nicenes.

Homoios (ὅμοιος): "like." Promoted by antimodalist Acacius of Caesarea. Homoeans tried to avoid the philosophically loaded term *ousia* and thus simply asserted that the Father and the Son were alike.

Anomoios (ἀνόμοιος): "unlike, dissimilar." Employed by Heteroousians Aetius and Eunomius. Unfortunately, the designation "Anomoeans" misrepresents the position of Aetius and Eunomius. They did not deny *any* likeness between the Father and the Son but only their *essential* likeness.

Heteroousios (ἑτεροούσιος): "other or dissimilar essence." It is a term of Aetius and Eunomius for distinguishing between the Father and the Son. The Father and the Son (and the Holy Spirit) are of a different nature.

On the scale of *homoousios* ↔ *heteroousios*, the four terms should be positioned as follows:

homoousios	*homoiousios*	*homoios*	*heteroousios* or *anomoios*

The imperial preferences for certain of these terms was designed to establish religious uniformity:

- *Homoousios*—Constantine; Council of Nicaea, AD 325
- *Homoiousios*—Constantius II, in 340s
- *Homoios*—Constantius II, in AD 359; Council of Constantinople, AD 360; Valens after Athanasius's death in AD 373; Valentinian II and his mother empress Justina after Gratian's death, in late 380s
- *Anomoios*—Constantius II, allegedly expressing his intention shortly before his death in AD 361
- *Homoousios* (again)—Theodosius; Council of Constantinople, AD 381; Gratian; Council of Aquileia, AD 381

Introduction to the Three Charts

While studying patristic Trinitarian theology, I constantly made charts, comparisons, and definitions for myself. Doing this helped me to learn. Even when I got things wrong and had to redo them, such schematic exercises helped me to clarify the issues and to correct my mistaken understandings. So, out of these sketches and scribbles, I have developed a few charts and a wordlist. My expectation is that these aids will facilitate the learning of those who take and read. Even for teachers, the charts and lists may suggest an idea or two, which they in turn could develop into a more elaborate presentation of Trinitarian theology. I recommend the *process* of creating charts. Composing such schematic presentations forces us to think the material through comparatively—and it certainly helps us to remember the material.

The idea of a chart with three titled columns (with their subdivisions) is taken from Novatian's daring comparison: "Indeed the Lord is crucified, as it were, between two thieves, ... and so he was exposed on either side to the impious revilings of the heretics" (*De Trinitate* 30). Creating rhetorical opposites for the purposes of refutation was a widespread practice in the patristic period. Hilary of Poitiers used the strategy of postulating the two extremes, Sabellians and Ebionites, in the middle of which he could then find Trinitarian orthodoxy (*Trin.* 1.26). Likewise, Gregory of Nazianzus understood his (orthodox) position as being the middle ground between modalists and Arians (*Or.* 20.5–6). Even though M. Barnes correctly calls such pro-Nicene juxtapositions "ahistorical summaries of the two rejected extremes" (in Fitzgerald 1999, 33), for the purposes of learning, it is indeed important to figure out the "other" against which a given theological trajectory defined its position.

So, what is one supposed to learn from the three charts? Above all, these charts provide a synoptic view of the search for Trinitarian orthodoxy throughout the centuries. They map the "landscape" of the Trinitarian beliefs of the early church. Well-known theologians and synods represent larger and internally diverse theological trajectories. The representative "boxes" are placed in relation to each other, so that their position on the created scale from oneness to threeness or from sameness to distinctness can be grasped at a glance. For example, the juxtaposing of the respective "boxes" helps us to see that Marcellus insisted on the sameness of the Father and the Son, and Eusebius on their distinctness. The charts depict theology rather than (strict) chronology. This means that various "boxes" often present contemporaneous theological positions. For example, Athanasius, in the second row of Chart Two, also conducted the Synod of Alexandria in AD 362, which is placed in the fourth row. The charts also show how radical one's position was. For example, Aetius and Eunomius represent an extreme trajectory that insisted on the essential unlikeness of the Father and the Son. On the other hand, Basil of Ancyra diverges just a bit from what came to be acknowledged as Trinitarian orthodoxy.

Next, readers are asked to pay attention to the changing titles of the columns in the three charts (Oneness—One and Three—Threeness; Sameness—Sameness and Distinctness—Distinctness; Sameness—Equal Divinity—Unequal Divinity). The issues shift from oneness or threeness to the sameness or distinctness of the three divine persons. In other words, the charts illustrate the shift from the issue of God's oneness to the issue of God's productivity. This shift can be observed from the diagonal movement: the early centuries provide more material for the left side of the charts, and the fourth century for the right side.

The titles in the central columns of all three charts ("One and Three," "Sameness and Distinctness," and "Equal Divinity of the Father, Son, and Holy Spirit") designate the positions that were eventually acknowledged as orthodox. The rejected views are found to the left and right of the orthodox positions. However, the positions presented on the left and right were seldom blunt heresies that disturbed the doctrinal quiet of the apostolic orthodoxy. Rather, they were expressions of alternative views and, as such, were equally part of the intra-ecclesiastical Trinitarian debates. Doctrinal orthodoxy "was created by argument and counter-argument" (Young in Mitchell and Young 2006, 452).

During controversies theological pronouncements are hardly ever perfectly balanced and cautiously nuanced. That which is said is polemical and pointed rather than pondered over and systematic. Accordingly, the central columns—the backbone of the three charts—are also not a completely straight vertical line. The central columns consist primarily of the professed beliefs of the first two ecumenical councils, which captured the Christian attempt to understand God's self-revelation as the Father, Son, and Holy Spirit. Depending on what position was corrected, the boxes in the central columns inevitably shift left and right. This takes us to the delicate issue of orthodoxy and heresy.

Orthodoxy and heresy are both *theological* categories. They concern doctrinal matters. Orthodoxy stands for rightness and normativity, heresy for deliberate and harmful falseness. For a secular "objective" observer, the whole issue of orthodoxy and heresy makes little sense and seems utterly strange and misguided. Yet, it matters for Christians and especially for seminarians who are going to be pastors, priests, and teachers in the Christian church. The very fact that the Niceno-Constantinopolitan Trinitarian theology is still taught in seminaries shows the continuous importance of orthodoxy. Concern for right doctrine is evident already in the writings of the New Testament (Rom 16:17; Gal 1:6–8; Titus 1:9). Not every teaching was welcomed in the name of greater inclusiveness, and tolerance was not mistaken for doctrinal relativism. True and false were true categories. Arguably, some false teachings were rejected for legitimate theological reasons, although political and ideological reasons often hid behind these theological reasons.

Some scholars think that the seminal Trinitarian orthodoxy found occasional recognition in various controversies until it finally blossomed at Nicaea. Such reading of the early theology prefers to begin with the Apostolic Fathers and detect progress in the subsequent provision of theological building blocks (technical terms, distinctions, and arguments). In this scheme of things, later theologians almost have to be better (meaning more orthodox, often less Platonist, and always more articulate) than earlier theologians, although all of them defended the already existing Trinitarian orthodoxy.

Others, including the author of this book, think that it is anachronistic to speak about Trinitarian orthodoxy before the end of the fourth century. They reject the view that orthodoxy and doctrinal unity were there before heresies challenged these. In other words, it was not that the church somehow knew Trinitarian orthodoxy before AD 381 and that its best sons and daughters only had to fight off heretical contesters after the apostolic period. Hanson (1988, 870) writes, "It should be perfectly clear that at the outset nobody had a single clear answer to the question raised, an answer which had always been known in the church and always recognized as true, one which was consistently maintained by one party throughout the whole controversy." One would indeed be hard pressed to find any early theologian whose deliberations about the Trinity would match exactly with the post-Constantinopolitan standards of orthodoxy. Thus, we can only say *in retrospect* that some beliefs were orthodox and others heretical. Because of such an understanding of things, in the charts, those who proved to be "heretics" are not placed outside the parameters of Christianity. "Heretics" as much as the orthodox were part of the process that led to the establishing of Trinitarian orthodoxy.

The three charts present the "Search for Trinitarian Orthodoxy and Rejected Extremes." It is a variation of the title of Hanson's (1988) magnificent monograph. I have borrowed (a part of) his title because the word "search" is extremely relevant for perceiving the emergence of Trinitarian orthodoxy. Namely, during the first four centuries, there was no established "patristic consensus" regarding the doctrine of the Trinity—unless patristic theology is reduced to the views of some in the central column. There were many competing arguments and alternative exegetical proposals for constructing the doctrine of the Trinity. In short, "search" seems to be the right word for the period under investigation in this textbook.

I also mention some problems I faced in composing these charts, because a reader will face the same problems in using these charts. First, historical reality is always more complex than a neat chart of that reality. Any schematic summary of the patristic Trinitarian debates in a form of charted boxes inevitably imposes more unity to the selected trajectories than is justified. For example, although

Hilary of Poitiers and Marius Victorinus were both pro-Nicenes, their theological positions were not identical. Hilary should be more on the right and Victorinus more on the left. But making the more subtle distinctions would require a separate box for each representative. Perhaps my grouping of the more-or-less similar theological positions into one box flies in the face of the contemporary tendency to diversify the theological groups and to deconstruct these as mere polemical constructs. However, grouping the more-or-less similar theological positions into one box and discussing just one or two of their representatives seems a legitimate pedagogical device.

Second, charting the early Trinitarian debates compelled me to create clearly identifiable boxes with no shadowy overlaps. Yet the similarity between the two figures in different boxes is often more significant than the difference. For example, the two Dionysii agreed that modalist views of the Trinity were incorrect. Despite all differences and mutual dislike, their Trinitarian theologies were much closer to each other than the separate boxes imply.

The options for teaching Trinitarian theology are either to provide short, simplified, and recognizable units, or to present the history of theology in its full messiness and never reach a presentation that can be grasped, understood, and remembered. Assuming that the former is a better option for instruction, I have charted theology despite the above-mentioned problems (cf. Bertrand de Margerie and his "Trinitariograms" [1982]). In a textbook I consider it more beneficial to move gradually away from the simplified black-and-white understanding of the subject matter than to be hopelessly confused from the very beginning.

Finally, the naming of the charted boxes has presented a major problem because many labels reflect bias and most often the pro-Nicene bias. For this reason I have decided to use the names of persons rather than the conventional names of the given theological positions. There are a few exceptions, though, such as the two types of Monarchianism and Latin Homoeans, because these designations are descriptive rather than pejorative. The only pejorative label that is retained is "Pneumatomachians" (Spirit-Fighters). If they are not named after their early leader Macedonius, no neutral name is really available for them. The designation "Pneumatomachians" at least indicates the issue that was debated—the full divinity of the Holy Spirit. A brief analysis of naming, an "Excursus on Naming," is provided in the commentary on Chart Two.

Charts

*Search for Trinitarian Orthodoxy
and Rejected Extremes*

Chart One: The First Three Centuries

	Oneness	One and Three, Triunity		Threeness
Non-Christian mono-theism		**Justin Martyr** The pre-existence of the Logos **Theophilus** *Logos* in the mind and *Logos* expressed (*logos endiathetos* and *logos prophorikos*) **Irenaeus** The doctrine of recapitulation (*anakephalaiosis*) defended both the oneness of God and the unity of God's threefold economic activity.		Non-Christian poly-theism
	Monarchianism 1. *Modalist* Oneness at the expense of the hypostatic difference (Sabellianism/ Modalism/ Patripassianism) **Praxeas, Noetus** The Son is a "mode" of the Father	**Origen** In God, there are three *hypostaseis;* the Son is eternally begotten from the Father		
	2. *Dynamic* Oneness at the expense of the divinity of the Son (Adoptionism/ Psilanthropism) **Paul of Samosata** The Son is a divinely powered human being.	**Tertullian** God is One substance and three persons (*una substantia in tribus coharentibus*) **Novatian** God is one; the Son is the "second person" (*secunda persona*) after the Father		
		Dionysius of Rome Father, Son, and Holy Spirit are *not* three *hypostaseis* (substances)	**Dionysius of Alexandria** Accused of promoting unbalanced Origenist subordinationism, he rejected *homoousios*.	

Chart Two: From the 320s to the 360s

	Sameness	Sameness and Distinctness		Distinctness	
Non-Christian mono-theism		**Alexander of Alexandria** The Father and the Son are coeternal. *Council of Nicaea* (325): The Son is of the same nature (*homoousios*) with the Father, not of a different *hypostasis* or *ousia*.		**Arius** The divine Son is the first created being.	Non-Christian poly-theism
	Marcellus of Ancyra The Father and the pre-existent Son are one *hypostasis*. *(Western) Synod of Sardica* (342/343)	**Athanasius** There are no distinctions between the Father and the Son on the level of nature (*ousia*)	**Eusebius of Caesarea** Emphasis on the hypostatic distinction within the Godhead. *Synod of Antioch* (340–341)		
		Cyril of Jerusalem The Son is eternally begotten from the Father.			
	Synod of Alexandria (362): *homoousios.* **Hilary of Poitiers** The Father and the Son are of the same nature. **Marius Victorinus** Three subsistences (*subsistentiae*) are of one substance (*substantia*) "to be": *homoousios.*	*Fourth Synod of Sirmium* (359) **Basil of Ancyra** Father and Son are of like nature: *homoiousios.*	**Acacius of Caesarea** Father and Son are alike: *homoios.*	**Aetius and Eunomius** Father and Son are of unlike nature: *hetero-ousios* or *anomoios.*	

Chart Three: The Second Half of the Fourth Century

Sameness	Equal Divinity of the Father, Son, and Holy Spirit		Unequal Divinity of the Father, Son, and Holy Spirit		
Late "nameless" Sabellians condemned at the Council of Constantinople	*Council of Constantinople* (381) **Basil of Caesarea** **Gregory of Nazianzus** **Gregory of Nyssa** "one nature, three hypostases" (*mia ousia treis hypostaseis*)		"Pneumato-machians" (Macedonians): The Son is consubstantial with the Father but the Holy Spirit is not.		**Aetius and Eunomius** Both the Son and Sprit are "unlike" (*anomoios*) the Father's nature, which is unbegotten (*agennētos*).
	Ambrose of Milan The common operation testifies to the substantial unity of the Godhead. **Augustine of Hippo** Father, Son, and Holy Spirit are coequal by nature and distinguished by relations; their operation is inseparable.			Latin Homoeans: The Father, Son, and Holy Spirit are of "like" (*similiter*) nature.	

Introduction to Commentary
on the Charts

The classical Trinitarian theology was established by working out the implications of the Christian faith given in *scriptural witness* and *daily worship*.

First, it was necessary to present adequately the biblical testimony concerning Father, Son, and Holy Spirit. The task was to maintain the divinity of the Son and the Spirit without giving up the monotheism Christianity inherited from Judaism (Mark 12:29; Rom 3:30). Speaking about God, the New Testament as well as the Apostolic Fathers and the Christian apologists made use of triadic formulas (e.g., Matt 28:19; Rom 15:30; 1 Cor 6:11; 12:4–6; Heb 10:29; 1 Pet 1:2; *1 Clement* 46.6; 58.2; Ignatius, *To the Magnesians* 13; *To the Ephesians* 9; Justin, *1 Apology* 13). These triadic formulas were the raw material for the emerging doctrine of the Trinity. Yet the mere existence and piling up of these formulas does not explain the emergence of Trinitarian theology; a case for the Trinity had to be made before one could speak about Trinitarian theology in the proper sense of the word.

Second, *lex orandi, lex credendi*; the rule of prayer lays down the rule of faith! Christians "revere and worship him [the Father], and the Son, . . . and the prophetic Spirit" (Justin, *1 Apol.* 6). The fact that the Son and the Spirit were worshipped together with the Father needed a theological justification, because to worship anything besides God or less than God was idolatry.

Scholars often assert that while the Scriptures and worship provided the data for Trinitarian theology, the *philosophy* of the day provided the conceptual means for explicating the belief in the Triune God. Philosophy no doubt helped the early Trinitarian theologians to spell out their beliefs. But philosophy had a much more basic role in the formation of Trinitarian theology than merely lending its discourse for articulation. It contributed to the greater coherence of theological statements.

On the other hand, the search for adequate theological language was relativized by belief in God's transcendence. Ever since Clement of Alexandria, it was emphasized that any language, be it biblical or philosophical, came radically short in disclosing God (*Strom.* 5.12). To say that God was "dazzling" or "beautiful" was as inadequate as to say that God was "one *ousia* and three *hypostaseis*." Augustine's apophatic maxim put it this way, "If you comprehend something, it is not God" (*Sermo* 117.5). Yet, as mentioned in Part 1, our object of study is not the Triune God in Godself, but the *doctrine* of the Triune God. Although the former is incomprehensible, the latter should be comprehensible.

On Chart One

The First Three Centuries

Chart One represents the early phase of the search for Trinitarian orthodoxy under three titles "Oneness," "One and Three," and "Threeness." The Christian discussion of the Trinitarian theology took place in the historical context of non-Christian monotheism and polytheism, as indicated by the marginal columns.

God's Oneness

There were several *non-Christian monotheisms*, but in emphasizing God's oneness, Jewish monotheism (belief in one God) and pagan henotheism (belief in one supreme God among the lesser gods) were the closest to Christianity.

Jewish Monotheism

At least since the time of David and Solomon, the Israelites called YHWH "one" (Deut 6:4) and "[God] alone" (Deut 32:12). God was wholly other and utterly distinct from all other beings. Monotheism is not henotheism. Monotheism denies the existence of other gods. "I am God, and there is no other; I am God, and there is no one like me" (Isa 46:9). "This is our God; no other can be compared to him" (Bar 3:35). The *Shema* ("The LORD is our God, the LORD alone" [Deut 6:4]) was and is said by Jews every morning and evening. Pro-Nicene theologians labeled Arian and Heteroousian (see below) theology "Jewish" because they refused to acknowledge the divinity of the Son and the Spirit (e.g., Gregory of Nyssa, *C. Eun.* 1.15, 21).

Furthermore, only God has always existed. Everything else, including the creation and created spiritual beings, comes into being from nothing (*ex nihilo*; 2 Macc 7:28; Rom 4:17) and is therefore contingent. But God never comes into being or ceases to be. God eternally *is*.

Pagan Henotheism

From Platonism to Neoplatonism, many philosophers believed in the existence of one Ultimate Being above the other lesser divinities. Plato argued that there could be but one "First Principle," the Good (*Respublica* 505a–509b). Aristotle agreed, at least as far as the issue of God's oneness was concerned. Although his God, too, was impersonal, Aristotle argued that there was only one "Unmoved Mover," the divine Mind (*Metaphysica* 1072a21–27; *De anima* 430a22–23). The Neoplatonist Plotinus called the ultimate cause of everything "the One"(*Enn.* V.4.1). Belief in one ultimate cause of everything is henotheism (*hen* in "henotheism" means "one").

Readers should note an important difference between Jewish monotheism and pagan henotheism, even though both insisted on the oneness of God. The Greek Ultimate Being was *neuter* (*to on*; e.g., Plato, *Timaeus* 27d), whereas a Jewish Platonist Philo insisted that the God of Israel was *masculine* (*ho ōn*, Exod 3:14). The point was not that YHWH was masculine rather than feminine, but that YHWH was *personal* rather than *impersonal*.

Christian Trinitarian Monotheists

For Christians, in the three middle columns of the chart, the primary issue was: If God were one, how could God be the Father, Son, and the Holy Spirit? The obvious problem was to reconcile God's oneness—emphasized both by Jewish monotheism and pagan henotheism—with the divinity of the Son and the Spirit. This very problem shows that God's oneness was presupposed. So, in order to affirm the full divinity of the Son and the Spirit, a new and qualified case for the oneness of God had to be made, for Christians did not want to affirm "one God in an impious sense" (Hilary of Poitiers, *Trin.* 5.1). Apologist Athenagoras worded a resolution by saying that Christians "set forward God the Father and God the Son and the Holy Spirit and . . . declare both their power in unison and their distinction in order" (*Legatio pro Christianis* 10).

Monarchianism

I will begin my commentary on Christian Trinitarian positions from the second column from the left under the title "Oneness." First, consider the solutions to the problem of God's oneness that were rejected as inadequate.

Tertullian called the Christians who believed in God's undiversified unity "Monarchians" (*Prax.* 3 and 9; cf. Theophilus of Antioch, *Ad Autolycum* 2.4). The word "Monarchian" comes from the Greek word *monarchia*, from *monos* (alone) and *archē* (principle). Monarchianism was a predominately Western Trinitarian doctrine of the second–third century that came to be rejected by the so-called *Logos*-theologians (see below). Monarchianism emphasized the absolute oneness of God either at the expense of personal distinctions within the Godhead or at the expense of Christ's divinity. Accordingly, Adolf von Harnack, a great nineteenth-century historian of dogma, distinguished between two kinds of Monarchian: *modalist Monarchians* and *dynamic Monarchians*. Modalist Monarchians denied personal distinctions within the Godhead, while dynamic Monarchians denied Christ's divinity.

Two obvious but ultimately heretical solutions suggested themselves to some of the early Christian theologians who defended God's oneness against the Gnostics: either the Son was the Father (Isa 45:54; John 10:30), or the Son was inferior to the Father (John 14:28). In other words, either there was only nominal and not real difference between the Father and the Son, or there was a fundamental ontological difference between the Father and the Son. As Origen wrote:

> Many people who wish to be pious are troubled because they are afraid that they may proclaim two Gods. . . . They either deny that the individual nature of the Son is other than that of the Father, . . . or they deny the divinity of the Son and make his individual nature and essence as an individual to be different from the Father. (*Commentarii in evangelium Joannis* 2.16)

Both modalist and dynamic Monarchians had a legitimate and honorable task: to rescue the oneness of God, who was according to both the Scriptures and philosophy "the Most High God" (*ho theos hypsistos*). Even their critic Hippolytus commended them for being concerned with the legitimate task, "For it is right . . . to expound the truth that the Father is one God" (*Contra haeresin Noeti* 8). The protoorthodox theologians in the middle column agreed with the Monarchians' premise about God's oneness, but not with their conclusions. Later, Hilary of Poitiers pointed out that theologically misguided people "preach those doctrines which are to be denied by means of those doctrines that are not denied" (*Trin.* 7.1).

A caution: it is not at all clear what these early Monarchian dissenters actually taught. The authentic writings of theologians condemned as heretics are seldom extant. Refutations of their views are often the only evidence we have for what they actually taught, but citations for the purposes of refutation are impartial if not distorted. Also, the names of Monarchian theologians were used for labeling later heresies, and therefore their authentic positions were easily confused with later views. In addition, it is unlikely that Monarchians formed a "movement." And finally, the fact that these statements by "heretics" do not measure up with later orthodoxy does not necessarily make them some kind of theological villains. Monarchians of all kinds arguably did not try to teach distorted Trinitarian theologies, but once again, they were merely trying to defend the oneness of God.

Modalist Monarchians

Also known as Sabellians, the modalist Monarchians sought the solution to God's oneness on the side of God, within the Godhead. They refused to posit a separate divine being besides God the Father either from eternity or from the time of creation. Modalist Monarchians thought that by such refusal they salvaged both the oneness of God and the divinity of the Son and the Spirit. For them, the *Logos*-theology of Justin and Tertullian, which introduced plurality into the Godhead, seemed simply too Platonic, if not Gnostic. Modalist Monarchians taught that the one God had revealed Godself as Father, Son, and Holy Spirit. "The Father is the same, the Son is the same, the Holy Spirit is the same," asserted Sabellius (Epiphanius, *Pan.* 62.1.4). The names "Father," "Son," and "Spirit" referred only to the temporary *modes* of God's economic activity. They were not the eternal distinctions within the one Godhead (cf. "for as yet there was no Spirit"; John 7:39 in manuscripts $\mathfrak{P}^{66}$ and $\aleph$). Substantially speaking, God was one; nominally speaking, God was Father, Son, and Holy Spirit. Noetus, following John 14:10, "I am in the Father and the Father is in me," reportedly said that "Christ was the Father himself" (Hippolytus, *Noet.* 1). Noetus was not arguing against the divinity of Christ. Rather, he overdid the matter and identified Christ, the Son, with the Father. The Spirit in the incarnated Son *was* the Father (Hippolytus, *Refutatio omnium haeresium* 10.23). Indeed, did not John 4:24 assert that "God *is* Spirit"? (In Greek, the verb "is" is implied.)

"Patripassianism" is another name for the Monarchian doctrine that God the Father suffered in the "mode" of the Son. According to Tertullian, Praxeas was not able to distinguish the absolute Deity from the suffering *Logos*. Praxeas taught that God the Father was born, suffered, and died (Tertullian, *De praescriptione haereticorum* 7). This view was considered most ridiculous, because by definition God was understood as being impassible. Praxeas had "put to flight the Paraclete and crucified the Father" (Tertullian, *Prax.* 1).

Dynamic Monarchians

Dynamic Monarchians sought the solution to God's oneness on the side of Christ's humanity. Paul of Samosata seems to have taught that Christ was a human being who received the enabling divine power (*dynamis*, Acts 10:38; Rom 1:4). For him, the oneness of God was rescued by making the divinity of Christ an impersonal force empowering the human Jesus (cf. Ps 45:7; 110:3; Mark 1:10; please read!). Alternatively, Paul of Samosata may be understood as saying that the *Logos*, who was the one God, inspired the man Jesus.

Dynamic Monarchianism is also known as *Adoptionism* or *Psilanthropism* (*psilos anthrōpos*, "mere man"; Eusebius, *Historia ecclesiastica* 5.28.1–2). Adoptionism taught that Jesus was a human being uniquely chosen to be the divine "Son" (Luke 1:35; John 19:5; Acts 2:22, 36; please read these too!). Dynamic Monarchians/adoptionists were divided, however, over the question of whether Jesus, who became *Christ*, ever became *God* (Hippolytus, *Haer.* 7.23).

At least since the fourth century, the earlier dynamic Monarchians were accused of denying the preexistence of Christ. According to Eusebius, Paul of

Samosata taught that "Jesus Christ is from below" and that "the Son of God has not come down from heaven" (*Hist. eccl.* 7.30). Dynamic Monarchians further explained that Jesus' baptism was not the moment when Jesus Christ was *revealed* as the Son of God, but rather the moment when Jesus *became* the Son of God (Ps 2:7; Luke 3:22, which in some old Latin manuscripts reads, "Today I have begotten you"). Countering such understanding of things, Christmas, the Feast of the Incarnation (December 25), had to be separated from the Feast of Epiphany, which commemorated Jesus' baptism (January 6).

To recapitulate, some of the early theologians tried to rescue God's oneness either by seeking the solution on the side of God (modalist Monarchianism, or patripassianism, or Sabellianism) or on the side of Christ's humanity (dynamic Monarchianism, or adoptionism). Both solutions came to be rejected. Against modalist Monarchians, it was pointed out that, by definition, God could not die, and that Jesus did not address himself when he prayed to his Father. Against dynamic Monarchians, it was asserted that even a death of an extremely empowered prophet could not atone for the sins of humankind.

The two equally unsatisfactory forms of the Monarchian doctrine of the Trinity caused the early protoorthodox theologians to look for ways to express the distinctions within one God so that neither the oneness of God nor the divinity of the Son (and Spirit) was surrendered. The Christian God was understood to be "one in a new way," that is, including the Son and the Spirit (Tertullian, *Prax.* 31). A later author, Gregory of Nazianzus, worded this "new way" as follows: "As soon as I begin to contemplate the Unity, the Trinity bathes me in its splendor. As soon as I begin to think of the Trinity, I am seized by the Unity" (*Or.* 40.41).

Gnostics

Gnostics do not appear in Chart One because their primary problem was neither God's oneness nor threeness but matter (including Jesus' physical body). The (Christian) Gnostics argued that the supreme spiritual God could not have had a direct contact with matter. Therefore, *Gospel of Philip* 75 asserted that an inferior creator-God rather than the supreme God made the material world, and he made it by "mistake." The material world as a "mistake" was dualistically severed from the divine realm called "fullness" (*plērōma*), and the supreme God from the creator of the material world (the Demiurge). Irenaeus complained:

> They [Gnostics] dream of a nonexistent being above the true God, believing that they have discovered the great God, whom no one can know, who does not communicate with human beings, and who exercises no direction over earthly affairs. (*Haer.* 3.24.2)

Consequently, Gnostics needed to postulate the existence of certain hierarchical emanations or aeons, which mediated between the transcendent supreme

God and the created world. Hippolytus spoke about "their Trinity," by which he meant the Gnostics' tripartite understanding of the universe (*Haer.* 5.12). Thus, at least some Gnostic Christians can be placed, theologically not chronologically, into the third column in Chart Three: "Unequal Divinity of the Father, Son, and Holy Spirit." The Valentinian *Tripartite Tractate* spoke about the monadic Father as "the root of all totality," "the first one," "unbegotten," "incomprehensible," and "over the Totalities" (51–53, 63; cf. *Eugnostos the Blessed*, 1.71–73); and about the Son as "from the beginning," "comprehensible," and "partaking of the Totalites" (57, 63). As the beginning of multiplicity and aeonic emanations (notice that Heb 1:3 calls the Son "effulgence" [*apaugasma*]), the Son is neither the Father nor equal to the Father. The "third" in this Valentinian Gnostic Trinity, however, is not the Holy Spirit, but the [aeon] Church (57).

Another Gnostic treatise, *Apocryphon of John*, mentioned an alternative aeonic Trinity: "I [am the Father], I am the Mother, I am the Son" (1.2). This Trinity evolved from the ineffable Monad (2–4; Irenaeus, *Haer.* 1.29.1). The Father was contemplating himself and thus produced multiplicity, the (hypostatic) aeon Mother (or Wisdom or "the First Thought"; 4–6). The Son, the "only-begotten of the Mother-Father (*mētropatōr*)," was generated as the third member of the divine triad, who "created everything" through lower emanations (14, 16 and 7–8).

Because the supreme God could not have had a direct contact with matter, some Gnostics insisted that the Savior Jesus only seemed (*dokeō*) to have a human body (cf. Rom 8:3, God sent his Son "in the *likeness* of sinful flesh" [emphasis added]). Savior Jesus in no way submitted to the "enemy" who was responsible for the creation of the material world (cf. 1 John 4:2; 2 John 7)! Rather, he came to save us from material existence, from bodies. (It is a rather curious position because if you really believe thus, you should kill yourself!) According to Gnostic docetists, the spiritual Jesus merely entered into the human Jesus at his baptism, without ever assuming flesh, and left it at his crucifixion. The docetic doctrine was the key to the Scripture "My God, why have you forsaken me?" (Matt 27:46; cf. *Gospel of Philip* 68). The *Gospel of Peter* described Jesus as crying out, "My power, . . . you have forsaken me" (19). *Acts of John*, in turn, reported the words of Christ, "Nor am I [the man] who is on the cross. . . . I have suffered none of these things which they will say of me" (99–101). "For I did not die in reality but in appearance" (*Second Treatise of the Great Seth* 55). Curiously, even the canonical Heb 2:9, according to various minuscules and patristic quotes, mentions the man Jesus dying "apart from God [*chōris theou*]."

Now, the absolute oneness of God, at least in its traditional sense, seemed to be threatened by the opening statement of the Fourth Gospel: "The Word was with God, and the Word was God" (1:1). As an early critic of Christianity, Celsus pointed out that worship of Jesus, the divine Word, was simply inconsistent with monotheism (Origen, *Cels.* 8.14). Philo, who hardly had Christians in mind, wrote nevertheless that the *Logos* served as (the ultimate) God for those who were not "fully enlightened" (*Quaestiones et solutiones in Genesin* 3.34).

As already pointed out, chronologically speaking, the first Trinitarian problem was, "How can the one God be both Father and Son? How can God be both one and many?" Curiously, even in pagan philosophy and Judaism, there were notions that suggested the existence of certain plurality within the one God. Hence, I introduce the middle column through the wider contextual margin, working with the column on the far right.

God's Threeness

In antiquity, there were many forms of non-Christian polytheisms. The hierarchical organization of various gods in polytheistic religions was one of the wider religious contexts for the emerging Trinitarian theology. However, pagan polytheisms do not provide a close comparison to the Christian concept of the Triune God because Christianity was/is a monotheistic religion. Therefore, I will consider only the non-Christian but monotheistic or henotheistic thought-systems that nevertheless pondered about plurality in the one God.

Henotheistic Platonists

Perhaps surprisingly, henotheistic Platonists deliberated whether the Ultimate Being contained any plurality. Should the *arché* or the First Principle of all things be understood in a monist or a pluralist sense?

Plato assessed the concept of the One (*Hen*) as both a simple and a complex unity (*Parmenides* 142b–155e). He also recognized the analogy of numbers, which needed both unity and plurality (*Phaedrus* 96e–97b). The tendency for the hierarchical understanding of the Ultimate Principle can be seen in the *Timaeus*, where Plato suggested the existence of the Demiurge. In *Timaeus* 28c, Plato mentions God as "Father and Creator of all." Was he speaking of one being with two names, or two beings? Is there a Creator God the Father, or a supreme deity *and* a Demiurge?

Middle Platonist philosophers, in turn, affirmed the multiplicity in the first principle by conceptualizing the Ultimate God as the Mind (*Nous*) with reason/word (*logos*). The monad was the Mind which contemplated the ideas (*eidē*; Xenocrates, *Frg.* 16; Alcinous, *Didaskalikos* 9.3).

Plotinus, the Neoplatonist, tackled the problem of how the One could produce multiplicity that it did not contain (*Enn.* V.2.15). He "delayed" the problem by attributing both simplicity and multiplicity to the divine Mind as distinct from the absolutely simple, the One, which he rescued from all multiplicity. While the One was absolutely simple, the Mind included multiplicity, because thinking was distinct from the object of thought. Proclus, who indirectly influenced later Christian thought through Pseudo-Dionysius, also postulated entities which were "both one and not one" (*hen esti kai ouk hen, Stoicheiosis theologikē* Prop. 2 and 4; cf. Pseudo-Dionysius, *De divinis nominibus* 13.2). These entities or henads were distinct from the One, and also posterior (*deuteron*) to the One (Prop. 5).

Jewish Concept of God

The Jewish concept of God was monotheistic, as was the Christian concept of God. Yet, the problem of unity and plurality of God haunted also Jewish thinkers. In Judaism, there were personified divine attributes, such as Wisdom (e.g., Prov 8; Sir 24), the plural "we" (e.g., Gen 1:26), God's inner dialogue (e.g., Ps 110:1), mediating angels, and theophanies. The intra-Judaic interpretations of these cases varied. Nevertheless, such cases suggested the existence of some plurality within the one God. The Scriptures also included a reference to the plurality of thrones (Dan 7:9), and therefore the later Midrashic Merkavah mysticism developed a kind of "proto-Binitarianism" as it speculated about Metatron and the "Two Powers." Most important, Philo spoke about God's *Logos*, whom he also called "his own firstborn son" (*De somniis* 1.125). Philo purged the Stoic doctrine of *logos* of materialistic connotations and submitted it to a process of "hypostatization." He understood the *Logos* sometimes as a comprehensible aspect of God, and other times as a relatively independent *hypostasis*. Although Philo's deliberations on the *Logos* had only a limited value for Christians, later authors were quite convinced that Philo was a proto-Trinitarian, if not an "anonymous Christian." A fifth-century theologian, Isidore of Pelusium, wrote, "Philo, though a Jew, . . . gained a conception of the most royal (or highest) Trinity, . . . which is more unified than wholly discrete entities but richer than what is truly monadic" (Runia in Evans 2004, 83).

One and Three: Christian Trinitarian Monotheists

Christians affirmed the belief in the divinity of the Son (and the Spirit) without thereby denying the oneness of God. The doctrine of the Trinity was "imposed" on Christians by the fact of the resurrection of Christ. The doctrine of the Trinity was a postresurrection doctrine (Wilken 2003).

In the New Testament are several passages and variant readings that identify Jesus Christ explicitly as "God" (Luke 9:20; John 1:18; Col 2:2; 1 Tim 3:16; 2 Pet 1:2 [see the Greek]). Agreeing with John 1:1; 20:28; and the above-mentioned and supposedly anti-adoptionist textual variants, the author of *2 Clement* urged his readers, "Brethren, we must think of Jesus Christ as of God [*theos*]"

(1.1). Considering Christ as God, in turn, led to the discussion of God's productivity (the divine Father begetting the divine Son). It remained the main topic of discussion until the mid-fourth-century pneumatological controversy (the controversy about the full divinity of the Holy Spirit).

The so-called *Logos-theology* operated with the scriptural idea of the Son as the Word (*Logos*) of God. *Logos*-theology emerged as a response to strict Jewish monotheism and pagan henotheism. It continued as a response to Christian Monarchianism. The protoorthodox apologists understood that the unity and diversity within the Godhead had to be somehow kept together. Origen worded the difficult task, "But as our brethren take offense at the statement that there are two Gods, we must formulate the doctrine carefully, and show in what sense they are two and in what the two are one God" (*Dialogus cum Heraclide* 1). Yet, many non-Christians wondered together with "Epicurean and Stoic philosophers," who said after hearing Paul, "What on earth is he trying to say?" (a paraphrase of Acts 17:18).

In short, the task for the Christian theologians was to show in what sense God was one and in what sense God's oneness was manifold. The task was to show how the Father, Son, and Spirit were "one in distinction and divided in unity" (Gregory of Nazianzus, *Or.* 23.8). Assessing their own Trinitarian monotheism, Christians tried to find a way to introduce the principle of plurality into monotheism without ever going too close to polytheism. In the words of Gregory of Nazianzus:

> When I say the word "God," I mean Father, Son, and Holy Spirit: we do not speak of the Divinity as being spread out beyond them, lest we introduce a whole crowd of gods, nor as held within limits short of them, lest we be accused of being stingy with divinity—speaking like Jews by emphasizing the divine monarchy, or speaking like Greeks by emphasizing the divine abundance. (*Or.* 38.8)

Justin Martyr

A second-century apologist, Justin admitted that Christians worshiped a Triune God, "the most true God, the Father, . . . the Son, . . . and the prophetic Spirit" (*1 Apol.* 6; cf. Athenagoras, *Leg.* 10). The plurality of persons within the Godhead was manifested in the economy. In the economical order, the Son was "second" (*deuteros*) and the Holy Spirit "third" (*triton*; *1 Apol.* 13). Such economic "multiplication" was not dividing the one divine nature (*Dialogus cum Tryphone* 128). Rather, it was manifesting the eternal uniplurality of God. ("Uniplurality" is Bertrand de Margerie's neologism, which designates both the unity and the plurality of the Triune God.)

Justin insisted on the doctrine of the preexistence of the Son in order to protect the divinity of the Son, the "second" or "another [*allos*] God" (*Dial.* 56–62;

cf. Athenagoras, *Leg.* 10). He introduced the term *prohyparchein* (to preexist). Although it is a temporal designation (with the prefix *pro-*), the term *prohy-parchein* conveyed the truth that the Son existed eternally. Justin attempted to explicate philosophically what the Prologue of the Gospel of John stated poetically: the Son was the eternal God, although he was begotten and thus distinct from the Father. The Son (or the *Logos*) was the eternal offspring (*gennēma*) of the Father (*Dial.* 62).

> (Whether Christ's preexistence is implied in the letters of Paul, including Phil 2:6–11, has been a heated debate among contemporary New Testament scholars. However, the fact remains that, in the Christian canon, Paul's letters are read *after* the Gospel of John, and thus with an understanding that "the Word was with God" and "the Word was God.")

There is another interesting assertion of Justin that later enabled Arius to appeal to an ancient tradition: the Son is said to have been "begotten of the Father by an act of will [*toi patrikoi boulēmati*]" (*Dial.* 61). Unlike Arius, however, Justin did not juxtapose will against nature so that one would exclude the other. All he was saying was that the eternal begetting of the Son, whatever else it was, was a volitional act.

Theophilus of Antioch

Another second-century apologist, Theophilus, seems to have been the first to use the (Greek) word *trias* for God, God's Word, and Wisdom (*Autol.* 2.15). The word *trias* denotes threeness, but unlike the Latin *trinitas*, it has no connotation of *unitas* and thus lacks the creative tension between threeness and oneness.

Theophilus distinguished between "the word in the mind" and "the word expressed" (*logos endiathetos* and *logos prophorikos*) as he applied the analogy of the mind and word to the Father and the Son (cf. Isa 55:11; Sir 24:3; Ignatius, *Magn.* 8.2b; Athenagoras, *Leg.* 10). In Stoicism, where this linguistic/epistemological distinction originated, it was never applied to theology. According to Theophilus, like a word in the mind, the *Logos* was in God and yet distinct from the Father (*Autol.* 2.10). Furthermore, the expressed *Logos* did not empty the Mind of the *Logos* (*Autol.* 2.22). This was important, because God had to be eternally wise and rational (God always had to have his *Logos*).

In time, the mind/word analogy proved to be a fruitful yet controversial comparison. It could be interpreted either in a modalist, Arian, or orthodox sense. First, the noncontroversial aspect of this analogy: it guaranteed the causal priority of the Father. Theophilus pointed out that the Father's mind functioned as the "governing principle" (*archē*) in regard to the Word (*Autol.* 2.10). However, some controversial implications were also discerned in the analogy of the word as thought and expressed. On one hand, a word as a mind-dependent reality could obscure the reality of the Word having its distinct subsistence. The concept of *logos endiathetos* could deny the Word's individual *hypostasis*. Consequently, all kinds of modalists found this analogy quite helpful. On the other hand, the analogy of internal and expressed word could suggest the subordination, inferiority, and even the mere potential existence of the Son. Arians and other subordinationists welcomed these implications. Thus, eventually the distinction between *logos endiathetos* and *logos prophorikos* became suspect in the eyes of the orthodox. In fact, Irenaeus, Ambrose, and Athanasius rejected the analogy, and it was explicitly condemned at the Council of Sirmium in AD 351. Nevertheless, the analogy continued to be employed in a qualified sense by some orthodox authors, such as Augustine.

Irenaeus

This leading second-century theologian posited his theology of God against both Gnostic hierarchical ordering of the divine realm and their differentiating God the Father from the Creator God. Irenaeus emphasized that there was but *one* God the Creator (*Haer.* 2.1.1; 3.9–10). This one God the Creator became manifest as Father, Son (or Word), and Spirit (or Wisdom) in economy. To be anachronistic in the use of terminology, Irenaeus explained that the "theological Trinity" was revealed as the "economical Trinity." In economy, God in Godself became known as Father, Son, and Holy Spirit.

One of the reasons why Irenaeus rejected the *logos endiathetos* and *logos prophorikos* analogy was precisely that it seemed to do justice to cosmology and economy, but not to *theology* (to the "theological Trinity"). As we have seen, the Stoic nontheological distinction had some unwanted implications when applied to the generation of the Son from the Father, such as posteriority and inferiority (the Son being later and less than the Father; *Haer.* 2.13.8; 2.28.5). Because of his anti-Gnostic polemic, Irenaeus avoided anything that threatened the unity of God, even if by implications.

Irenaeus called the Son and the Spirit "the two hands of God" (*Haer.* 4.20.1; 5.6.1; a combination of Ps 119:73 and Gen 1:26), which were "instrumental" in creating the world. He did not thereby consider the Son and Spirit lesser divinities or some kind of Gnostic subordinate emanations. Rather, the Son and the Spirit were part of the internal life of God. How exactly this was the case remained beyond human comprehension. Irenaeus did not speculate about the "theological Trinity."

Instead of speculating about "theological Trinity," about God in Godself, Irenaeus proposed a soteriological argument for defending both the oneness of God and the unity of God's threefold economic activity: a doctrine of recapitulation (*anakephalaiōsis*; cf. Eph 1:10; Phil 2:9–11). True, the verb *anakephalaioomai* was only occasionally used as a designation of God's being one, for its primary use was to denote the consummation of salvation history. The economy required the operation of the Father, Son, and Holy Spirit (*Haer.* 3.6.1). Human beings, both body and soul (*Haer.* 5.6.1), were created by the Father through his Word and Wisdom, and brought back to God by the incarnation of the Son and deification by the Spirit. To simplify: in the "theological Trinity," the movement is from the Father through the Son and to the Spirit, but in the "economical Trinity" the movement is from the Spirit through the Son to the Father. "The Spirit prepares the human being through the Son of God, the Son leads him to the Father, and the Father gives him incorruption in eternal life" (*Haer.* 4.20.5). This is recapitulation (*anakephalaiōsis*) and also an affirmation of the unity of God's threefold economic activity.

In connection with Irenaeus's theology of God, it is proper to make an important observation. In patristic theology there was really no abstract metaphysical discussion of God in Godself; there was virtually no discussion of "onto-theology" apart from economy, soteriology, and other theological doctrines. Thus, we should not read back into patristic theology the situation where "the Trinity has become an abstract concept that seems to say something about God but does not affect any other Christian doctrines" (Lorenzen, 1999, 2).

Origen, Tertullian, and Novatian

Despite their differences, what unites these second-generation *Logos*-theologians is the shared anti-Monarchian context. The chart places them in the middle column, as defenders of the emerging protoorthodox doctrine of the Trinity. Even so, a reader should resist the urge to force these early theologians to utter something pro-Nicene. The "rule of faith" (*regula fidei*) taught them that God was Father, Son, and Holy Spirit, and they started to see the implications of this conviction for the doctrine of God. Origen, Tertullian, and Novatian did not get everything "right" in the Niceno-Constantinopolitan sense of the word, for many aspects of the orthodox Trinitarian theology remained to be sorted out. In other words, Origen, Tertullian, and Novatian did not have the privilege of assessing their Trinitarian deliberations from the point of the later conciliar orthodoxy.

Although Tertullian (d. ca. 220) lived a bit earlier than Origen (d. 253), it might be helpful to consider his anti-Monarchian Trinitarian theology after looking at Origen's Trinitarian theology; arguably, in this way certain issues can be comprehended more easily. Here the chart follows the order of discussion rather than the strict order of chronology.

Origen

Origen's theology is an important milestone, because comparable Trinitarian "systems" of Christian theology emerged only in the fourth century. This delay may be partially due to persecutions. Origen distinguished between the three divine *hypostaseis* (*Comm. Jo.* 2.75), argued for the doctrine of the monarchy of the Father (*De principiis* 4.4.1), and assigned the three *hypostaseis* their "special activities" (*Princ.* 1.3.7–8). Nevertheless, he balanced all this with the doctrine of the eternal generation of the Son (*Princ.* 1.2.4; *Homiliae in Jeremiam* 9.4–5). Precisely because Origen coupled his causal subordinationism (see below) with the eternal generation of the Son, he can be placed with protoorthodox theologians in the middle column of the chart.

The basic postulate in Origen's Trinitarian theology was the affirmation of the one God (*heis theos*; *Princ.*, Pref. 4; *Dial.* 3). However, "one God" did not only mean that there were no other gods and that God and the Father of Jesus Christ were the same God; it also meant that God was simple and indivisible. Those who introduced divisions into God (e.g., Marcionites and Valentinians) missed the point that, in simple realities, parts came after the whole (*Princ.* 1.1.6). They also missed the fact that "God is spirit" (John 4:24) and that spiritual or incorporeal realities could not have parts. Only material entities could be compound (they can consist of parts), and only in compound realities do parts come before the whole.

Consider the philosophical context: a Platonist philosopher, Alcinous, had explained that the supreme God was "partless, by reason of the fact that there is nothing prior to him" (*Didask.* 10.7; cf. Plato, *Parm.* 137c). A Neoplatonist, Plotinus, in turn established the "Principle of Prior Simplicity" (to use O'Meara's 1995 phrase), which stated that composite realities derived from that which was not composite. "What is not simple is in need of those which are simple in it so that it may be from them," argued Plotinus (*Enn.* V.4.1).

For Origen, the fundamental doctrine of God's simplicity had certain qualifications, however, because the simple God was not a simple concept. Echoing certain philosophical discussions about the complex (but not composite) unity of God, Origen argued that the Christian discussion should neither separate the three divine persons according to their nature nor collapse them into one being (*Comm. Jo.* 2.16).

Together with Irenaeus, Origen asserted that the complex unity (the uniplurality) of the one and simple God became evident in economy (cf. Matt 11:27). The one God "becomes many things" (*polla ginetai*) in order to redeem the creation (*Comm. Jo.* 1.119). The important thing here is again that the uniplurality of the one God was not established in incarnation but *became manifest* in incarnation. Origen was adamant in insisting that the eternal God had always existed as Father, Son, and Holy Spirit. In other words and antimodalistically, the three divine *hypostaseis* were distinct from eternity and not only for the sake of creation and economy, which revealed God as the Trinity. Ormerod (2005, 13) puts it succinctly: "Unless the distinctions we encounter in the economy are real distinctions in God's own being, then God has not really revealed Godself to us."

To conceptualize the Triune God, Origen, just like the early apologists and/or Clement of Alexandria, entertained the idea of God being the Mind (*Nous*; Origen, *Princ.* 1.1.6; *Comm. Jo.* 1.277). This idea suited well with the scriptural designation of the Son as "the Word." The Son as the Word was with the Father before he was "uttered" (cf. John 1:1; *Princ.* 1.2.3). The fact that the Mind was thinking/uttering the Word indicated some kind of plurality in the unity of God. The Word had to be distinguishable from the Mind which uttered it, and it had to be distinguishable not only notionally.

Origen also investigated what exactly was implied in the biblical names "Father," "Son," and "Holy Spirit." Evidently, modalist Monarchians did not think that a different name or "conception" (*epinoia*) implied a different reality, but Origen's Stoic theory of language required such a conclusion. He did not consider the names to be conventional but natural (*Cels.* 5.45). This means that, at least in their original imposition, names corresponded to realities. Father, Son, and Spirit were not just different names for one and the same reality, but names that designated the somehow distinguishable three realities.

To emphasize the actual distinctions within the Godhead against modalist Monarchians, Origen employed the term *hypostasis* respectively to the Father, Son, and Holy Spirit (*Comm. Jo.* 2.75). Such application of a would-be technical term requires special attention. Although the term *hypostasis* highlighted the three divine persons as distinct realities, it did not yet have the fourth-century connotation of personal relation. Thus, there is a danger to read too much into Origen's assertion that there are three *hypostaseis* in the Trinity. The word *hypostasis* meant "reality of subsistence" as opposed to a mere mental notion or conception (*epinoia*; *Comm. Jo.* 10.246). Origen insisted that the three divine subjects had their own subsistence. He was not providing a proto-Constantinopolitan formula of God as "three persons [*hypostaseis = prosōpa*]." But Origen's affirmation of the hypostatic existence of the *Logos* is significant nevertheless in light of the fact that, in Plotinian Neoplatonism, *logos* as an aspect of the divine Mind was denied a separate *hypostasis*. *Logos* was a mere "transfer from the Divine Intellectual Being to the third Hypostasis of the World Soul" (Gericke 2000, 106).

After distinguishing between the Father, Son, and Holy Spirit according to their *hypostaseis*, Origen also affirmed the equal divinity of the Father, Son, and Holy Spirit. Now, because the semantic realm of the terms *hypostasis* and *ousia* overlapped in the third century, there is an additional danger to understand Origen as suggesting the existence of three divine substances. In *On Prayer* (*De oratione*) 15.1, Origen indeed wrote that the Father and Son were distinct in *ousia* and (!) *hypokeimenon* (= *hypostasis*; see "Trinitarian Terms" above). Yet, Origen did not teach the existence of three divine substances or three Gods but one consubstantial God in three *hypostaseis*. Within the Godhead, there are no hierarchical gradations of divinity. If not an interpolation, the text of *The First Principles* (*De principiis*) reads that in the Trinity (and in the substantial sense), it is not permissible to call anything "greater or lesser" (*maius minusue*; *Princ*. 1.3.7). Origen in *Fragmenta ex homiliis in epistulam ad Hebraeos* 93 adds that the Son "is born from the very nature [*substantia*] of God." On the other hand, in *Comm. Jo.* 20.157, Origen explicitly denied the possibility of the Son's birth from the divine essence (*ousia*). But it seems that in his Gospel commentary, Origen was not discussing the sharing of the divine essence by the Father and the Son. Rather, he was worried that if the word "essence" was understood in a materialistic sense, it became inapplicable for describing the birth of the Son from the Father. The Father was in no way diminished in his divinity or emptied of his *ousia*, since the Son was eternally begotten from the Father.

As we try to understand Origen's use of theological vocabulary, it might be good to keep in mind that he was active at a time "when theological language was being worked out to express the fundamentally inexpressible Christian mysteries" (Berthold, in Daley 1992, 446).

In making his case for the consubstantiality of the divine *hypostaseis*, Origen further argued that the Son's existence was intrinsic to what God was, because "father" and "son" were correlative terms (*Princ*. 1.2.2). God had always been the Father. To assert the contrary was to deprive the Christian notion of God of something important. Since God was not only eternal but also immutable, God's productive capacity had to be eternal. Put differently, if God were Father and also immutable and eternal, then God always had the Son.

However, if Origen taught the eternity of the creation—using the same logic that the immutable and eternal God had always to be the creator—his notion of the eternal generation of the Son becomes more problematic (*Princ*. 1.2.10).

If God always had the Son, the Son had to be begotten *eternally*. Origen commented that in Ps 2:7, "You are my son, today I have begotten you," the word "today" stood for "always," because God existed in eternal "present" (*Comm. Jo.* 1.204). There was "never a time when the *Logos* was not" (*Princ*. 1.2.9; 4.4.1). Proverbs 8:25 (LXX) used the present tense of *gennaō*, "Before all the hills he begets me," as opposed to the other aorist verbs in the passage. For Origen, this grammatical nuance confirmed that the generation of the Son was indeed eternal (*Hom. Jer.* 9.4–5).

Another way to affirm the eternity of the Son was to say that since God was eternally wise, the Son (or Wisdom) had to be coeternal with the Father; 1 Cor 1:24 speaks about Christ as "the wisdom of God." It was absurd to think of God without wisdom at some point of God's existence.

But Origen's anti-Gnostic and antipagan concerns cautioned him against speaking about the Son's eternal generation without certain qualifications. As hinted above, the problem was that generation could be perceived as emanation. For instance, certain automatic flow was implied in the traditional metaphors of heat coming from fire and a ray from the sun, as these metaphors were applied to God the Father and the Son (cf. Wis 7:26; Heb 1:3). Therefore, Origen explicitly rejected the possibility of perceiving the generation of the Son as emanation (*Princ.* 1.2.6; 4.4.1; cf. Tertullian, *Prax.* 7).

Furthermore, Origen needed to deal preemptively with the argument that the Father arbitrarily decided to have a Son and that thus the Son was not intrinsic to what God was. Origen emphasized the fact that the generation of the Son involved the will (*boulē*) of the Father. Begetting the Son was the Father's voluntary act and not a mere automatic emanation. This move was later picked up by Arius, Arians, and Heteroousians (see below), who thought, in turn, that begetting from the *will* of the Father excluded the possibility of begetting from the *nature* of the Father. For Origen, will and nature were not necessarily mutually exclusive entities. It was not only possible but also quite likely that being born from nature included not only the begetter's nature but also the begetter's will.

But what about the substantial equality and coeternity of the Holy Spirit? In his *First Principles*, Origen dedicated a whole chapter to the Holy Spirit. He wondered how a Christian "could have even a suspicion of the personal existence of the Holy Spirit" (1.3.1). Although the Holy Spirit and the other divine *hypostaseis* have their own "special activity (or ministry)," Origen emphasized their unity of action (1.3.7–8). The unity of action implied the unity of nature, at least as far as the *divine* actions and nature were concerned. Furthermore, Origen asserted that the Holy Spirit was "united in honor and dignity with the Father and the Son" (*Princ.* Pref. 4). Perhaps the coeternity of the Holy Spirit is stated most strongly in Origen's *Commentarii in Romanos* 6.7.19: "The Spirit . . . is always with the Father and the Son; and he always is, was, and shall be, just like the Father and the Son."

If one is to believe the authenticity of Pamphilius's citation of Origen's commentary on Hebrews, Origen was also the first mainstream writer to use the famous word *homoousios* (same nature) in connection with the Trinity. According to this fragment, Origen contended that the Son's "coming forth" or "effluence" (*aporreusis*) from the Father implied that the source and the effluence were *homoousios* (*Frg. Heb.* 93). But the word *homoousios* does not fit well into Origen's theology.

1. The word *ousia* could still mean *hypostasis*. One of the reasons why later "Origenists" disliked the would-be-orthodox term *homoousios* was precisely that it was simply too close to "one *hypostasis*." Stating that the Father, Son, and Holy Spirit were *homoousios* could obscure the fact that they had their own subsistence. Arius pressed this connotation further and rejected the term *homoousios* altogether.

2. In Hermetic texts (the first–third-century religious texts attributed to Hermes Trismegistus), the word *homoousios* described the coming forth of the *Logos* from the *Nous* as emanation (*Poimandres* 6 and 10). Although the Latin fragment of Origen's commentary on Hebrews arguably employed the word *homoousios* in the Hermetic sense (*Frg. Heb.* 93; cf. *Comm. Rom.* 7.13.9), in

other writings Origen clearly rejected the possibility of perceiving the birth of the coessential Son as emanation.

3. It is plausible that Origen had yet another reason for disliking the term *homoousios*. He considered God to be beyond *ousia*. Plato's *Republic* 509b stated that "the Good is not being, but superior to it in rank and power." For Origen the Platonist, to use the term *homoousios* was to assume the knowledge of the being of God and to assert that something was identical with it as a species of a generic class. But this was an impossible assumption! Even so, Origen as a Christian could not escape the phrase in Exod 3:14, "I AM WHO I AM" (LXX: *ego eimi ho ōn*). The Scripture as such is a (positive) kataphatic discourse, and thus Christian apophaticism can never be absolute. Besides, apophatic statements always say something!

In Chart One, Origen's "box" is partially under "Threeness" because his Trinitarian theology was often perceived as subordinationist. Why? After securing God's oneness and the coeternity and substantial equality of the Father, Son, and Holy Spirit, Origen added a balancing doctrine of the "monarchy of the Father." This doctrine safeguarded the distinct *hypostaseis* and the causal hierarchy within the Godhead. "Monarchy of the Father" means that there is a sense in which the Father is indeed superior to the other divine *hypostaseis*. The Father alone is "the very God" (*autotheos*) and the "unbegotten" (*agen[n]ētos*) God (*Comm. Jo.* 2.2; 2.75). Even though Origen called also the Son *agenētos* (*Cels.* 6.17), the word does not need to be translated as "unbegotten." Since in Origen's time the terms "to bring to existence" (*genesis*) and "begetting" (*gennēsis*) functioned as synonyms, *agenētos* could well be translated as "uncreated."

Origen explained that God the Father was the "root" (*hriza*) and "source" (*pēgē*) of everything that existed (*Fragmenta in evangelium Joannis* 69). Did the Scriptures not state, "The Father is greater that I" (John 14:28; cf. Eph 4:6)? For Origen, more was involved in this verse than merely the incarnational limitation of the Son. The Father was "*the* God" (*ho theos*), while the Son was "God" (*theos*; *Comm. Jo.* 2.13–18; cf. John 1:1). (Latin has no definite article; Westerners could *not* operate with such a distinction.) But notice: instead of insisting on the unqualified monarchy of God, Origen stressed the monarchy of the Father *within* the Godhead. He taught that God the Father was the *archē*, the source and principle of causation within the Godhead.

Origen explicated that the Son derived his *ousia* eternally from the Father, who alone was the Uncaused Cause. In pagan philosophy the name "Father" was applied to the First Principle to designate it metaphorically as the ultimate cause of all existence (e.g., Plato, *Tim.* 28c; Alcinous, in *Didask.* 10.3). Precisely in this causal sense, one should understand Origen's assertions that the Son was "less than the Father" and the Holy Spirit was "still less" (Origen, *Princ.* 1.3.5). Causation explains *how* rather than *what* the divine persons are.

Origen preserved the *causal* priority of the Father without affirming the *temporal* priority of the Father. "For he [Christ] is not later than the Father, but from the Father" (*Comm. Rom.* 7.13.9). Origen even did not hesitate to call the Son a "creation" (*ktisma*; *Princ.* 4.4.1; cf. Prov 8:22), but once again, the word "creation" should be understood as "caused." The Son was not "created" in the same sense as the creation was created (*Princ.* 1.2.10). The same logic applies to the Spirit. The following statement of Origen should be read in a causal and nontemporal sense, although Arius might have read it in a substantial and temporal sense: "We admit, as most pious and true, that the Holy Spirit is the most honored of all things made through the Word, and that he is [first] in the rank of all things, which have been made by the Father through Christ" (*Comm. Jo.* 2.75). Despite writing that the Spirit was "made" (*genomenōn*), Origen arguably meant that the Spirit was caused (*Comm. Jo.* 2.75).

Because Origen distinguished between the three divine *hypostaseis* and promoted the doctrine of the "monarchy of the Father," many have been quick to label Origen's Trinitarian theology "subordinationist." Yes, his teaching was subordinationist, but it was subordinationist in a very special sense. The Father was the "cause" and the Son was the "effect." But in God, cause and effect were "simultaneous," because cause and effect were not temporal but eternal (*Princ.* 1.2.2; 1.2.11). In other words, Origen argued for a caused but nontemporal origin of the Son. There was no temporal gap between the Father and the Son. The Father as the divine Mind was only logically prior to the Son as the *Logos*, which the Mind thought and uttered. The Mind could be only logically prior, because the divine Mind and the divine Word were both eternal.

Causality also offers a key to understanding Origen's notorious expression "second" or "another God" (*deuteros* or *heteros theos*), with which Origen named the Son in *Dial.* 2.3 (cf. *Cels.* 5.39). Yet, even this phrase does not provide material for convicting Origen as "nothing but a Platonist" and perhaps even as a tritheist. It is true that Plotinus titled the first tractate of book V of his *Enneads* as "On the Three Primary Hypostases" (*Peri tōn triōn arhikōn hypostaseōn*) and that Porphyry considered the word *hypostasis* to have a connotation of a product of a lower emanation. Perhaps for these reasons any mention of a "second God" was perceived as a mere pagan postulation of two unequal gods. But Origen seems to have had something different in mind than postulating two unequal Gods. The Son was "second" because he was caused; the Son was logically "second," not because he was less than divine.

However, Origen's causally subordinationist language was later borrowed by Arius and Arians, who neglected his balancing doctrines of the coeternity and consubstantiality of the three divine *hypostaseis*, and the eternal generation of the Son. Therefore, Origen's Trinitarian theology became suspect and seriously misconstrued in time. "As a result of the Arian controversy, Origen's formulation of the Son's relationship to the Father occasioned a serious misunderstanding, not yet dissipated, which obscures his contribution to the history of Christian doctrine" (Trigg 1998, 23).

Tertullian

This second–third-century North African theologian was the first to use the Latin word *trinitas* (*Prax.* 2). Despite sharing the inadequacy of any predication of God, the word *trinitas* wonderfully captured the plurality (*tres* or *trias*) and unity (*unitas*) of what it named. The Christian faith (*regula fidei*) taught one God, who was Father, Son, and Holy Spirit. In fact, the *unity* of God was grounded on the distinction between the three names. If the Father were identical with the Son, and the Son identical with the Holy Spirit, instead of unity, there would be uniformity, sameness, and redundancy in the Godhead. Tertullian's comment on John 10:30 ("The Father and I are one") was that Christ and his Father were *unum* (neuter, designating "substance") and not *unus* (masculine, designating "person"; *Prax.* 25; cf. 1 John 5:7; Novatian, *Trin.* 27).

Just like Origen, Tertullian asserted that the *Logos* was "second" (*secundus*) and that the Holy Spirit was "third" (*tertius*; *Prax.* 3, 8, and 13). It was "the mystery of *oikonomia*, . . . which distribute[d] the unity into a Trinity" (*Prax.* 2). By *oikonomia* Tertullian arguably meant the eternal "self-organization" of the Godhead rather that God's *ad extra* activity in time. To say that there was a "second" and a "third" within the Godhead was not to assert that the Son and the Spirit were some kind of later and lesser Gods. It was to say that the Father, who was without origin, was the source of the eternally originated Son and Spirit and yet that all three were God (singular; *Prax.* 13). "The Trinity . . . does not at all disturb the monarchy, while it, at the same time, guards the state of the *oikonomia*" (*Prax.* 8). "It is precisely this conviction that the divine life is not single or alone that comprises the principal core of Tertullian's attempt to redefine the divine monarchy" (McCruden, in *SJT*, 2002, 330).

Tertullian further maintained that the Godhead was "one undivided substance" (*Prax.* 12). Father, Son, and the Holy Spirit were one "by unity of substance" (*per substantiae scilicet unitatem*; *Prax.* 2). Even though Tertullian spoke about the Father as "the entire substance" (*tota substantia*) and the Son and Spirit as "a derivation and portion of the whole" (*derivatio totius et portio*; *Prax.* 9), his statements should be understood in line with Origen's distinction between the uncaused *ho theos* and the caused *theos*. To strengthen the argument for the substantial unity of God, Tertullian contended that the three *personae* were one in power (*potestas* or *virtus*), which implied the unity of substance (*Prax.* 2 and 22). Despite the fact that the word "power" (*dynamis*) is missing from the creeds of Nicaea and Constantinople, the deduction "one power, one substance" became an important argument for the post-350s pro-Nicenes (M. Barnes 2001).

Substantia, however, proved not to be a very happy choice of a word. It was one of the close equivalents to Greek *hypostasis*. When (the Greek) *hypostasis* came to mean "person" and was distinguished from the word "nature" (*ousia*), many were bound to misunderstand the Latin word *substantia* and consequently Latin Trinitarian theology. The word *substantia* could be taken to denote either the unity or the diversity of the Triune God. *Una substantia* could be misunderstood as God being "one person," and *tres substantiae* could be misunderstood as God being "three substances." Indeed, the Latin rendering of the Nicene Creed read *substantia* as a translation of *hypostasis* (= *ousia*).

In addition, the word *substantia* as "stuff" or "matter" had a certain philosophical (Stoic) connotation, which made it unsuitable for designating the immaterial God. In fact, few besides Tertullian understood God as consisting of a very refined "spiritual" matter (*Prax.* 7). Nevertheless, Tertullian's antimodalist point was that the *substantia* of the three divine persons was "something" (*aliquid*) rather than "nothing" (*nihil*). His assumption was that something was not real unless it had some (material) substance. Anything without substance would be a sham. Thus, in employing the analogy of the mind and a word, Tertullian insisted that the uttered Word, the Son, was "an actually existing thing" (*substantiva res*; *Prax.* 26). Such assertion was his response to modalist Monarchianism.

Tertullian contended that the three divine persons were not three in their divinity (not three *substantiae*) but in "degree" (*gradus*), "form" (*forma*), and "aspect" (*specie*; *Prax.* 2). Antimodalistically, he insisted that "the Father is other than the Son . . . as he who begets is other than the begotten" (*Prax.* 9). Distinction was not a division, though. Father, Son, and Holy Spirit were undivided as far as their *substantia* was concerned. In *Against Praxeas* 12, Tertullian famously asserted that Father, Son, and Holy Spirit were *una substantia in tribus coharentibus* (one substance in three coherent [persons]), which is a Latin alternative to the later Greek formula "one nature three persons" (*mia ousia treis hypostaseis*). However, because of the ambiguity of the word *substantia*, Tertullian's formula cannot be seen as a direct precedent for the expression accepted in the (Greek) Nicene Creed.

Although the earliest Christian discussions of God were often Binitarian rather than Trinitarian, Tertullian the Montanist did not forget to emphasize the divinity of the Holy Spirit, the Paraclete. (Tertullian had become a Montanist while he wrote *Against Praxeas*.) It has been recently argued that Montanists actually kept the issue of the Holy Spirit alive while the larger church focused more on the relationship between the Father and the Son (McGowan, in *JECS*, 2006).

Novatian

A third-century Roman presbyter, Novatian was the author of the first Latin treatise on the Trinity (ca. AD 250). Jerome thought that Novatian's treatise was "an epitome . . . of the work of Tertullian" (*De viris illustribus* 70). In the

Middle Ages, Novatian's *On the Trinity* (*De Trinitate*) was indeed transmitted as a work by Tertullian. Novatian's authorship of this treatise was reaffirmed only in the sixteenth century.

Novatian's approach to the doctrine of the Trinity was traditionally apophatic, at least as far as the knowledge of the "superior God" was concerned (cf. Rev 19:12). Long before Augustine, he wrote, "For whatever could be thought concerning him [God] must be less than himself" (*Trin.* 2). Yet, this "superior God" did reveal himself, and this very fact enabled Novatian to continue his Trinitarian deliberations kataphatically (cf. Gregory Thaumaturgos, *Fragmenta de Trinitate*). Interestingly, though, Novatian never used the word *trinitas* in his treatise.

Novatian, too, took his lead from the *regula fidei*, which mentioned Father, Son, and Holy Spirit. Yet, despite the presence of his chapter 29 on the Holy Spirit and a statement about the "divine eternity" (*divina aeternitate*) of the Spirit, Novatian's whole discussion of the Christian concept of God seems almost Binitarian. Clearly, the question of the full divinity of the Spirit was not yet an issue: the focus was almost exclusively on the relation between the Father and the Son.

Novatian saw both the dynamic and modalist Monarchianism as misguided attempts to rescue God's oneness. Accordingly, he had to emphasize the oneness of God as well as the distinctness of the divine persons. "They [the Monarchians] thought that they could not otherwise hold such an opinion than by supposing that it must be believed either that Christ was only man, or really God the Father" (*Trin.* 30).

Against dynamic Monarchians/adoptionists, the notion of the oneness of God helped Novatian to argue for the full divinity of the Son. He offered a beautiful soteriological argument for the Son being God by citing Hos 1:6–7, "The LORD said, . . . 'I will save them by the LORD their God.'" This text suggested to Novatian that Christ as the Savior had to be God (*Trin.* 12). Furthermore, the Son was clearly distinguished from the creation, for "according to his divinity the Word proceeded from the Father before every creature" (*Trin.* 21). Novatian even developed a three-chapter-long anti-adoptionist "litany," which repeatedly asked, "If Christ was only man, how . . . ?" (*Trin.* 14–16). He also employed the already-traditional argument from the correlativity of the names "Father" and "Son." Without really postulating the theory of eternal generation, he theologized that the Son had always been in (and from) the Father (*Trin.* 31). Interestingly, in arguing against dynamic Monarchians/adoptionists, Novatian did not make a case for the consubstantiality of the Father and the Son as Tertullian did, although Novatian did name Christ explicitly as having the "divine substance" (*substantia divina*; *Trin.* 31) and argued that Christ existed substantially (*in substantia*) before the creation of the world (*Trin.* 16). Instead, he acknowledged the oneness of the Father and Son "in agreement, in love, and in affection" (*Trin.* 27).

While countering modalist Monarchians, Novatian affirmed their premise of God's oneness (cf. Gal 3:20). He also agreed that God as a simple nonmaterial being "contains no differentiation of parts" (*Trin.* 6). The Father was "simple and without any corporeal commixture" (*Trin.* 5). But Novatian did not deny the plurality of the divine persons as his opponents did. Father, Son, and Holy Spirit were not the modes of one God, but the three eternal persons of the Triune God. This means that Novatian could not affirm God's oneness without qualification. "[The Son] is God . . . but God in such manner as to be the Son, not the Father" (*Trin.* 15). He was not teaching two Fathers or two Gods or one God with two names; he was teaching that the Son was divine without "taking from the Father that characteristic that He is one God" (*Trin.* 31). The Son was "second person [*secunda persona*] after the Father" (*Trin.* 26).

Novatian sometimes used puzzling language that can be interpreted either in the direction of orthodoxy or heresy. Here a sympathetic explication is proposed. In chapter 16 he stated that "Christ is greater than the Paraclete," because the Spirit received what the Spirit declared from the Son. Similarly, in chapter 27 he called the Son "inferior to the Father," for Christ, too, received sanctification from his Father (John 10:36). If he was speaking according to the economical order, hardly anyone could disagree. (The editors/translators of *ANF* [see "Abbreviations," in Part 3] have actually inserted the word "economy" into the text!) Yet even if Novatian meant something more than economy, his assertions can be interpreted in an orthodox sense. He affirmed that the Son was "in the Father" "before" (logically before) he was "with the Father" (*Trin.* 31). In other words, the Son was caused by the Father; again, the prepositions "in" and "with" in his treatise need not be understood as denoting *temporal* sequence. The last chapter of Novatian's treatise, which includes the words "from God," "source," and "head," suggests causality rather than temporality.

God's Threeness

The category of threeness is mentioned again because some Christian theologians were also accused of being tritheists. To those located in the left column in Chart One, the theologians in the middle column always looked like the "right wing" tritheists or polytheists. Tertullian complained, "They are constantly throwing out against us that we are preachers of two gods and three gods" (*Prax.* 3). It is implausible that any Christian theologian deliberately taught three Gods. But it became conventional to condemn tritheism anyway (e.g., the 27 anathemas attached to the Creed of Sirmium, AD 351).

Dionysius of Alexandria versus Dionysius of Rome

In the middle of the third century, bishop Dionysius of Alexandria had a controversy with bishop Dionysius of Rome. Dionysius of Alexandria was

invited to Syria to assess Monarchian theology. Countering modalist Monarchianism—and this might be crucial for understanding his position—Dionysius
insisted on the existence of three distinct *hypostaseis* within the Godhead. For his
Roman namesake, however, the Alexandrian's doctrine of three divinities
(*theotētes*) sounded like subordinationism, or even tritheism, and a blunt betrayal
of orthodoxy (Dionysius of Rome, *Fragment* [*against the Sabellians*] in Athanasius, *Decr.* 26). Dionysius of Alexandria dismissed the charges (Athanasius, *Decr.*
25; *De synodis* 43 [his citations may be inauthentic, however]). Athanasius, too,
defended his fellow Alexandrian by insisting that Dionysius's critics were "hunt-
ing merely stray expressions, while passing over the truth to be found in his other
letters" (Athanasius, *De sententia Dionysii* 4). Despite Athanasius's attempts to
defend the orthodoxy of Dionysius of Alexandria (in the work just cited),
Dionysius's teachings remained dubious for Basil of Caesarea (*Ep.* 9) and for
generations of theologians after him.

One of the reasons for the accusation of tritheism was that the Alexandrian
Dionysius did not employ the magic word "consubstantial" (*homoousios*). Yet next
to the dubious case of Origen's usage of the term, the controversy between the
two Dionysii was actually the first time the key Nicene term *homoousios* designated specifically the relationship between the Father and the Son. (Though
Paul of Samosata also argued that Christ was *homoousios* with the Father
[Athanasius, *Syn.* 43], it is not at all clear what he meant by this word.)

Another major reason for accusing Dionysius of Alexandria of tritheism
was that his language of three *hypostaseis* was probably misunderstood by his
Roman namesake as three substances (= *ousiai*). Furthermore, the Alexandrian
Dionysius called the Son "creature" (*poiēma*), "handiwork" (*cheiropoiēton*), and
depicted the Son as being "alien in substance [*ousia*]" to the Father (Athanasius,
Dion. 4 and 21).

The Roman Dionysius objected to all of that. He instructed that both
extreme positions, modalism and tritheism, had to be avoided. The Roman
bishop contended that the verb "created" (*ektisen*) in Prov 8:22 (LXX) had to be
interpreted in the light of the verb "begets" (*genna*) in Prov 8:25, and distinguished from the word "creature/work" (*poiēma*; Athanasius, *Decr.* 26). The Son
is "begotten," and "created" only in the sense of being caused. Yet there was
another statement of Dionysius of Alexandria that the Roman bishop seemed
to have missed. Namely, Dionysius of Alexandria also asserted that the Son "did
not exist before he was generated" (*ouk ēn prin genētai*; Athanasius, *Dion.* 4). This
indeed questions his orthodoxy and, in fact, also his "Origenism."

East-West Generalizations

The controversy between the Alexandrian Dionysius and the Roman
Dionysius seems to confirm the famous assertion of the nineteenth-century

scholar de Régnon (1898), who suggested that *subordinationism* was the characteristic of Eastern Trinitarian theology and *modalism* characteristic of Western Trinitarian theology (cf. M. Barnes, in *AugStud*, 1995). In other words, the East emphasized the distinctness of the divine persons and the monarchy of the Father, and the West stressed God's substantial oneness. Such characterization indeed makes some sense when we observe what theologies the protoorthodox theologians in East and West respectively opposed in the second and third centuries. Although de Régnon's generalization serves a pedagogical purpose of creating clear categories, he postulates these, unfortunately, at the expense of historical accuracy. If we apply his generalization to later Trinitarian theologies, for instance, to that of the Cappadocian fathers and Augustine, it becomes particularly misleading. Ayres (2004, 70) cautions, "In actual fact our knowledge of Latin Christology and Trinitarian theology between 250 and 360 is extremely limited and certainly not such that we can make any certain judgements about its overall character."

There is another problem with de Régnon's generalization: it operates with clear categories of East and West. But "'East' vs. 'West' is far too clumsy a tool of analysis for almost anything in the fourth century" (Ayres 2004, 123). Therefore, it may be best to put the word "Westerner" in quotation marks, because the designation includes, in fact, Greek-speaking thinkers living East from Rome and in North Africa. Likewise, the term "Easterner" begs a clarification: "East from what?"—unless it is made intentionally vague by the quotation marks. General categories of East and West may obscure the importance of large in-between and theologically active geographical areas, and of theologians who do not fit into this twofold division (such as Tertullian, Athanasius). It may also read later divisions of Christianity back into the formative period of Christian theology.

Because of the above-mentioned criticisms, our charts do not have a feature to distinguish between "Eastern" and "Western" trajectories. True, in Charts One and Three, the Greek-speaking and Latin-speaking theologians have their own boxes, but in Chart Two, for instance, the Synod of Alexandria is together with Hilary of Poitiers and Marius Victorinus. Additionally, the charts try to convey the theological overlap of various Trinitarian positions by placing the boxes in between the three columns and partially under each other.

On Chart Two

The First Half of the Fourth Century

The three titles in Chart Two are not the same as those in Chart One. In the first half of the fourth century, theological attention shifted away from the initial question of God's unity and plurality ("Oneness" and "Threeness") to the question of the essential sameness and/or distinctness of the three divine persons. Hence, the titles in Chart Two are: "Sameness," "Sameness and Distinctness," and "Distinctness."

A correlating task was to reconcile the two traditional convictions:

1. God as an ingenerate being. Some theologians were "such partisans of the Father that [they] end up canceling his Fatherhood" (Gregory of Nazianzus, *Or.* 20.6).
2. God as an eternally productive being. Other theologians insisted that the Father had his Son from eternity.

Yet, what does it really mean for a monotheistic religion to say that God had a Son?

In Chart Two the contextual marginal columns are retained but not discussed. It suffices to mention that, in the fourth century, neoplatonic philosophy began to have its impact on Christian theology.

Distinctness of the Divine Persons

Arius and Controversy

This time we begin from the right side of Chart Two, because it was the teaching of Arius that caused the Trinitarian controversy in 320s and the summoning of the Council of Nicaea. In his directory of heresies, Epiphanius announced, "Arius . . . stirred up a cloud of dust against the church" (*Pan.* 69.2.1). The more recent scholarship has demonstrated, however, that Arius was not as important a figure for the fourth-century Trinitarian controversies as several textbooks make him to be. You may wonder, Why such a long section on Arius, then, if the whole thing is really not about Arius? The reason is that Arius continues to be considered as one of the key antifigures in the early Christian Trinitarian controversies. The presumption of his importance has still not been universally contested. Furthermore, Athanasius considered his various opponents indiscriminately as one monolithic group of Arians. Because of his influential rhetoric, "the assumption that it is possible to identify a theological position that can in some sense be described as 'Arian' remains highly pervasive" (Gwynn 2007, 7). For these reasons, Arius cannot be ignored.

Arius's theology is known from his three letters. Some (redacted?) fragments of his acrostic *Thalia* are also preserved in the writings of Athanasius. But most of what we know about his Trinitarian theology comes from his opponents' many treatises. In one of his articles, Kannengiesser (in *TS*, 1983, 459) summarizes the situation of the sources: "(a) Arius is cited by Athanasius for strictly polemical purposes; (b) most of the quotations are fragmentary; (c) they are transmitted out of context, and exposed to arbitrary changes at the convenience of the citer."

Now, a certain dose of sympathetic attitude is always required for the understanding of someone or something. We should not suspend critical thinking and orthodox convictions, but we should suspend premature judgments about Arius. Countering the prevailing anti-Arian bias, Maurice Wiles (1996) has argued that Arius's appeal to the tradition and the Scriptures was indeed genuine. Arius was not a theological "outsider" who came to destroy everything precious in Christian theology with his "ten thousand blasphemies" (Epiphanius, *Pan.* 69.12.1). Presumably, his intention was not to teach a false doctrine that "no one before him had ever suggested" (Sozomen, *Historia ecclesiastica* 1.15). Rather, Arius was an insider, a churchman, an antimodalist, who ended up promoting rather peculiar Trinitarian teachings that were eventually considered heretical. He found significant following precisely because he built his theology on certain elements of the common Christian tradition and on certain passages of the Scriptures.

Using Tradition. Tradition supplies a hermeneutical key for interpreting the Scriptures. Once again, Arius did not deliberatively ignore the traditional faith, as Athanasius wanted everyone to believe. Instead, Arius wrote to Alexander that his faith was "from our forefathers, which we have learnt from you" (Arius, *Ekthesis pisteōs* [*Ep. Alex*]). There is no reason to prejudge that such an appeal was merely deceptive rhetoric. For Arius, tradition meant the tradition of Alexandria, which he defended against his superior's (Alexander of Alexandria's) "misinterpretation" of it. A former bishop of Alexandria, Dionysius of Alexandria, had written that God was "unoriginate" (*agenētos*; *Fragment, Against Sabellius* in Eusebius, *Praeparatio evangelica* 7.19), and Arius evidently concluded that therefore a begotten/originated Son could not have been God in the true sense of the word. Athanasius in turn offered an orthodox reading of Dionysius of Alexandria (*On the Opinion of Dionysius*) precisely because in doing so, he tried to prevent Arius's appeal to the Alexandrian tradition. He compared Arius's appeal to the Alexandrian tradition with the Jews'(!) appeal to Abraham (Athanasius, *Dion.* 3).

Without going into all possible parallels between Arius and his Alexandrian predecessors, we should once more focus on the contribution of Origen. As far as Arius and Athanasius are concerned, we have a debate between two interpretations of the theological tradition of Alexandria, a debate between two kinds of "Origenists." Origen was indeed "all-present in Christian theology" (von Balthasar 1984, 5). His speculative theological proposals in *On First Principles* were ambiguous enough to enable the parting of ways between his interpreters. Everyone used Origen's conjectures selectively as their proof texts.

To simplify and to adopt the orthodoxy versus heresy scheme, the Alexandrian tradition divided up as follows:

> —**Arius** (emphasizing the essential difference between the Father and the Son)
>
> Clement—Origen—Dionysius
>
> —**Alexander** —**Athanasius** (emphasizing the essential sameness of the Father and the Son)

Origen had explained that the Father alone was *autotheos* (the very God) and *agen(n)ētos* (unbegotten). Jesus' words "The Father is greater than I" (John 14:28) suggested that whatever the Father was, the Son was in a lesser sense. However, the subordinationist implications of Origen's Trinitarianism manifested themselves in an amplified form in the teachings of Arius. For Origen, the eternity and essential immutability of the Father meant that the Son's generation from the Father could not be an event *in time*. It had to be eternal (outside time), just like God's being the Father was eternal. Arius, on the contrary, seems to have emphasized the Son's being caused over the eternity of the Son. In his handling of the Alexandrian heritage, the Son's causal subordination became also the Son's *temporal* subordination and *essential* inferiority.

Precisely because the Son was a caused being, Arius concluded that God was not always the Father. "Father" and "Son" were not necessarily correlative terms, and consequently the Son was not intrinsic to what God was. This meant that God became a Father in begetting the Son, who was created out of nonbeing (*ex ouk ontōn*; Arius, *Epistula ad Eusebium Nicomediensem* 1.5; cf. Rom 4:17; Heb 11:3; Alexander of Alexandria, *Henos sōmatos* [*Ep. om.*]). Later Arius seems to have dropped this assertion. The Son was "made" like the rest of the creation yet before the rest of the creation (Ps 110:3 [109:3 LXX: "I produced you out of the womb before the morning star"]; Prov 8:22; Col 1:15). In philosophical discourse, the word *genētos* meant capacity of previous nonexistence (Aristotle, *De caelo* 1.6.281b.25) and Arius understood the generation of the Son accordingly. To be born was to have a beginning; and for the Son to have a beginning meant that God's fatherhood also had a beginning. We can state the difference thus:

for Origen, God was "first" the Father and "then" the Creator; for Arius, God was first the Creator and then the Father. Athanasius quoted his opponent(s), "When the Son came into existence and was created, only then was God called his Father" (*Decr.* 6).

To emphasize the fact that the Son came to be, Arius asserted that the Son came to be through the *will* (*boulē* [*boulēsis*] or *thelēma*) of the Father (Arius, *Ep. Alex.*; *Ep. Eus. Nic.* 1.4; Athanasius, *C. Ar.* 1.29). But though Origen, to refute the Gnostic idea of emanation, made the point of the Son being a product of the Father's will, Arius used the same point to deny the Son's coming forth from the essence (*ousia*) of the Father. The Son was willed into existence as was the rest of the creation (Prov 8:22–25 combined with Gen 1:1 and John 1:1).

Consequently, Arius rejected the controversial and "unbiblical" term *homoousios*. The Son could not share the Father's ingenerate *ousia*, or otherwise there would be two uncaused causes. Had not Athenagoras and Justin already argued that to be God was to be *agen(n)ētos* (Athenagoras, *Leg.* 4; Justin, *1 Apol.* 14)? For Arius, it was indeed possible to appeal to the ancient Alexandrian and even to the wider Christian tradition.

Using Scripture. Arius's appeal to the Scriptures has to be taken seriously too, even if the results of his exegesis were ultimately rejected. Böhm contends that "Arius could have understood most of his statements in biblical terms" (in Kannengiesser, vol. 2, 2004, 696). Arius himself confessed to Emperor Constantine that he had received his faith "from holy Gospels" and that his teaching regarding the Father, Son, and Holy Spirit was in accordance "with what the Scriptures (on which we rely in all things) teach" (*Epistula Constantinum*).

As an exegete, Arius had to tackle an old problem: how to reconcile monotheism with all that the Scriptures said about Jesus. In several places the would-be-canonical New Testament itself differentiated between the elevated status of the Father and the subordinate status of the Son. Was not the Father the God for the Son (John 20:17)? Was not God "the head of Christ" (1 Cor 11:3)? Because of such passages, Arius's theologizing was guided by a strong conviction of the Father's superiority. Hilary of Poitiers summarized Arius's and his colleagues' theological quest into a phrase: "They have magnified only the divinity of the Father" (*Trin.* 4.8).

In his letter to bishop Alexander, Arius confessed, "We acknowledge one God, alone unbegotten, alone everlasting, alone unbegun, alone true, alone having immortality, alone wise, alone good, alone sovereign." Wiles (1996), among others, points out that the first three "alones" ultimately come from Greek philosophy. They are notions that Christian theologians had accepted long before Arius: God is without origin, eternal, and without temporal beginning. The "alone true" is taken from John 17:3, "the only true God." "Alone having immortality ... and alone sovereign" come from 1 Tim 6:15–16. The "only wise" comes from the doxology of Rom 16:27, "the only wise God," and the "alone good" derives from Jesus' words to the rich young man in Mark 10:18, "No one is good but God alone." But after listing these scriptural designations, Arius made his crucial theological move: he attributed these eight "alones" exclusively to God *the Father*. (No sufficient distinction was yet made between the *ousia* of God and the *hypostasis* of the Father!) Once again, while affirming certain apophatic designations of God, such as "inexpressible" (*arrētos*), "invisible" (*aoratos*), and "ineffable" (*alektos*), Arius reserved these for the Father only (Arius, *Thalia*; cf. Clement of Alexandria, *Quis dives salvetur* 23; *Strom.* 5.11). "The Son is excluded from any share in them," remarked Hilary of Poitiers (*Trin.* 4.9).

Arius's theology was apparently warranted by several other scriptural designations of the Son. In the Prologue of John, the Word (*logos*) was said to be both "God" (*theos*) and "with God" (*pros ton theon*; v. 1). Verse 14 added that the Son was the "only-begotten" (*monogenēs*), which Arius probably understood as "unique." All this could mean that the Word/Son was God, but God in a qualified and lesser sense: he was the *only-begotten* God. God the Father was *unbegotten*; God the Son, however, was *only*-begotten. The only-begotten Son participated in the unbegotten God in a unique way (Athanasius, *C. Ar.* 1.9). Accordingly, in his letter to Eusebius of Nicomedia, Arius employed a carefully constructed phrase, *plērēs . . . theos monogenēs* (literally, "full . . . God only-begotten"), to speak about the Son (1.4). The title "only-begotten" seemed to emphasize both the dissimilarity of the Son with the Father and the uniqueness of the Son as compared with the rest of the creation. The Son was "a creature of God, but not as one of the creatures" (Arius, *Ep. Alex.*).

Proverbs 8:22–25, which sparked the fourth-century Trinitarian controversy (Epiphanius, *Pan.* 69.12.1), spoke explicitly of the origination of Wisdom: "The LORD created me at the beginning of his work [or, 'as the beginning of his work'], the first of his acts of long ago. . . . Before the beginning of the earth, . . . I was brought forth." The Greek text (LXX) said that Wisdom was created (*ktizō*) and born (*gennaō*). The parallelism of the Hebrew poetry suggested that these verses were actually saying the same thing: Wisdom derived its existence from God. Thus, according to Arius, the verb "to create" (*ktizō*) in Prov 8:22 was considered to be the key to understanding the verb "to beget" (*gennaō*) in Prov 8:25. Job 38:28, for instance, used the verb "to beget" in a sense of "to create." It is not, however, that Arius refused to employ the word "to beget" as he was speaking about the Son. Rather, he understood the verb "to beget" to mean "to create." For him, there was no fundamental difference between the designations "begotten" and "created," because both indicated the coming into existence from the Father's will. Reportedly Arius asserted, "The Unbegun made the Son a beginning of things originated" (Arius, *Thalia*).

But there was a subtle qualification to Arius's exegetical conclusion: the Son, the "perfect creature" (*ktisma teleion*), had a beginning, and yet he was begotten "timelessly" (*achronos*; Arius, *Ep. Alex.*; *Ep. Const.*). Evidently entangled in temporal terms, Arius tried to say that the Son's existence had a beginning (the Son "did not exist prior to his begetting"), but the begetting of the Son was "before" anything, including time (*chronos*), was created (cf. 1 Cor 2:7; Col 1:17;

Ps 55:19 [54:20 LXX, with the phrase "before the ages," *pro tōn aiōnōn*]).
According to Hilary's summary of Arius's point, "He [the Son] was not before
he was born, but was born without time before everything" (*Trin.* 4.13; cf.
Alexander of Alexandria, *Henos sōmatos*). This means that Arius affirmed
Christ's "preexistence" in a relative sense. Edwards puts it succinctly: "Arius postulated not an eternal but timeless generation" (in Mitchell and Young 2006,
563). The phrase about the Son being "begotten from the Father before all ages"
(*pro pantōn tōn aiōnōn*)—in the writings of Arius, the Eusebian Creed considered by the Nicene fathers, and also the Creed of Constantinople (AD 381)—
could be read in a sense that the Son was created before the rest of creation,
including time. Therefore, the Dedication Creed of 340–341 (see below) could
easily condemn those who asserted that "there either is or was a time or moment
or age before the Son was begotten" and still held on to the belief that the Son
had a beginning.

There were other scriptural passages that guided the course of Arius's argument. For instance, 1 Cor 8:6 says, "There is one God, the Father, from whom
are all things, . . . and one Lord, Jesus Christ, through whom are all things." The
question here is the relation between the "one God," "one Lord," and "all things."
If "one Lord" stands outside the "all things" that come from the one God, then
there is another reality alongside the one God. For Arius, such a solution probably looked like giving up traditional monotheism. In his letter to Alexander,
Arius pointed out that all things were "from him [God]" (Rom 11:36) and that
Jesus himself asserted that he came "from God" (John 8:42; Arius, *Ep. Alex.*).
The phrase "beyond your companions" in Ps 45:7 (44:8 LXX) also seemed to
imply that the Son belonged to the world of companions, to the class of the created "things." Therefore and once again, Arius insisted antimodalistically that
one should not confuse the Father with the Son by thinking of them as coeternal and essentially equal beings. The Father and the Son were "nonmixable"
(*anepimiktoi*), "foreign" (*xenos*), "alien" (*allotrios*), and "unlike" (*anhomoioi*; Arius,
Thalia; Athanasius, *C. Ar.* 1.17). The Scriptures called the Son "the image of the
invisible God" (Col 1:15), and by definition an image was not isomorphic with
its prototype. The same text also called the Son "the firstborn of all creation,"
and the genitive case could indicate association, that the Son was a preeminent
creature, yet one *of* the creatures. For Arius, the cumulative exegetical effect was
clear: the Son was the first creature who began to be.

Arius thought the philosophical defense of the transcendental One to be
compatible with the scriptural data about God the Father. The Christian neoplatonic tradition stressed the unchanging transcendence of the Father. In addition, the Christian *Logos*-theology focused on the mediating role of the Word
in creation. All this fit well with Arius's understanding of things. God the Father
had to be one and simple; the Monad (*monas*) had to be left untouched by the
dyad (*duas*; Arius, *Thalia*). Arius was not at all silenced by his opponents' insistence on the scriptural phrase "The Father and I are one" (John 10:30), because
the essential unity of the Father and Son simply did not follow from this text.

Did not Jesus also pray that his followers "may be one as we are one" (cf. John 17:21)? No one would argue that his prayer implied an essential unity between Christians and their Lord. The unity prayed for could only be a *moral* unity, and thus the "being one" of the Father and the Son also meant a moral unity.

Finally, some biblical passages indicate that the title "Lord" was conferred on the Son as a direct result of his faithfulness: Phil 2:5–11 includes the forceful "therefore" (*dio*) and thus suggests that the exalted status of the Son was the *result* of his obedience rather than his ontological birthright (cf. *dia touto* in Ps 45:7 [44:8 LXX]; Heb 1:8–9).

There are indeed intrinsic difficulties and ambiguities within the canonical data of the Scriptures about the ontological status of the Son. (For convenient lists of the debated scriptural texts, see Gregory of Nazianzus, *Or.* 29 and 30; Hanson 1988, 832–38; Vaggione 2000, 383–95.) Therefore, it would be unfair to condemn Arius hastily as "unbiblical." One may not agree with his exegesis, and many did not already in the fourth century, but a blunt and unqualified dismissal of his exegesis as a misguided philosophical venture is just too easy and unfair to be recommended.

This intentionally positive appraisal of the "heretic" Arius's theology tries to show that the process which led to Nicaea was truly a *search for orthodoxy* (to use again Hanson's wording), rather than a defense of the already-established true doctrine of the Triune God. In other words, the fourth century tells us the story of how orthodoxy was reached, not of how it was maintained and defended after the apostles. In retrospect, Arius's Trinitarian theology appeared as heretical, but it took about half of the fourth century to prove that.

An Excursus on Naming

Giving labels to groups, trajectories, and movements has been part of rhetorical strategy in any controversy. Naming something identifies and even partially creates the reality observed. Naming can be a means to control, build a bias, and exclude—hence the difficulty in finding neutral names for the participants in the search for the orthodox doctrine of the Trinity. Even the vague names "pro-Nicene" and "anti-Nicene" express the assumption that the Trinitarian controversy was a debate between two opposing groups: pro-Nicene/Athanasian/orthodox and anti-Nicene/Arian/heretical. Gwynn (2007, 106) warns that "to envisage the fourth-century Church in terms of organized ecclesiastical and theological 'parties' is to underestimate the polemical nature of the sources from which this interpretation of the 'Arian Controversy' and its divisions has derived."

Like almost all religious signifiers, "Arianism" originated as a term of abuse. Therefore, one should use it with reservation or even put it within quotation marks. It was the post-Nicene reaction of the anti-Arians that led to the invention of "Arianism." Initially the name "Arian" labeled the anti-Alexandrian/anti-Athanasian Egyptian bishops. Only after the Council of Nicaea did it take on a more theological (and less ecclesiastical) coloring as it designated "Eusebians" (which is another polemical label; see below). Still later, Athanasius limited the name "Arian" only to Homoeans and Heteroousians (see below). "Arianism" has ever since been applied to any position that does not confess the full divinity of the Son. It became a pejorative name of "family resemblance" for various subordinationist Trinitarian theologies. Thus, throughout church history, Arianism is looked upon as the "archetypal heresy" (the title of Wiles's book [1996]) and Arius as the heretic of the worst sort.

As just mentioned, the name "Arian" was coined by pro-Nicenes (such as Athanasius and Marcellus), and it was coined after Arius's death. "The Alexandrian presbyter was now hardly even marginal" (Chadwick 2001, 201). "Arius was dead before Athanasius embarked on any large scale theological debate of the issues that Arius had raised. And then his real quarrel was with the living. The dead Arius was not even a whipping boy, but a whip" (Wiles, in Barnes and Williams 1993, 43). The mode of Arius's death, a day before he was to be restored to the communion, indicated divine disfavor—and anti-Arians were quick to earn dividends on this perception (Athanasius, *Epistula* 54; Rufinus, *Hist. eccl.* 10.14). Gregory of Nazianzus wrote that Arius "paid the penalty of his unbridled tongue by his death in a profane spot" (*Or.* 21.13). "The latrine where he died was shown as a sort of tourist point" (MacMullen 2006, 47).

In short, after his death in AD 336, Arius had become a liability. Even the so-called Arians, that is, Eusebians, clarified, "We have not been followers of Arius—how could bishops, such as we, follow a presbyter?" (Athanasius, *Syn.* 22). Western bishops Palladius and Secundianus, who were scrutinized in AD 381 because of their alleged Arianism, denied any knowledge of Arius. Hilary of Poitiers, who wrote a 500-plus-page refutation of Arianism (*On the Trinity* [*De Trinitate*]), mentioned Arius only twice. This means that Arius was never the single "founding father" for those who came to be called after his name. His person faded relatively quickly into the background of the increasingly international debate about the full divinity of the Son of God.

The obvious reason for calling many dissenting theologians "Arian" was that, after his condemnation at Nicaea, the name "Arian" carried guilt by association. Several controversialists could not resist employing such an attractive polemical tool. Everyone loved to hate the heretics! Furthermore, "conflating all anti-Nicene factions as 'Arians' gives him [Athanasius] an opportunity to accuse his opponents of inconsistency" (Anatolios 2004, 177).

In operating with labels such as "Arianism," we should keep in mind at least three things:

1. Naming a movement after a person (as with "Arianism") attributes a more significant role to a single founding figure than is often justified. Arius was just one of the more extreme subordinationist who combated the Alexan-

drian/Athanasian Trinitarian doctrines. (Chart Two unfortunately does not inform the reader about the fact that Arius and Eusebius of Caesarea, for instance, lived at the same time.)

2. Inventing heresiological labels, composing typologies, and creating all kind of new "-isms" tends to postulate unified movements that are easier to learn about, but that do not match the full complexity of the historical reality. R. Williams (2002, 82) writes, "'Arianism' as a coherent system, founded by a single great figure and sustained by his disciples, is a fantasy—more exactly, a fantasy based on the polemic of Nicene writers, above all Athanasius." Lienhard's (1999, 31) judgment is similar: "'Arianism' is a shorthand designation for a possible doctrinal deviation rather than judicious description of a historically verified movement."

3. Orthodox faith is apostolic faith. To associate a movement with a particular nonapostolic name is to suggest that the given movement is not apostolic. Accordingly, to call a theological position "Arian" is to show *whence* and *from whom* this nonapostolic "heresy" started. Athanasius wrote, "The Arians, having left the Church in the time of Alexander, exchanged the name of Christ for that of Arius" (*C. Ar.* 1.2–3).

Consequently and for centuries, Arius has not been considered even a Christian. Alexander of Alexandria wrote, "These men, therefore, . . . have partly in public derided the Christian religion" (*Epistula ad Alexandrum* 14). Athanasius added that Arians were "no longer called Christians" (*Apologia de fuga sua* 27.1). A heresiologist Epiphanius topped them both, "Arius, then, was infused with the power of the devil" (*Pan.* 69.12.1). Some may still want to limit Christianity to the central column in our charts and consider everything else non-Christian. Yet it is incorrect to oversimplify the Arian conflict into a clear-cut conflict between those who acknowledged the full divinity of the Son and those who did not. Such distinction would perhaps separate Christians from non-Christians, but it would not distinguish adequately Nicene Christians from Arian Christians.

Sameness and Distinctness of the Divine Persons

In Chart Two, the orthodox countertrajectory to that of Arius is represented by the Council of Nicaea and Alexander of Alexandria. Athanasius appears below the Council of Nicaea in Chart Two because much of his anti-Arian writing took place after AD 325.

Alexander of Alexandria

What complicates figuring out Alexander's convictions about the Trinity is that some of his doctrinal pronouncements may have been written by young

Athanasius. Nevertheless, in the early 320s, patriarch Alexander was disturbed that one of his subordinates, a priest named Arius, was teaching that there was a time when the Son did not exist. "I have stirred myself up to show you the faithlessness of these men who say that there was a time when the Son of God was not" (*Ep. Alex.* 2). Alexander evidently believed that the Father and the Son were equally eternal. "There is no interval between the Father and the Son" (*Ep. Alex.* 4). Denying the coeternity of the Son (Word, Wisdom) was equivalent to saying that "God was once destitute both of Word and Wisdom," which was absurd (*Ep. om.*). To emphasize the Son's eternal existence, Alexander insisted on the traditional Alexandrian/Origenist notion of the eternal generation of the Son. The doctrine of eternal generation allowed the admission that the Father was superior to the Son in a causal sense, without the Son's being less and later than the Father. "In this alone is He [the Son] inferior to the Father that he is not unbegotten" (*Ep. Alex.* 12). Consequently, Alexander denied that the Father and the Son had two different *physeis*, for the Son was an eternal and exact image of the Father (*Ep. Alex.* 9).

Alexander excommunicated Arius, and by doing so he unintentionally exported the controversy to the larger world.

Athanasius of Alexandria

Athanasius was one of the main opponents of Arius and Arianism. He was a significant figure in the shaping of the orthodox Trinitarian theology, although as a young deacon he was not able to be involved in the actual discussing of the Trinitarian dogma at the Council of Nicaea. Perhaps Adolph von Harnack exaggerated just a bit when he observed that Athanasius's "biography coincides with the history of dogma of the fourth century" (1997 [reprint], 3:139).

Building his anti-Arian case throughout the years, Athanasius argued for the full divinity of the Son and the Spirit. Father, Son, and Spirit are of the same nature (cf. John 10:30; 14:9). The three divine persons "are not an alliance of ontologically hybrid subjects" (R. Williams, in Barnes and Williams 1993, 153), but one God. To separate the Father from the Son and from the Spirit on the basis of a perceived difference in their respective natures was nothing but to postulate three Gods and to give up monotheism.

To emphasize the full divinity of the Son, Athanasius asserted that the Son was born out of the Father's (nonmaterial) *ousia*. The Son was neither a merely voluntary creation (Arius) nor involuntary emanation (Gnostics). Rather, the begetting of the Son was "natural," from the *ousia* of the Father. True, it was also voluntary, but will and nature were not mutually exclusive categories, as Arians contended. Put differently, the existence of the Son was not an "accident" but an eternally willed begetting of a "natural" offspring. The Son was not "from God" as everything else was, but once again, the Son was "from the essence" (*ek tēs ousias*) of God (*C. Ar.* 1.8; *Syn.* 36).

Since the Son was of the same nature with the Father, the "alones" that Arius had picked up from the Scriptures as the exclusive predicates of the Father had to apply also to the Son. The Son shared all the divine properties of the Father except paternity. "Everything that can be said of the Father can also be said of the Son, except his being called 'Father'" (*C. Ar.* 3.4). Arius had considered it possible to speak about God without thinking of God's fatherhood, but for Athanasius, such talk made no sense. For him, the name "Father" automatically implied the existence of the Son (*C. Ar.* 1.5–6; 3.6; *Decr.* 6). For Athanasius, "The word father signified that the divine nature was both inherently generative . . . and inherently relational" (Widdicombe 1994, 3).

Initially, Athanasius did not defend his central idea of the Son being from the *ousia* of the Father with the help of the term *homoousios* (consubstantial). In his *Orations against the Arians* (*Orationes contra Arianos*), written in the 340s, the word *homoousios* occurs only once (*C. Ar.* 1.9). But in the 350s, while writing *On the Decrees of the Council of Nicaea* (*De decretis*) and after the emergence of Homoeousians and Homoeans (see below), Athanasius began to pay more attention to this Nicene key word. Although an "unscriptural" term, *homoousios* nevertheless "contain[ed] the sense of the Scriptures" with regard to the divinity of the Father and the Son (*Decr.* 21). Athanasius turned to the term *homoousios* as a shorthand for the phrase "from the essence of the Father" (*ek tēs ousias tou patros*; *Decr.* 19; *Syn.* 51). He believed that both expressions reinforced each other.

Upholding the consubstantiality of the Father and the Son, Athanasius was in no way neglecting the difference between the Father and the Son. True, he was reserved about using the language of three *hypostaseis*—the words *ousia* and *hypostasis* were still more or less synonymous—but he never modalistically identified the Father with the Son. "The Father is Father and is not also Son, and the Son is not also Father; but the nature is one, . . . and he [the Son] and the Father are one in propriety and peculiarity of nature, and in the identity of the one Godhead" (*C. Ar.* 3.4). The very fact that John 1:1 said the Word to be "with (*pros*) God" indicated the difference between God and the Word. That which coexisted with another had to be, in some sense, distinct from the other (*C. Ar.* 2.38).

However, trouble came as many theologians thought that Athanasius was emphasizing the essential unity of the three divine persons more than their distinctness. What added to the problem was that Athanasius never distanced himself from Marcellus of Ancyra (see below) clearly enough and never condemned him (cf. Epiphanius, *Pan.* 72.4.4). Thus, in the minds of many, there was really no difference between the two "modalists" (Athanasius and Marcellus) who met in Rome in the 340s. In his letters to "Eastern" bishops, a pro-Nicene Pope Julius coupled Marcellus and Athanasius several times, and so, for the letter receivers, these two men became a "party" with one agenda and ideology. (Notice the vertical dotted line in the chart!) Later, however, when both theologians advanced their respective Trinitarian theologies, their ways parted, due to the following differences:

1. Athanasius employed both terms: *ousia* and *homoousios*; Marcellus preferred the term *hypostasis*.
2. Athanasius eventually worked for achieving the largest possible theological consensus and showed some theological and terminological flexibility; Marcellus wanted an unambiguous condemnation of Arianism and was not ready for compromises.
3. Athanasius accepted Origen's Trinitarian theology; Marcellus did not.
4. Pope Julius defended Athanasius enthusiastically but Marcellus rather unenthusiastically.
5. "Eastern" churches condemned Athanasius's behavior but Marcellus's doctrine.
6. Athanasius never quit; Marcellus tactfully withdrew when his theology was no longer accepted by his theological compatriots.

In summarizing the situation, D. Williams (1995, 16) has observed with significant rhetorical exaggeration, "Perhaps the only thing Athanasius and Marcellus ever had in common was their hatred of the Eusebians and the goal of being restored to their sees."

Athanasius's primary strategy in fighting for Trinitarian orthodoxy was not a philosophical rebuttal of Arianism. His main weapon was (theological) exegesis, for the battle itself was, to a significant extent, exegetical. T. Barnes (1993, 12) assesses, "Virtually everything that he [Athanasius] wrote is closely based on scriptural texts." Ernest (2004), in turn, has shown that the presence of biblical citations in Athanasius's dogmatic/polemical treatises is significantly greater than in his other works. (Athanasius never authored a commentary on a biblical book, however.) In his *Orations against the Arians*, in "a sustained refutation of Arian proof-texts" (Anatolios 1998, 87), Athanasius appealed to the Scriptures in more than 1,700 times. He seems to have considered his exegetical arguments so convincing that even his opponents were made to concede, "'Be it so,' they say, 'interpret these places thus, and gain the victory in reasoning and proofs'" (*C. Ar.* 3.59).

According to Athanasius, it was crucial to distinguish between texts that spoke about *theology* and texts that spoke about *economy*. This distinction was his exegetical rule of thumb. The mistake of the Arians was that they deduced the "theological" Trinity from the Son's economical limitations. But what was true about the *incarnated* Son was not necessarily true about the *preexistent* Son.

In connection with Col 1:15, "[Christ is] the firstborn of all creation," Athanasius contended that this verse referred to the incarnation rather than to the eternal begetting of the Son. The verse did not say that Christ was "the firstborn *of God*" (theological) but "the firstborn *of all creation*" (economical). Athanasius explained that the titles "only-begotten" and "firstborn" should be understood in different relations, the first referring to the Son's relation to the Father and the second to the Son's relation to the creation: "For the term 'only-begotten' is used where there are no brethren, but 'firstborn' because of brethren" (*C. Ar.* 2.62; cf. Rom 8:29; Col 1:18; Gregory of Nyssa, *C. Eun.* 2.8). For Athanasius, Christ was *begotten* as the only Son of God, and *made* as the "firstborn" Son of Man (cf. Rom 1:3–4). In addition, the verb "to beget" eliminated the implication that the Son was external (*exōthen*) to the Father, as a thing made was to its maker (*C. Ar.* 1.29). Athanasius's anti-Arian writings repeated almost like a chorus that the Son was the Father's "own" (*idios*); thus the Son was not "external" (*exōthen*) to the Godhead (e.g., *C. Ar.* 1.11–13; cf. Rom 8:32; Alexander, *Ep. Alex.* 14.32–33). "*Idios/exōthen* expresses the fundamental contrast between God and creature, between what belongs to the divine substance and what is created out of nothing" (Louth, in *SP*, 1989, 198.)

Likewise, the description of the creation of Wisdom in Prov 8:22 concerned the incarnation rather than the preexistence of Christ (*C. Ar.* 2.45). The Scriptures meant economy (including the incarnation) whenever it added a reason (e.g., Phil 2:7–8), and the Scriptures spoke about theology (the being of God) "when no 'why' is given" (e.g., Phil 2:6; *C. Ar.* 2.53; cf. 2.60). While the verb "to create" in Prov 8:22–25 was modified by "of the works," the verb "to beget" was unmodified. Well, Arians had a counterargument, for Prov 8:23 and 25 said that Wisdom was brought forth *before* the creation, and therefore the text could not refer to the incarnation, which took place *after* the creation. But Athanasius, in turn, labored to show that these verses referred to God's salvific activities, which were prepared *before* the creation of the world (*C. Ar.* 2.73–74).

For Athanasius, it was significant that the controversial text occurred in Proverbs. In Proverbs, things were "proclaim[ed] in a hidden manner" (*C. Ar.* 2.44; cf. Gregory of Nyssa, *C. Eun.* 1.22). A literary genre such as Proverbs often used words according to their improper supposition (figuratively). Accordingly, Athanasius surmised that the verb "to create" (*kitzō*) in Prov 8:22 was used in a figurative sense, and the verb "to beget" (*gennaō*) in Prov 8:25 in a literal sense (*C. Ar.* 2.3). In poetic parallel statements, the phrase that came later explicated the meaning of the previous phrase. Therefore, in Prov 8:22–25, the earlier word "created" should be understood in the light of the later word "begot." Since Athanasius considered the verbs "to create" (*kitzō*) and "to make" (*poieō*) synonymous (*Decr.* 26), he could connect Prov 8:22–25 with the Nicene "begotten not made" (*gennēthenta ou poiēthenta*). The Son was begotten from the Father, and thus he was "created" only in a figurative, causal, or economical sense. Athanasius also had to rescue Heb 3:2 from the Arian use, which with some linguistic justification read the text as "Jesus . . . being faithful to the one who made [*poiēsanti*] him" (*C. Ar.* 2.1). But again, the text was speaking about Jesus as our high priest (Heb 3:1), and thus it was clearly referring to economy.

Justifying his exegetical principles, Athanasius also argued that one should be able to perceive the difference between the linguistic attribution of God and of the creation. Whenever the Scriptures employed the term *gen(n)ētos*, it could not be univocal when applied to the Son of God and to the creation. "For all the creatures, though they be said to have come into being from God, yet are not from God as the Son is" (*Syn.* 35). Unfortunately, Athanasius did not yet make a distinction between *genētos* (created) and *gennētos* (begotten), which would have helped him to express the fact that the Son was caused yet eternally begotten from the *ousia* of the Father (*Ep. Serap.* 1.15; *Syn.* 46; cf. textual variants of *genēsis/gennēsis* in Matt 1:18, "Now the beginning/birth of Jesus Messiah"). Later, it became possible to say that the Father alone was *agennētos* (unbegotten); but Father, Son, and Holy Spirit were nevertheless *agenētos* (uncreated).

This might be a good place to introduce a crucial distinction that had important exegetical implications. It is the distinction between the *Creator* and the *creation*. This distinction was "the architectonic center of Athanasius's theological vision" (Anatolios 2004, 39) and the basis "of his construction of the 'Arian' heresy" (Gwynn 2007, 231). Although this distinction had been employed in Christianity since Athenagoras, its Trinitarian application was mainly a product of the fourth century (Ayres 2004). For Athanasius and his allies, there were only two distinct though related categories: the Creator-God (Father, Son, and Holy Spirit) and the creation. This distinction enabled them to spell out the fact that the Son was clearly on the side of the Creator-God and not somewhere between God and the creation. Athanasius (in *C. Ar.* 1.19) contended that the Son who participated in creating everything that existed (John 1:3) could himself not be created. "And if all things are through him, he himself is not to be reckoned with that 'all.'" The distinction between the Creator and the creation also enabled the deliverance of a "decisive" blow to the Arians: if the Son were a creature, then Arians were actually idolaters, for they worshipped that which was created (*C. Ar.* 2.24; *Ep. Serap.* 1.29).

The task for Athanasius was not only to clarify the status of the Son in regard to the Father but also in regard to the creation. For Arians, the title "only-begotten" implied the Son's difference from the "unbegotten" Father and the Son's difference from the rest of the creation; for Athanasius, the Son's title "only-begotten" implied a fundamental difference between the Son and the creation. He argued that the Father was not a higher solitary God who had to have the Son, a lesser God, in order to reveal himself and enable him to create and save the world. The incarnation of the Son was not a mediation of the ineffable *Agennētos* but *God*'s "becoming flesh." The divine-human person of the incarnated Son, rather than a semidivine Son, was the Mediator between God and humankind.

Athanasius clearly saw the tremendous soteriological implications of his distinction between the Creator and the creation. If the Son were fully God and not a second-rate mediating divinity, only then were Christians justified in believing that, in the incarnation, none other than *God* had come to save fallen humankind. Accordingly, the word "therefore" in texts such as Phil 2:6–11 and Ps 45:7 could not have indicated the Son's earning of his lofty status, because the incarnation and dying as a "lesser" God could not have had the redeeming effect. That is, it would not unite hypostatically the divine and human nature; it would not result in an archetypical deification (*C. Ar.* 1.37–38; 2.69–70). "A creature could never be saved by a creature" (*Ep. Adelph.* 8). Therefore, the incarnation was a *descent* of the fully divine Son rather than an *ascent* of the first created being. The Son as the "first creature" logically lacked the ability to deify other creatures. It is significant indeed that, in *Orations against the Arians*, Athanasius's dominant soteriological motif is deification (Hess, in *SP*, 1993).

For soteriological reasons, Athanasius also maintained that the elevation of the Son in Phil 2:9 had to refer to Christ *as a human being* (*C. Ar.* 1.41–43). To refute the Arian interpretation of "therefore" (*dio*) in Phil 2:9, Athanasius piled up all possible texts from the Hebrew and Christian Scriptures that indicated the preexistence of the Son and provided the theological preunderstanding necessary for comprehending this passage. Ernest (2004, 132) provides an example (*C. Ar.* 2.14) and writes, "Athanasius can . . . on occasion compose texts of his own by weaving language from all parts of the canon into concise summaries of the overall shape of the biblical metanarrative." Athanasius considered it very important that in interpreting ambiguous texts, the *skopos* of the Scriptures (its overall sense) and the "double account of the Savior" should be taken into account (*C. Ar.* 3:29).

However and interestingly, Arius did not think Athanasius's soteriological argument was the strongest because Arius did not understand salvation in terms of deification. As Gregg and Groh (1981) have contended, after accepting the Athanasian absolute distinction between the Creator and the creation, Christ, the "firstborn of all creation," was capable of change and spiritual development, and as such he set the example of obedience to be imitated by Christians. Arius's soteriology, if it can be reconstructed at all, was built on imitation (*mimēsis*) rather than on deification (*theōsis*). As it often happens in controversies, many "punches" are given that really do not hit the mark. It is not without cause that a historian Socrates called the Nicene controversy "a battle fought by night" (*His. eccl.* 1.23).

Finally, it was also Athanasius who defended the full divinity of the Holy Spirit by applying the word *homoousios* to the Spirit (*Ep. Serap.* 1.27). Doing so, he earned an accolade from Gregory of Nazianzus as the first true Trinitarian theologian (*Or.* 21.33). Athanasius believed that "there is one Godhead of the Holy Trinity" (*Ep. Serap.* 1.16). His elaboration enforced the classical Trinitarian doctrine of God:

> The Trinity is holy and perfect, confessed as God in Father, Son, and Holy Spirit, having nothing foreign or extrinsic mingled with it, nor compounded of creator and created, but is wholly Creator and maker. It is identical with itself and indivisible in nature, and its activity is one. (*Ep. Serap.* 1.28)

In the first treatise on the Holy Spirit in Christian history, in his *Letters to Serapion*, Athanasius argued that the Holy Spirit was not a creature but God. The divine work of the Spirit implied the divinity of the Spirit. Again, Athanasius's argument was soteriological, and it rested on the Creator/creation distinction: a Spirit which was not fully divine could not divinize. "Indeed, if we were merely united to a creature, we would still be foreigners to the divine nature, having no participation in it" (*Ep. Serap.* 1.24). And again, "The one who binds creation to the Word could not be among the creatures; . . . the one in whom creation is divinized cannot be extrinsic to the divinity of the Father" (*Ep. Serap.* 1.25). Athanasius further theologized that the Spirit proceeded eternally from God, yet not in a modalist sense, but so that the Spirit had its own (real) subsistence (*Ep. Serap.* 1.28). The Spirit was "from God" (1 Cor 2:12) as a caused being, but the Spirit was not thereby a lesser being. Like the Son, the Spirit was Father's *idion*; the Spirit was the Father's "own" Spirit. Following the example of John 15:26, Athanasius used the verbs "to send" and "to proceed" in such a way that the later economical/theological distinction in the proceeding of the Spirit could find a suitable proof text in the writings of this celebrated church father. He wrote that the Spirit "proceeded from the Father" (theological proceeding) and was "sent and given by the Word who is . . . from the Father" (economical sending; *Ep. Serap.* 1.20; cf. Origen, *Princ.* 1.2.12).

The Council of Nicaea (AD 325)

The increasingly international controversy between Alexander and Arius needed an imperial "taming" and an ecclesiastical settlement. Thus, in AD 325, the emperor summoned over 200 bishops to the Council of Nicaea. The traditional number of participants is 318, associated with the number of Abraham's servants in Gen 14:14. A Coptic source counts 319, adding the Holy Spirit to the traditional number! Constantine made it rather clear that the only option the council had was to establish doctrinal unity (Socrates, *Hist. eccl.* 1.8).

Despite the fact that seventeen bishops were on Arius's side as the council began (Sozomen, *Hist. eccl.* 1.20), or twenty-two according to an anti-Nicene historian Philostorgius (*Hist. eccl.* 1.8), Arius's views had already been condemned before the meeting by hundreds of bishops. Many of them had participated in the Synod of Antioch (AD 324–early 325), which issued the earliest example of a synodal creed. It rejected the propositions that the Son was a creature (*ktisma*) created out of nonexistence (*ouk ek tou mē ontos*), and that the Son was the product of the Father's will (*thelēma*).

Contrary to the Synod of Antioch, which avoided the *ousia* language, the Council of Nicaea affirmed the eternal generation of the Son from the Father's *ousia*. Father and Son were said to be "consubstantial" (*homoousios*). The term *homoousios* was not a breathtakingly exact designation of Christ's full divinity, but a relatively novel and suspicious item in the church's vocabulary. (The only occurrence of the word *ousia* in the New Testament is the hapax legomenon *epiousion* in the Lord's Prayer; Matt 6:11.) Anatolios (1998, 96) remarks, "The *homoousios* is not to be understood so much as a positive statement telling us something about God's being, but rather as a negative one, indicating what the *Logos* is not, namely a creature." Perhaps the "new" word *homoousios* was chosen because the term was despised by Arius and Arians, such as Eusebius of Nicomedia (Hilary of Poitiers, *Syn.* 83; Alexander of Alexandria, *Ep. om.*).

Hermetic and Gnostic theologians had employed the word *homoousios* while explaining the emanations of many from the One, of the word (*logos*) from the Mind (*Nous*). In the earliest Christian discourse, if the term *homoousios* was employed at all, it lacked the specific Trinitarian application. Even at Nicaea, it seems to have been a nuisance to almost everyone. Nevertheless, after consulting with Bishop Hosius (Ossius) of Cordova, Emperor Constantine suggested the use of the term *homoousios*. But in the beginning of the fourth century, it was far from clear what *homoousios* meant and what the theological implications of using it were to the three distinct divine persons. Hilary of Poitiers provided ample evidence about the debates concerning *homoousios* even after the Council of Nicaea. There were theologians who understood the term in a modalist sense, theologians who thought that it referred to a prior substance that the Father and the Son then shared, and theologians who believed that it designated a division of the Father's substance (*Trin.* 4.4; *Syn.* 67–69; cf. Sozomen, *Hist. eccl.* 3.14). Furthermore, while the Latin prefix "con-" in the word "consubstantial" implied distinctness or togetherness, the Greek *homos* in *homoousios* implied sameness, either relative or absolute sameness. In short, *homoousios*, just like any other term, was open to various interpretations. "The expression [*homoousios*] contains both a conscientious conviction and the opportunity for delusion" (Hilary of Poitiers, *Syn.* 67). Probably because of the strangeness and ambiguity of the word *homoousios*, it almost disappeared from the ensuing debates. Only when the Synod of Sirmium (AD 357) condemned the use of the term *homoousios* did it capture the real interest of the Athanasian pro-Nicenes. Rufinus, however, reports that as late as AD 359 the Latin bishops "did not know what the word *homoousios* meant" (*Hist. eccl.* 10.22).

Arguably, the intention of introducing the term *homoousios* into the Nicene Creed was to explicate what the phrase "from the essence of the Father" (*ek tēs ousias tou patros*) attempted to state. Arius could have signed everything before the phrase "from the essence of the Father" in the Nicene Creed. For instance, he did not have any objections to the biblical designation "only-begotten"—if it was understood as "unique." But he could not agree with the clarifying clause stating that the Son was "from the essence (*ousia*) of the Father." Together with the clause "from the essence of the Father," the title "only-begotten" seemed to mean much more than being unique among the creatures. It meant the Son's consubstantiality with the Father.

The choice of the preposition *ek* (from) in the phrase *ek tēs ousias tou patros* (from the Father's essence) had its own significance. In the Nicene Creed, the biblical "*from/by/beside* the Father" (*para tou patros*) of John 15:26 became "*from* ... the Father" (*ek tou ... patros*). Supposedly, the change of the preposition differentiated the council's *theological* statement from the evangelist's *economical* statement. (The use of prepositions is complicated. For instance, John 8:42, "I came from God," employs the preposition *ek* and refers nevertheless to economy. [The following phrase "and now I am here" makes this clear.] However, the NEB still translates it in both theological and economical senses: "God is the source of my being, and from him I come.") In addition, perhaps the preposition *ek* in the Nicene Creed also brought out the notion of causality more clearly than the preposition *para*.

To recapitulate, the introduction of the term *homoousios* was intended to safeguard at least three convictions:

1. The fully divine status of the only-begotten Son. The Nicene Creed confessed the Son to be "true God from true God" (*theon alēthinon ek theou alēthinou*). The Son was also called "Lord" (*kyrios*).
2. The unity and oneness of the Christian God. The idea of using the term *homoousios* was to make sure that affirming of the full divinity of the Son was not giving up monotheism.
3. The fundamental difference between the divine Son and the creation. The Nicene Creed stated that the Son was "begotten not made" (*gennēthenta ou poiēthenta*). In anathemas, the council emphatically rejected the phrases "there was time when he was not" (which Arius had rhymed as *ēn pote hote ouk ēn*) and that the Son came into being "from things that were not" (*ex ouk ontōn egeneto*). (In the earliest extant text of the Nicene Creed [in Athanasius's *Appendix* to *De decretis* 4], those who said that the Son was "created" [*ktistos*] were also condemned. Yet, Athanasius may have inserted the word into the text of the Creed [Wiles, in *SP*, 1993]).

When the term *homoousios* was applied to the Father and the Son, it became important to clarify that it implied neither the divisible materiality of God nor the existence of two first principles. Socrates explicitly stressed that the presiders of Nicaea understood the word *homoousios* in a nonmaterial sense (*Hist. eccl.* 1.8). The accusation that calling the Father and the Son *homoousios* was postulating two first principles was dodged, in turn, perhaps by the statement that the Son was "from the Father" (*ek tou patrou*). However, the phrase that was supposed to provide the analogy for determining the correct sense of the novel term *homoousios*—"light from light"—was not effective in disallowing either of the two implications: of emanation or of materiality of God's nature (*ousia* as the "stuff" shared).

Statements made during controversies—yes, even the conciliar statements—are usually one-sided. The Nicene bishops were preoccupied with emphasizing the equal divinity of the Father and Son, and consequently they somewhat underemphasized the distinction between the divine *hypostaseis*. There were really no defenses in the Nicene Creed against a modalist reading of it. On the contrary, one of the anathemas, or legal condemnations of the Nicene Council, confusingly denounced the position that the Son was of another *hypostasis* or (!) *ousia*. Accordingly, many suspected that the Nicene key word *homoousios* was, at least by implication, modalist. Some 250 Arian/Eusebian bishops actually condemned the term *homoousious* already at the Synod of Nicomedia in AD 327. Later even an orthodox Basil of Caesarea had to concede, "But the term *homoousion* [is] ill received in certain quarters" (*Ep.* 52.1). The suspicions about Nicene "modalism" were substantiated by Marcellus's arguments for the sameness of the Father and his Word (see below).

On the other hand, the fact that most Eusebians signed the Nicene Creed indicates that the council was not an overwhelming victory of the Alexandrian/Athanasian alliance either, although it looked like that in retrospect. Curiously, the Nicene condemnations could also be read in an anti-Marcellian sense, condemning the position that there was no *hypostasis* of the Son before his birth from Mary (Parvis 2006).

A footnote on later development: adding to the terminological "mess" of equating *hypostasis* and *ousia* in the Nicene condemnations, the Synod of Sardica (AD 342/343) under the direction of Marcellus soon preferred the expression *mia hypostasis* to the Nicene *homoousios* (Theodoret, *His. eccl.* 2.6). In the middle of the fourth century, Cyril of Jerusalem could still write that God was "uniform in *hypostasis*" (*Catecheses* 6.7). Furthermore, an early sixth-century Monophysite text reported an earlier Egyptian oracle as saying that Father, Son, and Spirit "are three, but they are only one nature [*mia physis*]" (anon., *Theosophia* 1.43). The point of these three examples is to illustrate the semantic overlap of the terms *ousia*, *hypostasis*, and *physis* in the fourth century (and, occasionally, even after that). Thus, it was altogether not clear what the Nicene Creed asserted. Ayres summarizes, "The seemingly precise terminology was thus actually used without agreement on its sense" (in Young, Ayres, and Louth 2004, 427). To use Farrelly's (2005, 79) phrase, the terms *ousia*, *hypostasis*, and *physis* still suffered from the "ambiguity of underdevelopment."

Contrary to the expectations of the Alexandrian/Athanasian alliance, the Council of Nicaea did not bring about an unconditional condemnation of Eusebians, though some people indeed were exiled. Within a year after Nicaea, the Eusebians/Arians gained the upper hand again due to the political influence of Eusebius of Nicomedia, a former fellow student of Arius, and due to the prestige of Eusebius of Caesarea. This meant that soon after Nicaea, the leading pro-Athanasian theologians were all deposed or exiled for theological and not-so-theological reasons. This quick change of tide, among other reasons, may explain why the Nicene Creed together with its suspiciously "modalist" term *homoousios* did not figure prominently in the theological treatises and debates for about the next fifty years. Even for Athanasius, it took some twenty–thirty years to figure out the real implications of the word *homoousios* and the significance of the Nicene statement. It was only in AD 362 that he wrote about the Nicene Creed, "Nothing more was to be written concerning faith, but that one was to be satisfied with the faith confessed in Nicaea by the fathers, because it lacks nothing, but is full of piety" (*Tomus ad Antiochenos* 5). Despite the fact that Pope Liberius asked Constantius to confirm the Nicene Creed as an ecumenical orthodox confession in AD 354, the Creed had to wait for its decisive reaffirmation by the Council of Constantinople in AD 381.

In short, before the second half of the fourth century, the Nicene Creed was not perceived as something final, universal, and cast in stone forever. It "did not halt debate but set terms for a new, more vigorous stage of dispute" (Wilken 2003, 83–84). In other words, the Nicene Creed caused a series of theological "aftershocks." Bishops constantly composed new creeds with the intent to improve the Nicene doctrine of the Trinity. A few decades after Nicaea, Acacius reportedly commented, "Since the Nicene Creed has been altered not once only, but frequently, there is no hindrance to our publishing another [the Creed of Seleucia, AD 359] at this time" (Socrates, *Hist. eccl.* 2.40). Ayres (2004, 85) observes: "The idea that the [Nicene] creed would serve as a universal and precise marker of Christian faith was unlikely to have occurred to anyone at Nicaea simply because the idea that *any* creed might so serve was as yet unheard of."

The Council of Nicaea slowly acquired its authority only after its "modalist" interpretation(s) were refuted and after the Homoeans had provoked a more sophisticated defense of the Nicene position. Despite its slow acceptance, the much-debated *homoousios* became a litmus test for orthodoxy by the end of the fourth century. Vaggione (2000, 365) comments somewhat sarcastically about the Council of Nicaea,

> Now, suddenly, within a relatively short period of time, formularies that had been resisted throughout the region for more than a generation were identified as ancestral faith: it turned out that they had "always" been Nicene. . . . And that, truly, is the Nicene victory—the capacity to see an inherited faith in formularies that had previously been thought to exclude it.

What we can say in retrospect, however, is that the Nicene *homoousios* at least restricted the tendency to explicate the Christian doctrine of the Trinity in the neoplatonic categories of hypostatic hierarchy, which was a tempting option for several theologians. And although the new formularies were coined, they were coined to explicate the convictions that were not new. Christians had worshipped the Son as God from the very beginning of their existence. After all, councils were convened "not to invent doctrine, but to confess it" (Nassif, in *ChrCent*, 2005, 35). So in retrospect, the Nicene Creed is regarded as the orthodox statement of the classical orthodox Trinitarian theology.

Sameness of the Divine Persons: Marcellus of Ancyra

Even though Marcellus of Ancyra was a leading anti-Arian and one of the creators of Arianism, he shared the fate of Arius in becoming an oft-condemned stereotypical theological villain. Marcellus and Arius are commonly perceived as the two heretics of opposite ends. (The Library of Congress cataloging system still places both gentlemen unambiguously among heretics!) The subordinationist theologians called Marcellus a "Sabellian" and considered him "a more abominable plague than all the other heretics" (Hilary of Poitiers, *Contra Valens and Ursacius* 1.2.2). Marcellus returned the favor by blessing the subordinationists with the name "Arian."

In Chart Two, Marcellus is placed in the left, nonorthodox column because he was formally condemned at the Council of Constantinople in AD 381 (Canon One). Marcellus's opponents considered him to be a modalist or Sabellian, despite the fact that he never promoted the idea of the Father *becoming* the Son. On the other hand, Marcellus was also a participant at the Council of Nicaea, a fighter against subordinationism and for the full divinity of the Son. The "Western" bishops declared at Sardica (342/343) that "his faith was found to be correct" (Theodoret, *Hist. eccl.* 2.6). So, what was he?

We should give Marcellus a fair hearing, for he was arguably one of the most respected and influential theologians of his time (Parvis 2006). When the anti-Arian churches condemned a modalist Photinus, Marcellus was not condemned together with his student. Athanasius, too, refused to denounce him. At the same time, Marcellus's theology provoked a lot of reaction, which in turn became the impetus for the making of much of the fourth-century Trinitarian theology. Reaction to his "modalism" became a real catalyst for the emerging orthodox doctrine of the Trinity.

Marcellus was a representative of the "miahypostatic" theological tradition (Lienhard's term [1999]). The Synod of Antioch of AD 324/325 stated that the Son was "of the *hypostasis* of the Father" (*tēs patrikēs hypostaseōs*; cf. Heb 1:3). Following the synod's lead, Marcellus chose the expression *mia hypostasis* to guard the unity (*monas*) of the Father and his *Logos* (*Fragment* 97). He insisted that in God there was one *hypostasis* (= *ousia*), just as the condemnation of Nicaea had said! As we have seen, this confusing condemnation demonstrated clearly that there was yet no universally established difference between the theological uses of the terms *ousia* and *hypostasis*. This caused much misunderstanding. Marcellus adamantly denied that one could speak about two (or three) *hypostaseis* in God. Such talk would postulate two Gods, or alternatively, deny the full divinity of the Son. Saying that anything was "two" in the Godhead (e.g., *ousia*, *hypostasis*, or *prosōpon*) scandalized Marcellus and provoked his celebrated-but-mostly-lost response to Arians (his treatise *Against Asterius*).

To explain the (eternal) relationship between the Father and the Son/*Logos*, Marcellus turned to the Stoic distinction between the "word in the mind" (*logos endiathetos*) and the "word uttered" (*logos prophorikos*) (cf Ps 45·1; 44·2 LXX)· "My heart brings forth a good word [*logon agathon*]" (Theophilus, *Autol.* 2.10–22). Trusting the analogy to the point of neglecting the difference—at least according to Eusebius (*De ecclesiastica theologia* 2.15)—Marcellus opined that, in the mind of the Father, the *Logos* was without its own *hypostasis*. Referring to John 10:30, 38, and 14:9, Marcellus confessed, "I have learned from the Sacred Scriptures that the Godhead of the Father and of the Son cannot be differentiated; . . . the Son is indistinguishable and inseparable [*adiairetos kai achōristos*] from the Father" (Marcellus, *Confessio*, in Epiphanius, *Pan.* 72.3.2). The "nonuttered" mental *Logos* could not be differentiated from the Father's mind, just like a word could not be differentiated from the human mind that was thinking it. "For it is impossible . . . to separate the discourse [*logos*] of a human being . . . as a reality [*hypostasis*], for the discourse [*logos*] is one and the same with the human being" (Marcellus, *Frg.* 87). Marcellus did not mean thereby that the *logos endiathetos* existed only potentially in the mind. The eternal *Logos* existed in the Father's mind not as a mere potency but as a realized act, because the Father was never without reason, word, and wisdom. God the Father was never only *potentially* wise! Yet, even as a realized act, the "nonuttered" Word did not have a *hypostasis* different from that of the Father.

Now, the eternal *Logos* in the Father's mind was uttered for the sake of the creation and the incarnation. The "uttered Word" had indeed its distinct *hypostasis*. Building again on the human analogy, Marcellus argued that a word had its hypostatic existence only *when* uttered and only *while* uttered (Eusebius, *Contra Marcellum* 1.1.4). The uttered word had a *temporal* hypostatic existence because it existed as long as it sounded, as long as its material medium (sound waves) existed. Marcellus concluded that, likewise, the Son/Word was hypostatically distinct from the Father/Mind only in the incarnation. Even the scriptural designation "image" (*eikōn* in Col 1:15) did not imply that the *Logos* was eternally distinct from God, because the word "image" did not concern the eternal *Logos* at all. It concerned the *incarnated* Son. The image had to be different from the archetype: "The image is image not of itself but of something different" (Marcellus, *Frg.* 114); above all, it had to be *visible* (*Frs.* 53–55). Thus, for Marcellus, the word "image" was an expression of *economy*, of Christ's flesh, rather than of *theology*, of the eternal preincarnated *Logos*. Likewise, Arians failed to understand that Prov 8:22, "The LORD created me at the beginning of his work," was not about the preexistent Wisdom (Marcellus, *Frg.* 28). The preexistent Wisdom/Word was "neither created nor made" (*ou ktistheis, ou poiētheis*; Marcellus, *Conf.*). "The Word . . . is always with the Father and has never had a beginning" (*Conf.*). It followed that it was the incarnated Son whose *hypostasis* was created in the beginning of his economic activity.

Marcellus postulated a crucial distinction between the *Son* and the *Word*. The "uttered" or incarnated *Logos* was the Son (*Frs.* 85, 97; *Conf.*), while the "nonuttered" or preexistent *Logos* was the Word (Marcellus, *Frg.* 3). The Son was begotten from Mary (*Frg.* 59; John 1:14), but the Word was always in God (*Frs.* 68, 76; John 1:1). To be precise, Marcellus did not always consistently follow the Word/Son distinction: at times he also called the preexistent Word "Son" (as in *Frg.* 38; *Conf.*). Nevertheless, this very distinction between the incarnated Son and the preexistent Word got Marcellus into trouble. It brought him trouble even though he emphasized that the incarnated Son and the eternal Word were not unrelated. Marcellus's basic soteriological idea—the Word was the subject of the incarnated Son—was actually quite orthodox (*Frs.* 5, 28). Yet his insistence on the indistinguishable status of the preincarnate Word/Son in the mind of the Father made most theologians quite wary. It can be seen, ironically, from the fact that the phrase "there was time when he was not," which Nicaea condemned as Arius's theological mistake, was later turned against Marcellus. The "Eastern" bishops at Philippopolis (AD 342/343) condemned those who taught that "there was time when he was not"—and they meant Marcellus's view that the Son began to exist from Mary (cf. Hilary of Poitiers, *Syn.* 34)! Eventually, the twenty-six anathemas of the First Sirmian Creed (AD 351) rejected the mind/word analogy precisely because an uttered word had no distinct existence before being uttered and because it ceased to exist after the utterance was over (Hilary of Poitiers, *Syn.* 46; *Trin.* 2.15).

Another phrase in the Nicene-Constantinopolitan Creed, "of his kingdom there will be no end," came to be known as a stock anti-Marcellian phrase. However, perhaps the creed did not consider the changes in Marcellus's theology adequately enough (cf. Hilary of Poitiers, *C. Valens and Ursacius* 1.3.6.). Marcellus figured that since the enemies of God were not yet subjugated at the feet of Christ, the kingdom of Christ was "partial [*meros*]" (*Frg.* 106; cf. 1 Cor 15:24–28 and in v. 25 the word "until [*achri*]"!). This "partial" kingdom would yield to the "full" kingdom when Christ reigned with the Father. Marcellus later indeed argued that the temporal kingdom of the Son would be part of the Father's kingdom, which would have "no end" (*Frg.* 106; cf. Theodoret, *Hist. eccl.* 2.6; Ps 145:13; Luke 1:33; Eph 1:10).

It remains to be said that Marcellus, the signer of the Nicene *canons*, never became a proponent of the Nicene *Creed*. The Nicene Creed included several pronouncements that did not please him, such as the use of the *ousia* language, and statements that facilitated an understanding of the distinct existence of the preincarnate Son. (The word *homoousios* never occurs in the extant fragments of Marcellus's writings.) Since Marcellus's defense of the full divinity of the Son of God was not accompanied by a clear affirmation of the distinct hypostatic subsistence of the preincarnate Son, many thought his distinction between the Father and Son seemed merely nominal. Eventually his teaching was considered heretical. Gregory of Nazianzus, for example, complained about "theories that honor the unity of God more than is appropriate" (*Or.* 20.10). As Lienhard (1999, 68) summarizes, Marcellus "can call God a Triad but cannot say what is triadic in God."

Distinctness of the Divine Persons (The Second Row)

Next, consider the middle-right column in row two, Chart Two. Eusebius of Caesarea was among the main opponents of Athanasius and Marcellus. Grouping certain like-minded theologians (e.g., Eusebius of Caesarea, Asterius, and Eusebius of Nicomedia) together as "Eusebians"—just as Athanasius did (*Apologia secunda* [*Apologia contra Arianos*] 87; *Decr.* 1)—is not to ignore their theological differences, but to identify a larger group of like-minded theologians that would fit into our chart. Antimodalistically, Eusebians defended that part of the Origenist heritage that emphasized the monarchy of the Father and the subordination of the three divine and distinct *hypostaseis*. Athanasius, however, wanted the world to believe that the Eusebians (named after Eusebius of Nicomedia) behind his condemnation at the Synod of Tyre in AD 335 were Arians. Athanasius was quite convinced that the battle was between orthodoxy (Athanasius) and heresy ("Eusebians" = "Arians"; Athanasius, *Epistula encyclica* 2; Gwynn 2007).

Eusebius of Caesarea

Eusebius was one of the notables attending the Council of Nicaea and after that, one of the leading opponents to the Athanasian interpretation of the theology of that council. Eusebius was an erudite church historian who "pleased Constantine with his imperial interpretation of salvation history" (Lyman 1993, 82) and who considered the acts of Alexander of Alexandria against Arius "to be that of a pastor unfamiliar with advanced theology and scholarship" (Chadwick 2001, 196).

In his theological works, Eusebius avoided mentioning Arius, but Asterius's influence on his work connects the two. Eusebius and Asterius both authored their respective refutations of Marcellus (their treatises *Against Marcellus*). To revisit our simplified scheme and to follow Athanasius's postulation of two opposing groups (e.g., *Decr.* 20), the "afterlife" of the Alexandrian tradition consisted of anti- and pro-Nicene trajectories:

> — (anti-Nicene) **Arius**
> —Asterius
> —Eusebius of Caesarea
> Clement—Origen—Dionysius
> — (pro-Nicene) **Alexander** —**Athanasius**

Eusebius and Marcellus appear in Chart Two at opposite ends. Both of them said things that proved to be orthodox, and things that proved to be unorthodox. Both theologians struggled to find the best *locus* for affirming the plurality in one God. As we have seen, Marcellus proposed that the plurality should be sought in the incarnation. Eusebius, in turn, suggested that it should be sought in the distinct *hypostaseis* of the divine persons; in what the names "Father," "Son," and "Holy Spirit" signified. Because of this difference, Eusebius thought that Marcellus's major mistake was to deny the Son his own *hypostasis* before the incarnation and to argue that the Son existed as a distinct *hypostasis* only during his incarnation (*C. Marc.* 2.4.21). For Eusebius, Marcellus's "miahypostatic" position was nothing but blunt modalism (*Eccl. theol.* 3.6).

As a consequence, Eusebius considered it his theological duty to secure the affirmation of the preincarnate hypostatic distinction of the divine persons. He was resolute in insisting that there had always been three *hypostaseis* in the Godhead. (*Hypostasis* was still not clearly distinguished from *ousia.*) In his profession of faith in Nicaea, Eusebius said that "each one of these [Father, Son, and Spirit] exists and subsists [*einai kai hyparchein*], the Father truly [*alēthōs*] [existing as] Father, the Son truly as Son, and the Holy Spirit truly as Holy Spirit" (Eusebius, *Confessio*, in Athanasius, *App. Decr.*). The Son had his own (*idiōs*) existence apart from the Father (Eusebius, *Dem. ev.* 4.3). Marcellus's denial of the hypostatic preexistence of the Son was due to his erroneous consideration of the Son being a "mere word" (*psilos logos*; Eusebius, *C. Marc.* 1.1.4; cf. Basil of Caesarea, *Ep.* 125.1). But the Son could not have been a "mere word" because the Scriptures did not say that the Son was "*in* God" but that he was "*with* God" (John 1:1). The latter expression presupposed the distinct *hypostaseis* of the Father and the Son.

Marcellus wanted to read all the scriptural passages about the hypostatic distinctness and inferiority of the Son as pertaining exclusively to the incarnation. But Eusebius deliberated that there was more to the Son's hypostatic distinctness and subordination than his being incarnate. The Son's being distinct from and subordinate to his Father had to be affirmed both on the ontological level and before the incarnation. Did not the scriptural designation of the Son as "image" (Col 1:15) imply both the Son's derivation from his archetype (from the Father) and the Son's distinct hypostatic preincarnate existence (*Eccl. theol.* 2.23)?

Defending the hypostatic existence of the preincarnate Son, a subordinationist Eusebius also guarded against the alleged modalism hiding behind the Nicene Creed. He appealed to his colleague Asterius's teaching on two wisdoms which, in turn, countered the argument that God had to be rational (that God had to have his wisdom eternally) and therefore that the Son/Wisdom had to exist eternally. Asterius concluded that there were *two* Wisdoms, one of which was eternally with God, and the other of which was the Son (Asterius, *Fragment* 1 [see Athanasius, *Syn.* 18]; cf. Arius's *Thalia* and Arius in Athanasius, *Dion.* 23). This way God could always be rational and there could also be the time when the Son/Wisdom did not exist. He took 1 Cor 1:21–24 to be the supporting text. It seemed to postulate a distinction between God's wisdom and Christ as God's power and wisdom. The phrase identifying Christ as God's power and wisdom did not use a definite article before the word *theos* (v. 24), as Asterius astutely observed (*Frg.* 64). Thus, Asterius concluded that the text did not speak about the wisdom and power of the ultimate God the Father (Origen's *ho theos*), but about Christ as God's power (*dynamis*) and wisdom (*sophia*) in a secondary, derivative, and qualitatively different sense (*Frg.* 74).

Accepting this "two powers/two wisdoms" doctrine, Eusebius distanced himself from the idea of the Son being born from the Father's essence (*Eccl. theol.* 1.8). The Son was truly from (*ek*) the Father but not from the essence (*ek tēs ousias*) of the Father in the Athanasian sense of the word (*Conf.*; *Eccl. theol.* 1.8). When Eusebius indeed wrote that "the Son alone is Son of God by nature" (*to monon einai physei tou theou huion*), he wanted to say that the Son reflected the Father's essence in a unique way (Eusebius, *Dem. ev.* 5.4). His intention can be surmised from the fact that he quickly added an explanation: As the image of the Father, the Son received his divinity from his Father, and therefore the Son was not a self-subsistent Unbegotten God (*Dem. ev.* 5.4). The Son did not have his divinity, so to speak, "from himself." The begotten Son, the form and image of God (Phil 2:6; Col 1:15), reflected the Father's essence without being the unbegotten Father or equal to the unbegotten Father. To prove it, Eusebius provided an interesting Christological variation on Isa 45:14–15 (LXX): "In Thee shall they pray, because God is in Thee, and Thou thyself art God, the Savior of Israel. . . . God is in Thee, and there is none beside Him" (*Dem. ev.* 5.4).

Eusebius made absolutely sure that the uniqueness of God the Father was maintained whenever the divinity of the Son was affirmed. The Father alone was "unbegotten" (*agen[n]ētos*). The Father and only the Father was the "first God" (*prōtos theos*; *Dem. ev.* 5.4). The Son was begotten and thus "not the same as the Unbegotten" (*Dem. ev.* 5.1). Eusebius regarded the Son as the "second [being]" or "second God" (*deuteros theos*) in the sense that the Son was a God who began to be (*Dem. ev.* 5.3, 30; cf. Origen, *Dial.* 2.3).

What does it mean, then, that the Son is divine and yet has a derived existence? Together with his theological compatriots, Eusebius contended that the Son came to be by "the Father's transcendent and inconceivable will [*boulēs*] and power [*dynameōs*]," and by Father's "intention [*gnōmēn*] and choice [*proairesis*]" (*Dem. ev.* 4.3). The Son was the "sole-begotten of his will" (*monogenē tēs autou boulēs*; *Dem. ev.* 4.5). It was not that the Son was created out of nonbeing (*ex ouk ontōn*); that would have obscured the crucial difference between the Son and the creation (*Dem. ev.* 5.1; *Eccl. theol.* 1.9). The case of the only-begotten Son was unique. Being born out of the will of the Father and not being created out of nonbeing made the Son unlike the Father and unlike the creation.

To defend the correctness of his theological understanding, Eusebius appealed to the traditional doctrine of the monarchy of the Father. However, unlike his "teacher" Origen, Eusebius concluded that the monarchy of the Father meant both logical *and temporal* priority of the Father over the Son. "But the Father precedes [*prohyparchei*] the Son, and has preceded Him in existence" (*Dem. ev.* 4.3). Here is a curious contradiction: on one hand, Eusebius asserted that human analogies of begetting were not adequate to illustrate the ineffable begetting of the Son; on the other hand, he took the very same analogies quite literally and insisted that "a father must exist before and precede his son" (*Dem. ev.* 5.1; cf. *Hist. eccl.* 1.2). Be this as it may, Eusebius asserted that "the Son was certainly not . . . without beginning" (*Dem. ev.* 5.1). He elaborated that the "begotten" God could not be eternal (*aidios*), because only the "unbegotten" God was eternal (*Eccl. theol.* 2.3). A "coeternal" (*synaidios*) Son would be isomorphic with the Father, and such understanding would, in turn, undermine monotheism (*C. Marc.* 2.4.24).

At the same time, the trick was to say that the "'later'-than-the-Father" Son was "earlier" than time, because time was something that was created through the Son. Postulating a "pretemporal" time, Eusebius confessed that the Son was born "before all ages" (*pro pantōn tōn aiōnōn*), "before" time was created (*Conf.*; *Eccl. theol.* 1.8; cf. Prov 8:23 LXX, *pro tou aiōnos*). One can see how Eusebius struggled to put this idea into words, piling up qualifying expressions (in the end of *Dem. ev.* 4.3): the begotten Son existed "before eternal time [*pro chronōn aiōniōn*], and [was] preexistent [*proonta*], and ever with the Father as his Son, and yet not Unbegotten, but begotten from the Father Unbegotten, being the Only-begotten."

It remains to be said that Eusebius signed the Nicene Creed, but with some serious reservations. The wording of the creed that he himself proposed at the council was changed in several ways. For instance, Eusebius's phrase "God from God" was retained but also elaborated into "true [*alēthinos*] God from true God," and some of his phrases were altogether omitted (such as "firstborn of all creation" and "begotten from the Father before all ages").

Some Interim Synods

Out of the many synods (*synodos*, Greek for "assembly" or "council") between the Councils of Nicaea and Constantinople, we have selected four: the synods of Antioch, Sardica, Sirmium, and Alexandria. These four interim synods offer a sampling of creeds from the main theological trajectories.

A note on chronology: the temporal overlap between the many persons and synods in Chart Two is not as evident as it should be. Many theologians found in this chart were the key figures at several synods. Thus, readers do well to keep in mind that the primary purpose of the chart is to locate the persons and synods on a three-column scale depicting the Trinitarian views under the titles "Sameness," "Sameness and Distinctness," and "Distinctness."

Synod of Antioch

Eusebians (of whatever kind) conducted the Synod of Antioch (AD 340–341) in response to Pope Julius's proposal to reconsider the deposition of

Athanasius and Marcellus. The Synod of Antioch was "the last theological word of the Eusebian alliance proper" (Parvis 2006, 173). Their appeal to the Scriptures was no less sweeping than that of their opponents. The so-called Dedication Creed of the Synod of Antioch (AD 340–341) asserted, "For we believe and follow everything that has been delivered from the Holy Scriptures by the prophets and apostles truly and reverently" (Socrates, *Hist. eccl.* 2.10).

Asterius was the major ideologue behind the Dedication Creed of the Synod of Antioch. Countering the Athanasian Trinitarian theology and the alleged modalism of Marcellus, this synod affirmed the three *hypostaseis* of the Father, Son, and Holy Spirit; it defended certain hierarchical subordination within the Godhead. Since these two beliefs *could* be interpreted in a pro-Nicene way, the creed was considered acceptable by some theologians of Athanasius's persuasion (e.g., Hilary of Poitiers, *Syn.* 32–33). However, some ninety "Eastern" bishops admitted that their theology was compatible with Arius's theology, even though they were not *followers* of him (Athanasius, *Syn.* 22). So, perhaps the creed's compatibility with Arianism needs to be exposed.

The Dedication Creed confessed that "the Lord Jesus Christ [was] . . . the exact image of the essence . . . of the Father's divinity [*tēs theotētos ousias . . . tou patros*]" (Athanasius, *Syn.* 23). The Son being an "image" (Col 1:15), even if an "exact image," arguably affirmed the essential difference between the Father and the Son. The creed named the Father as "fashioner and maker . . . of everything [*tōn holōn*], from whom are all [things] [*ta panta*]" (Athanasius, *Syn.* 23). The word "everything" could include the Son, since it came *before* the mentioning of the Son (cf. John 1:3; Acts 17:24–25). The word "everything" did not occur again when it was said that "all things" (the rest of the creation?) came to be "through" (*dia*) the only-begotten God. While being completely silent about the Nicene term *homoousios*, the creed employed Arian stock phrases: "Father's divinity [*theotēs*]," "only-begotten God [*monogenēs theos*]," and "the firstborn of all creation [*prōtotokos pasēs ktiseōs*]" (Col 1:15). It ended with a strong affirmation of the three *hypostaseis* of the Father, Son, and Holy Spirit and explained that "these names are not assigned casually or idly, but designate quite precisely the particular subsistence, the rank, and the glory [*hypostasin te kai taxin kai doxan*] of each of those named" (Athanasius, *Syn.* 23).

Synod of Sardica

The future division between the churches of East and West indicated itself powerfully at the Synod of Sardica (AD 342/343). The synod actually never convened as such. In their separate meeting, about ninety "Western" bishops acknowledged the orthodoxy of Athanasius and Marcellus and considered it credible that Eusebians were indeed Arians. Although the synod tilted toward the miahypostatic theology of Marcellus, Athanasius later claimed that they had no intentions of going beyond "the faith confessed by the fathers at Nicaea" (Athanasius, *Tom.* 5). What happened was that the "Western" delegates regarded it unacceptable to distinguish between the words *hypostasis* and *ousia*. They confessed the "oneness of essence [*hypostasis*]" of the Father and Son (Theodoret, *Hist. eccl.* 2.6; cf. the condemnation of the Nicene Creed). Consequently, they deemed it illegitimate to speak about the three *hypostaseis* in the Godhead. But the "Easterners" continued to speak about three *hypostaseis*. Therefore, the "Westerners" accused them of alienating the *Logos* from the Father and dividing the divine nature (Athanasius, *Apol. sec.* 49; *Tom.* 5). "The gang of heretics contends, that the substances (*hypostaseis*) of the Father and the Son and the Holy Spirit are different, and that they are separate" (Theodoret, *Hist. eccl.* 2.6).

This is a drastic example of how differently the words *ousia* and *hypostasis* were understood. It demonstrates a complete unwillingness to understand the other side! Marcellus probably meant *ousia* when he used the word *hypostasis*; the "Easterners," on the other hand, meant a "concrete subsistence" or "person." The "Western" creed indeed showed an awareness of the problem by admitting that "there is one substance [*hypostasis*], which the heretics themselves call 'nature' [*ousia*]" (Theodoret, *Hist. eccl.* 2.6). Barnard (1983, 84) observes, "The ability to understand the theological position of others is a rare phenomenon at any period."

The "Western" creed (an encyclical letter) was not intended as a formal confession by the "Western" bishops. Therefore, when the miahypostatic position became an embarrassment, Athanasius could dismiss the whole thing: "The council made no such definition" (*Tom.* 5). He also omitted the creed from his account of the Synod of Sardica in his *Defense against the Arians* (*Apologia secunda*) 36–50. Yet, the letter is extant, and its theology is open for everyone to assess.

The "Western" creed of Sardica condemned the views that the Son was God but not the *true* God (*alēthinos theos*), that the begotten Son had to have a beginning, even if "before time" (*pro aiōnōn*), and that the Father ever existed without the Son. "We as catholics condemn their [the 'Easterners'] foolish and deplorable view" (Theodoret, *Hist. eccl.* 2.6). To affirm the unity between the Father and the Son, the creed also affirmed that the Son *was* the very power (*dynamis*) of God and not a secondary divine power, as Arius had insisted (*Hist. eccl.* 2.6). "The theology of *dynamis* in the creed of Sardica is a complete repudiation of 'two-powers' theology and any understanding that *dynamis* is something other than very divinity" (M. Barnes 2001, 140). At the same time the accusation of modalism was dodged with a clear statement: "We do not say that the Father is the Son, or again that the Son is the Father" (Theodoret, *Hist. eccl.* 2.6).

On the other hand, some eighty or so "Easterners," who had recently learned that they were Arians, gathered in Philippopolis (342/343; cf. Socrates, *Hist. eccl.* 2.20; Sozomen, *Hist. eccl.* 3.11). They questioned the behavior of the deposed Athanasius as well as the orthodoxy of the deposed Marcellus; they wondered how Pope Julius could be in communion with those deposed trouble-makers (Athanasius, *Apol. sec.* 44–47). The "Easterners" reminded the "Western-ers" that their councils had no right to reverse the decisions of Eastern councils. Neither had they any right to restore the condemned Athanasius and Marcellus to the communion of the church. Thus, those who obstinately continued to be in communion with Marcellus and Athanasius were excommunicated. This list included Pope Julius(!) and Hosius (Ossius) of Cordova, who had suggested the word *homoousios* at Nicaea.

As far as Trinitarian theology was concerned, the "Easterners" protested against the Western alleged hypostatic identification of the *Logos* with the Father. In expressing their version of the orthodox faith, the bishops in Philip-popolis repeated the phrases "who was begotten from the Father before all ages" (which *can* be read in the Arian sense) and the anti-Marcellian "whose kingdom remains without the end forever" (Hilary of Poitiers, *Syn.* 34). Marcellus's friends protested, "He had never pretended, as they [the 'Easterners'] positively affirmed, that the Word of God had his beginning from the holy Mary, nor that his kingdom had an end" (Athanasius, *Apol. sec.* 47). Yet, there seems to be more to the story, because the "Western" bishops also had to defend Marcellus by say-ing, "What Marcellus had advanced by way of enquiry, they falsely represented as his professional opinion" (*Apol. sec.* 47). The condemnations, which the "East-erners" added to their creed, demonstrated their pointed anti-Marcellianism. Those believing that there was no Son before the ages or that the Father and the Son and the Spirit were the same *hypostasis*, "the holy and catholic Church anathematizes" (Hilary of Poitiers, *Syn.* 34).

Synod of Sirmium

There were several synods held in the imperial residence of Sirmium, in the "imperial creed factory" (Hardy and Richardson 1954, 341). The one selected for our chart is the Fourth Synod of Sirmium, AD 359, which produced the so-called Dated Creed (May 22). (Notice the ironic ambiguity of the word "dated"!) Emperor Constantius strove for religious unity, hoping to achieve it by elimi-nating the extreme positions (modalists/pro-Nicenes vs. Heteroousians) and endorsing the compromise between Homoeousians and Homoeans in the Homoean terms (see below). The emperor thought that it was easier to build doctrinal uniformity and to heal the East-West schism by summoning two dif-ferent synods: one in Seleucia for "Easterners" and one in Ariminum (Rimini) for "Westerners." He also decided to prepare a common document that would create the conditions for establishing doctrinal uniformity. Thus, a handful of selected bishops were summoned to draft the Dated Creed. It was written in Latin, but only a Greek copy is extant.

God, the Father Almighty, was confessed to be the "only and true God [*ton monon kai alēthinon theon*]" (Athanasius, *Syn.* 8). The only-begotten Son was "like [*homoion*] unto the Father who begat him" (*Syn.* 8). In the end of the creed, it was explained that the unscriptural word "essence" (*ousia*) has to be dropped altogether while mentioning the birth of the Son. It was sufficient to say that "the Son is like [*homoion*] the Father in all things [*kata panta*]" (*Syn.* 8). Before Basil of Ancyra signed the creed, he inserted a further note that "like *in all things*" included the Son's *essential* likeness to the Father (Epiphanius, *Pan.* 73.22.6–7). However, the scriptural phrase "all things" (e.g., Col 3:20), which was adopted for the final version of the creed, was by itself imprecise enough to enable various interpretations, including and excluding essential likeness. To distance itself from the more radical subordinationists, this creed also made a strong fourfold statement of the Son's preexistence. The Son was begotten "before all ages, and before all beginning, and before all conceivable time, and before all comprehensible essence" (Athanasius, *Syn.* 8).

Yet as it often happens with enforced compromises, the new creed failed to satisfy the theologians involved. On the one hand, "Easterners," meaning Homoeans and Acacius of Caesarea (see below), accepted a clearly subordinationist statement at Seleucia (cf. Athanasius, *Syn.* 29; Epiphanius, *Pan.* 73.25.1–73.26.2; Socrates, *Hist. eccl.* 2.40). On the other hand, a group of "Westerners," "bishops . . . of simple and unsophisticated ways," expressed their preference for the Nicene Creed at a split Synod of Ariminum (Rimini; Theodoret, *Hist. eccl.* 2.15; cf. Athanasius, *Syn.* 11; for the Creed of Ariminum, see *Syn.* 30; Theodoret, *Hist. eccl.* 2.18; Socrates, *Hist. eccl.* 2.41). Thus, the Dated Creed of AD 359 was modified once again before it was accepted at the Synod of Constantinople in AD 360. In a statement following the creed of AD 360, the term *hypostasis* was considered unacceptable for designating the Father, Son, and Spirit, and the phrase "in all things" (*kata panta*) was dropped after the assertion that the Father and the Son were "like" (*homoion*; Athanasius, *Syn.* 30). Homoeans had it their way until the Council of Constantinople (AD 381). The Eastern emperor Valens (364–378) made sure that the established Homoean "consensus" lasted. However, every enforced "consensus" provokes a reaction, and paradoxically the Homoean triumph also mobilized the Athanasian pro-Nicenes.

Synod of Alexandria

Another important event between the first two ecumenical councils of Nicaea and Constantinople was the Synod of Alexandria (AD 362), led by Athanasius himself. It took place a year after the death of Emperor Constantius, who had been sympathetic toward Homoeans. As a reaction to the imperial theological preferences, this synod mobilized the anti-Arian and anti-Homoean theologians into a more unified front. To make their theological position very clear, the synod condemned both Arians and modalists, together with Gnostics and Manicheans, . . . but curiously never Marcellus in person.

The synod also issued an encyclical letter (*Epistula Catholica*) that urged communion with all those bishops who accepted the Nicene Creed (Tetz, in *ZNW*, 1988). This letter affirmed the essential unity of the Father, Son, and Spirit by confessing that "the Trinity is consubstantial" (*homoousios hē trias*). The Son and the Holy Spirit were neither "creation" (*ktisma*) nor "work" (*poiēma*), since they were inseparable (*mēte . . . chōrizontōn*) from the Father.

Furthermore, the Synod of Alexandria sent a document to the "Easterners" (*Tome to the People of Antioch* [*Tomus ad Antiochenos*]). Being still haunted by the confusing condemnation of Nicaea (*hypostasis* or *ousia*), the authors of this document demonstrated willingness to accept those who insisted on the one *hypostasis* of the Godhead as something that enforced the Creator/creation distinction (Athanasius, *Tom.* 6). But to distance the synod from the Marcellian creed of Sardica, the *Tome* also acknowledged the (eternal) distinction between three divine *hypostaseis*. The hypostatic distinction was acknowledged so that it did not imply ontological subordinationism (Athanasius, *Tom.* 5).

The historic significance of the Alexandrian Synod is that it established the emerging pro-Nicene/Athanasian theology as the would-be universally accepted orthodox Trinitarian theology, and the Nicene Creed as *the* reference point for this orthodoxy. It brought about reconciliation with at least some Homoeousian bishops who had come to understand that the Athanasian pro-Nicenes were not teaching Marcellian "modalism." The *Tome* distanced itself from the embarrassing creed of Sardica, and this in turn enabled winning over some "Eastern" bishops. Last but not least, the synod also mobilized Rome behind the Nicene anti-Arianism. Having said all this, a reminder offered by Ayres (2004, 237) deserves accentuation: "The theologies that constitute pro-Nicene orthodoxy are not reducible to one point of origin or to one form of expression." The pro-Nicene theological spectrum was at least as diverse as the non- or anti-Nicene spectrum. These subtle differences defy charting, however, for otherwise a chart as a simplification no longer clarifies much of anything.

Sameness and Distinctness of the Divine Persons (Third and Fourth Row)

While studying the various trajectories of the fourth-century Trinitarian thought, one should not forget the conservative group, which is often the majority in the church even though it is not always that visible. Cyril of Jerusalem is chosen as an example of those who disagreed with the "cutting-edge" Trinitarian theologies of both Marcellus and Eusebians, but did not particularly like the Nicene *homoousios* either.

Cyril of Jerusalem

Cyril belonged among those bishops who were "without direct 'party' commitment" (Ayres 2004, 152). In fact, the existence of people like Cyril undermines Athanasius's polemical suggestion that the whole Arian controversy took place between the pro- and anti-Nicenes. Besides, Gregg (1985, 87) reminds the students of Trinitarian theology that in the fourth century "opposition to Nicaea ... did not of itself counter-indicate Arianism."

1. Against modalists and their beloved analogy of the Word thought and uttered, Cyril argued for the hypostatic subsistence of the Word before the incarnation (*Catech.* 11.10; cf. 4.8).
2. Against Eusebians, Cyril affirmed the Son's eternal begottenness from the Father (*Catech.* 4.7; 11.20). He also refuted the idea that the title "Lord" was conferred to the Son as a direct result of his (moral) faithfulness (cf. Phil 2:5–11; Heb 1:8–9). Considering it an important Arian teaching, Cyril opined that the Son "received not the Lordship by advancement [*ek prokopēs*], but has the dignity of his lordship from nature [*ek physeōs*]" (*Catech.* 10.5; cf. Athanasius, *C. Ar.* 1.37–38; *Syn.* 15). The Son's lordship had to be eternal, because the Son's priesthood was eternal (Heb 5:8–10). Because only God could forgive sins, a "promoted" Savior seemed like soteriological nonsense.
3. Against the Athanasian pro-Nicenes, Cyril acknowledged the need to affirm more clearly the causal superiority of the Father. Significantly, the Creed of Jerusalem (ca. AD 350), which Cyril preferred, ignored the allegedly modalist key word *homoousios* altogether. Cyril actually found nothing fundamentally wrong in saying that the Father and the Son were substantially alike (*homoios*; *Catech.* 11.4, 18). Perhaps because of this, Rufinus of Aquileia called him a man who "wavered sometimes in doctrine" (Rufinus, *Hist. eccl.* 10.24).

Many theologians before Cyril had asserted apophatically that the begetting of the Son was undiscoverable. Isaiah 53:8 (LXX) confessed, "Who could have imagined his origin?" (LXX has *genean*, Vulgate *generationem*). Irenaeus, for instance, ironically mentioned those who seemed to know the details of the birth of the Son: "As if they had assisted at God's birth, they talk largely about the production and generation of his first begetting" (*Haer.* 2.28.6). Likewise, to claim to have exact knowledge of the Son's generation was, according to Cyril, to go beyond what was revealed. No one should confuse the inadequate human analogies with the divine realities (*Catech.* 11.4). Cyril did not want to use the word *hypostasis* and even less the word *ousia*—although at times he did—in connection with the divine persons, because these terms pretended to convey some technical sense that was arguably not found in the Scriptures. If the technical terms had been in the Scriptures, "we would have spoken of [these]" (*Catech.* 16.24).

Remarkable is also Cyril's perceptive attention to the Holy Spirit, "the sanctifier and deifier of all" (*Catech.* 4.16). He urged his catechumens to "hold the same opinion concerning him [the Holy Spirit]" that they were taught to hold concerning the Father and the Son (*Catech.* 4.16).

Hilary of Poitiers

Next, I will turn to two Latin pro-Nicene theologians, Hilary of Poitiers and Marius Victorinus, as the orthodox group of representatives in row four, Chart Two. They are placed together with the Synod of Alexandria in order to represent the increasingly international pro-Nicene alliance that countered the Arian, Eusebian, Homoean, and Heteroousian Trinitarian theologies (see below). The Western emperor Valentinian (364–375) tolerated the Nicene Trinitarian theology, and this enabled the pro-Nicenes to group and to start rallying for their cause. Readers may keep in mind that Athanasius, placed in the second row in our chart, was still the leader of the pro-Nicenes. In short, the fourth row presents a later phase of the post-Nicene Trinitarian controversies.

In the beginning of the second half of the fourth century, Hilary of Poitiers authored a twelve-book *On the Trinity* (*De Trinitate*). Since Trinitarian debates took their lead from the Scriptures, Hilary's treatise was a rigorous exegetical analysis of the many relevant biblical passages. He had something important to say to the students of the Scripture of all times: "Now the Word of God . . . reveals a deeper meaning to the patient student than to the momentary hearer" (*Trin.* 1.6). Later Augustine paid him a compliment by writing that Hilary was "a man of no small authority in the interpretation of the Scriptures and the defense of faith" (*Trin.* 6.2.11). Hilary was one of the few in the West who came to know the Eastern Trinitarian controversies during his exile in Phrygia. After his return from the East, Hilary defended the pro-Nicene position at the Synod of Paris (AD 360/361). Because of his writings "all the darkness of heresy was driven from even the most remote and hidden corners" (Rufinus, *Hist. eccl.* 10.32).

While Hilary critically engaged Arius's *Confession* in his *On the Trinity*, his real battle was with the imperially supported Latin Homoeans—with the rather disastrous bishops Valens and Ursacius and the decisions of the anti-Nicene/anti-modalist Synods of Philippopolis (AD 342/343), Sirmium (AD 357; Hilary called it the "Blasphemy of Sirmium" [*Syn.* 11]), and Seleucia (AD 359). In other words, his refutation targeted those who "confess the likeness [*similitudinem*], but deny the equality [*aequalitate* of the Father and the Son]" (*Syn.* 74). Since the writings of Hilary often mention "Arians," readers need to remember that in antiquity it was common to refute traditional enemies as if they were the actual enemies.

Hilary's analysis is a rather typical mixture of theological apophaticism and exegetical kataphaticism. After calling Exod 3:14 "a *clear* definition of God," he says that this verse "spoke of the *incomprehensible* nature" of God (*Trin.* 1.4). Such paradoxical language seasons his whole discussion, almost tiring the reader. Take, for instance, the very fact that although Hilary rhetorically confessed that his "only knowledge of God consists in my worship of him" (*Trin.* 11.44), he managed to write a 500-page pro-Nicene exposition of Trinitarian theology. Just like Augustine several decades later, Hilary ended his treatise with a prayer that rhetorically expressed the utter impossibility of saying anything worthy of God: "My poverty of speech chokes the faith into silence" (*Trin.* 12.52).

Before proceeding, I will consider Hilary's use of theological terms. The Latin terms, such as *natura*, *persona*, and *substantia* began to find their eventually restricted meaning in his works. *Natura* came to designate what was common in the Triune God, and *persona* what was not common. *Substantia*, however, was still elastic enough to function as a synonym of both *natura* and *persona* (*Syn.* 12). Knowing both Greek and Latin, the bishop of Poitiers indeed struggled with translating the Greek documents for Gallican bishops: "Much obscurity is caused by a translation from Greek into Latin, and to be absolutely literal is to be sometimes partly unintelligible" (*Syn.* 9). Basil of Caesarea later remarked with a certain sense of superiority:

> The nonidentity of *hypostasis* and *ousia* is, I take it, suggested even by our Western brethren, where, from a suspicion of inadequacy of their own language, they have given the word *ousia* in the Greek, to the end that any possible difference of meaning might be preserved in the clear and unconfounded distinction of terms. (*Ep.* 214.4)

Hilary was a defender of the full divinity of the Son and the Nicene key word *homoousios*, a term he had learned about before returning from his exile (*Syn.* 91). Being well aware that the term *homoousios* was "unbiblical," Hilary believed that the controversial word nevertheless expressed the Trinitarian faith, which was indeed biblical: the Son was fully divine both eternally and by nature. "I believed this before I knew the word *homoousion*" (*Syn.* 88).

Hilary was also convinced that the alternative term *homoiousios* expressed basically the same conviction as the Nicene term *homoousios*. Both terms could be understood as affirming the equality of the Father and the Son. Thus, he was ready to accept the term *homoiousios* as long as it was interpreted by *homoousios* (*Syn.* 91). Because of such openness, Hilary should perhaps be placed a little right from Marius Victorinus, who categorically rejected the term *homoiousios*. (Such subtle divisions within the larger trajectories defy charting, however.)

To defend the notion of the Son being *homoousios* with the Father, Hilary investigated the correspondence between the acts of the Son and the divine nature. The "doings" of the Son (John 5:17, 19) enabled him to identify the Son as *homoousios* with the Father. "He [the Son] is able to do and to perform those things which are characteristic to God" (*Trin.* 6.34). In John 10:37, Jesus indeed challenges the agnostics: "If I am not doing the works of my Father, then do not believe me."

The Son was "from God," that is, the Son was born from the nature of God. In making this assertion, Hilary did not operate with the pair of exclusive opposites of God's *nature* and God's *will*. Rather, he postulated another primary pair of opposites: *generation* and *creation* (*Trin.* 3.4; 6.18). He distinguished between "generation through will" and "creation through will" (Meijering 1982, 86, 134). The Father willed the eternal *generation* of his Son, but the Father willed the *creation* of the world. By affirming God's will in the process of generation, Hilary was saying that the eternal begetting of the Son from the Father was neither an accident nor an automatic act. It was the Father's eternal and deliberate decision to have a Son. The Son was from both the Father's will and nature. But since the mode of the *homoousios* Son's begetting was controversial and often misunderstood, Hilary also clarified that "God is not from God by a division [*desectionem*], an extension [*protensionem*], or an emanation [*derivationem*]" (*Trin.* 5.37). There was no splitting of the divine nature, or transformation, or impersonal flowing out of something as the Son was eternally born from the Father.

As Hilary was refuting Arians/Homoeans and defending the Nicene *homoousios*, he also had to guard against promoting modalism. It was necessary to show that God was not just one (in a modalist sense), but that God was one in a new, uniplural sense. God was *unum* (a unity), not *unus* (one [person]; *Trin.* 2.23). Accordingly, Hilary pointed out that John 10:30 spoke of neither two Gods nor one person but of a unity of persons (*Trin.* 7.31). The text said that the divine persons "*are* one" and not "*is* one," and for Hilary, this grammatical nuance further proved the reality of the eternal hypostatic distinction between the Father and the Son (7.5). Confession of the identical nature of the Father and Son must not lead to a modalist denial of their individual *personae*. Attempting to affirm both the sameness and distinctness between the Father and the Son, Hilary spoke about the "unity of the inseparable and identical nature [*naturae inseparabilis adque indissimilis unitatem*]" of the Father and the Son (7.31).

The only adequate way for distinguishing between the equally divine persons of the Father and the Son was by their respective attributes "unbegottenness" and "begottenness" (*Trin.* 7.20). Hilary had to sort out the question of how the Father and the Son could be equal in nature if one was "unbegotten" and the other "begotten." He explained that the designations "unbegotten" and "only-begotten" were relational attributes and coined a memorable maxim: "The birth of the Son establishes the Father as the greater, but the nature of the birth does not allow the Son to be less" (9.56). As one can see from this quote, Hilary was familiar with the Alexandrian Trinitarian tradition and with the doctrine of the "monarchy of the Father." To be born and to have a father meant to be caused; but to be born and to have a father did not mean to be of a different or a lesser nature. In more technical terms, to be caused did not necessarily imply ontological inferiority. "The nature does not lose its nobility by its birth" (7.22). "The only-begotten God is from the one unbegotten God. There are not two gods, but one from one. There are not two unbegotten gods, because he is born from him who is unborn" (2.11).

Hilary reserved his assessment of the Arian key proof text, Prov 8:22–25, for the final chapter of his *opus magnum*. He colorfully called this passage "the most powerful wave of their storm" (*Trin.* 12.1). Hilary tied the passage to economy through the last phrase in 8:22 (LXX): "for [*eis*] his work(s)." He read Prov 8:22 in connection with John 14:6, which mentions the mediating task of the Son: "I am the way, and the truth, and the life. No one comes to the Father except through me"; and with Gal 4:4, "When the fullness of time had come, God sent his Son, born of a woman" (*Trin.* 13.44–45, 48). Accordingly, the words "at the beginning" in Prov 8:22 did not refer to the inscrutable eternal begetting of the Son but to the temporal beginning of economy, to the beginning of the salvific work of the Son. The mistake of the Arian exegesis was to turn an *economical* term "to create" into a *theological* term. They "use the text of the Scriptures to invent things that are not in the Scriptures" (*Liber II ad Constantium* 6).

Hilary also contended that the Holy Spirit was neither generated as the Son, nor created as the creation (*Trin.* 12.55). Like his predecessors, he focused primarily on the economic role of the Spirit, and the future issue of the *filioque* did not agitate him. Nevertheless, Hilary demonstrated awareness of the distinction between theological "begetting" and economical "sending" (6.34). Following the wording found in John 15:26, Hilary wrote, "The Spirit of truth *proceeds* from the Father, but he is *sent* by the Son from the Father" (*Trin.* 8.20; cf. 12.55). But once again, this statement should not be read anachronistically in the light of the later *filioque* controversy.

Although the full divinity of the Spirit was not a central point in the agenda of Hilary's *On the Trinity*, he assumed what the "creed of my rebirth" (*Const.* 11) had taught him: God was Father, Son, and Holy Spirit (Matt 28:19). The Father, Son, and Holy Spirit had "a perfect fullness of the Godhead in each of them [*plenitude in utraque divinitatis perfecta est*]" (*Trin.* 3.23). Hilary had employed an argument of the Son's divine works to prove the Son's consubstantial divinity with the Father. Now he employed the same argument to argue for the consubstantial divinity of the Holy Spirit: "I do not know why there is any ambiguity about it, since its cause, its manner of acting, and its power are clearly determined" (2.34).

Marius Victorinus

As a converted rhetorician, Marius Victorinus offered a rather distinctive philosophical defense of Nicaea by reasserting the validity of its key term *homoousios*. He regarded the common argument that this foreign term was difficult to understand an empty one, because those who rejected it (e.g., Basil of

Ancyra) certainly understood it (*Adversus Arium* II.9). The ultimate reason for the acceptance of the word *homoousios*, however, was that it conveyed what the Scriptures said about the Father, Son, and Holy Spirit. Rather than providing clumsy and misleading Latin equivalents of the Greek word, Victorinus was happy to go with the original *homoousios*, which provided "the maximum of meaning and the minimum of length" (II.12). The affirmation of the consubstantiality (*homoousios*) of the Father, Son, and Holy Spirit was indeed both the premise and the aim of Victorinus's Trinitarian deliberations.

Despite the fact that Victorinus focused on a sophisticated metaphysical justification of the doctrine of the Trinity, he took his guidance from the traditional proof texts. Victorinus concluded his first book *Against the Arians* with a confession: "Indeed, all that I say is said by the Holy Scripture and comes from the Holy Scripture" (IA.46). This is something that Jerome refused to acknowledge, as he dismissed Victorinus in his short vita: "Victorinus . . . in the manner of dialecticians, wrote some extremely obscure books against Arius, understood only by the learned" (*Vir. ill.* 101). Jerome was known for his dislike of Victorinus's exegesis, and much of the contemporary scholarship has unfortunately sided with Jerome in reducing Victorinus to a mere Neoplatonist metaphysician. The quality of his exegetical Trinitarian theology has yet to be properly acknowledged.

What characterized Victorinus's exposition was that he used biblical texts indicating the subordination of the Son to the Father (e.g., John 14:28) to signify the differentiation between the divine persons, and the texts indicating oneness (e.g., John 5:19; 1 Cor 1:24) to signify their substantial sameness.

Victorinus refuted all possible non- and anti-Nicene positions, just as a rhetorician was used to doing. He seems to have been less worried about how all his refutations cohered into a consistent theological position than about a metaphysical deconstruction of every possible heretical assertion. In his anti-Arian writings, he often concluded a paragraph as if he had to win a case in court: "Therefore . . . *homoousios*." Victorinus's goal in composing literary refutations of Arianism, its historical variations, and deduced abstract metaphysical implications was to show that, in the final analysis, all this was nothing but bad philosophy. For instance, since the divine *substantia* was simple, the *substantia* of the Father and the Son could not be "alike." In fact, Homoeousians and their leader Basil of Ancyra did not correctly perceive the metaphysical implications of their doctrine: if the Father and the Son were *homoiousios*, God was not simple and substance was confused with quality. "Likeness" was applicable to the shared qualities of different substances. Substances could only be the same or different, but qualities could be similar and dissimilar (*Adv. Ar.* IA.21–22). In this respect (in postulating by implication different substances of the Father and Son), there was really no fundamental difference between the assertions of Homoeousians and Heteroousians (IA.43).

Victorinus's preferred analogy of the Trinity was "to be" (*esse*), "to live" (*vivere*), and "to understand" (*intelligere*; cf. John 17:3), although he was acutely aware that it was "not possible to find a name worthy of God from those things which we know [from the created sensible world]" (*Ad Candidum Arrianum* 28). The above-mentioned neoplatonic analogy provided him a triad, which was essentially the same but distinguishable only through its characteristic movements of action: "'To be,' 'to live,' and 'to understand' are three in such a manner that they are always one and contained in 'to be'" (*Adv. Ar.* III.4). (Some modern Orthodox theologians have considered the Western Trinitarian theology [of Victorinus, Augustine, Boethius, Aquinas] as "essentialist," because God's essence is said to be "being" rather than "relation.")

Nevertheless, to understand Victorinus's discourse, we have to start precisely with the notion that God *is* existence. "To be" (*esse*) is God's substance (*substantia*). "This 'to be' in God, the learned call substance" (*Hymnus* 1). As such, "'to be' is the foundation for the rest [for 'to live' and 'to know']" (*Adv. Ar.* III.4). Here is Victorinus's variant of the doctrine of the monarchy of the Father. "To be" is the Father in the superlative sense of the word (IV.19), and accordingly, "'to be' is a principle for others" (III.7). "To be" has causal priority over its revelatory acts or movements.

At the same time, "to be" has only a *causal* superiority. According to Victorinus, Arius was just wrong as he confused causal superiority with temporal/ontological superiority. Victorinus explained that the Father was "to be" in potency; the Son was "to be" in act (*Cand.* 14). But in the eternal and simple reality of God, potency and act were "simultaneous" (*Adv. Ar.* IA.4). Within the Godhead, act did not follow potency in the *temporal* sense, for there was no becoming in the Godhead. It was a matter of something being hidden and revealed rather than God having a mere potency and then realizing it as an act. Thus, in the case of God, the distinction that mattered was not that between the "simultaneous" potency and act, but between "to be" in a *nonmanifested* act and "to be" in a *manifested* act (IA.31). Put differently, the Father is the *internal* act and the Son is the *external* act of the same substance "to be" (IA.33). Father is "inactive action" (*actio inactuosa*), while the Son reveals the eternal action already present in God's potency (IA.13; IB.55). "For up there 'to be' does not differ from 'to act'" (*Cand.* 19).

Distinguishing between the Father, Son, and Holy Spirit was indeed a tricky thing. It was extremely hard to find proper expressions or terms for indicating the perceived distinction. According to Victorinus, the Latin functional equivalent to the Greek *hypostasis* was *subsistentia*. The common *substantia*, the "to be" (*esse*), was differentiated by *existentia* as three *subsistentiae*. This means that *subsistentia* was *substantia* with a form (with *existentia*; *Adv. Ar.* II.4). (A form particularizes a given substance.) In the Godhead, the three subsistences (*subsistentiae*) were from one substance (*substantia*; II.4).

Marius Victorinus also defended the full divinity of the Holy Spirit and the Spirit's being *homoousion* with the Father and the Son (*Adv. Ar.* IV.33). Yet his philosophical ponderings had no immediate impact on the development of pneumatology, primarily because the "Easterners" simply did not know his writings. Yet Victorinus's understanding of the procession of the Holy Spirit indeed paved the way toward the Latin doctrine of *filioque*. He explained that because of the consubstantiality of the Father and Son, the Holy Spirit proceeded from them as from a diversified single principle. Furthermore, the Son and the Spirit proceeded from the Father as a twofold movement of life and knowledge, acting externally and internally (III.14). The substantial unity of the Trinity relativized both the "three" in the Trinity and the distinction between the theological proceeding and economical sending.

Distinctness of the Divine Persons (Fourth Row)

Next, consider the several anti-Nicene Trinitarian theologies. Alongside the notorious but orthodox key word *homoousios*, three other terms were proposed for expressing the Father's relation to his Son:

1. *homoiousios* (the like essence)
2. *homoios* (like)
3. *anomoios/heteroousios* (unlike/other nature)

Groups operating with or designated by these three terms were no marginal noisemakers. Homoeans (the supporters of the term *homoios*), the most significant group among the anti-Nicenes, were arguably as important as Homoousians (the Athanasian pro-Nicenes). The great appeal of the Homoean teaching was that it looked like an authentic teaching on the Trinity. As we have seen, many "Easterners" were allergic to modalism. Therefore, they preferred to have a more emphatic hypostatic distinction between the Father, Son, and Spirit than the Nicene Creed granted. But ultimately none of the terms besides the Nicene *homoousios* were taken to express the orthodox doctrine of the Trinity.

Basil of Ancyra and Homoeousians

Homoeousians considered their belief—rather than that of the Athanasian pro-Nicenes—to be the "royal middle way" of orthodoxy between the two heresies: modalism (left on the chart) and Arianism (right). For instance, the condemnations of the Synod of Ancyra (AD 358) include both anti-Marcellian and anti-Arian clauses. One of the leaders of Homoeousians, Basil of Ancyra, explained: "It is our purpose to give an accurate description of the catholic church's faith in the holy Trinity" (*Epistula* in Epiphanius, *Pan.* 73.2.7). The *Letter of George*, too, which Basil supposedly coauthored, began its confession with the words, "We of the catholic church, however, have taken our confession of faith from the Sacred Scriptures" (*Ep. Geo.* in Epiphanius, *Pan.* 73.14.1). Homoeousians took pride in being scriptural and also *pre*-Nicene(!). God was old, truth was old, the Scriptures were old, and purportedly so was the Trinitarian belief of Homoeousians!

Basil of Ancyra employed the term *homoiousios* (the like essence), which first appeared in the Creed of Sirmium (AD 357) in a Latinized form (*homoeusion*). The perceived difference between the terms *homoousios* and *homoiousios* was that the prefix "like" (*homoios*) in the compound *homoiousios* enabled a clearer distinction between the divine *hypostaseis* without at the same time suggesting the Son's identification with the creation. In other words, it seemed to affirm the monarchy of the Father without implying that the Son was a created being. For several "Eastern" bishops, it made better sense to say that Father and Son had the "likeness of essence" (*homoios kata tēn ousian*) rather than the "*same* essence" (*homoousios*; Basil of Ancyra, *Ep.*). The problem with the Nicene term *homoousious* was precisely that it could be understood as *tautoousios* (same or identical essence; *Ep.*). But to speak about essential identity was appropriate only in regard to *material* things (*Ep.*; Sozomen, *Hist. eccl.* 3.18). To say that the Father and the Son were *homoousios* could be heard as if God's essence were material and therefore passible; as if the divine begetting were the same as the human begetting (Basil of Ancyra, *Ep.*; cf. Athanasius, *Syn.* 41). Therefore, it was better to say that the Father, Son, and Spirit were of "like essence" (*homoiousios*).

The term *homoiousios* was shorthand for the phrase *homoios kata tēn ousian*. This phrase was the "cornerstone of our [Homoeousian] faith" (Basil of Ancyra, *Ep.*). Alternatively, it could be said that the Son was "like" the Father "in all respects" (*homoion kata panta*; *Ep. Geo.*). Indeed, Basil signed the confession of the Synod of Sirmium (AD 359) with a caveat: "I assent to the foregoing by confessing that the Son is like the Father in all respects. But in all!" (*Ep. Geo.*).

Despite the Homoeousians's initial dislike of the "innovator" Athanasius, some of them were eventually won over by the pro-Nicenes at the Synod of Alexandria (AD 362). (Hence the partial overlap of the chart's boxes representing the theologies of Athanasius and Basil of Ancyra.) The imperial pressure to accept Homoean theology, among other things, might have facilitated the Homoeousians' inclination toward the pro-Nicene position. At the end of his life, Athanasius called Homoeousians diplomatically "brothers, who mean what we mean, and dispute only about the word [*homoousios*]" (*Syn.* 41). Athanasius was ready to accept the followers of Basil of Ancyra, if they added the words "without any difference" to their key phrase "like essence" (*Ep.* 9.3; cf. *Syn.* 38). "For the first time he [Athanasius] acknowledges the possibility that a Christian might hold a different theology to his own, and yet not be 'Arian'" (Gwynn 2007, 43). The new fragile alliance between pro-Nicenes and Homoeousians was about to guarantee the slow decline of all forms of Arian theology.

Acacius of Caesarea and Homoeans

One of the leading Homoeans was Acacius of Caesarea. He was a successor of Eusebius of Caesarea and the author of another treatise titled *Against*

Marcellus. His adherents proposed yet another term, *homoios* (like), to speak about the Father and the Son. The biblical word "like" was common. But this common word was invested with particular theology, and it became an identity marker for a particular anti-Nicene theology. Gregory of Nazianzus, for instance, understood well the appeal of the biblical word "like" and therefore warned: "The phrase 'like, according to Scriptures' was a bait to the simple, ... a boot fitting either foot, ... gaining authority from the newly written villainy and device against the truth" (*Or.* 21.22).

According to Homoeans, however, the perceived terminological advance was that *homoios* avoided the discourse about the ineffable essence (*ousia*) of God. Some perplexed seminary students would probably agree, for their own reasons, with the sentiment of a Latin Homoean Creed of Niké (AD 360). It banned the troublesome words *ousia* and *hypostasis* altogether from theological vocabulary:

> But the word *ousia*, which was simplistically put down by the Fathers, being unknown to the people, has become a scandal; because the Scriptures do not contain it, we have decided [it] should be removed and that there should be absolutely no mention of it at all.... For neither should *hypostasis* concerning the Father, the Son, and the Holy Spirit be used. (Athanasius, *Syn.* 30)

Homoeans were happy to simply say that the Son was like (*homoios*) the Father. Emperor Constantius also liked the proposed simplification, evidently because this vague term had the wonderful promise of creating some religious unity. Pro-Nicene theologians, however, refused to accept anything less than the assertion that the Father and Son were of the same essence (*homoousios*). Victorinus reminded those who said that the Son was like the Father that King David found no one *like* God (Ps 35:10; Marius Victorinus, *Adv. Ar.* II.2).

The concept of "likeness" derived from the biblical term "image" (*eikōn*; Col 1:15; 2 Cor 4:4). Father and Son were *homoios*: what the word "like" exactly meant was rather conveniently left in the air. It was clear, however, that "likeness" had to be found in the activity and power of the Father and the Son, or even "in all things," except their respective mode of origination (Acacius, *Fragmenta contra Marcellum* in Epiphanius, *Pan.* 72.7.4–8). The Father was "unbegotten" (a self-existent without origin), and the Son was "only-begotten."

Homoeans thought that John 5:19 supported their case—whatever the Father did, the Son did "likewise" (*homoiōs*). If the works were "like" rather than the "same," the natures performing these works were also alike rather than the same. Furthermore, if the Son were the image (Col 1:15) of the Father, the Son had to be both like and unlike the Father. Images, in all their likeness, were not identical with their prototypes. An image "displays otherness, but otherness as though it were likeness" (Acacius, *Frg. c. Marc.*). Accordingly, as the "exact living image" of the Father, the Son was nevertheless a caused/begotten being and had his distinct existence, his own *hypostasis*. Here the supporting Scriptures asserted, "Just as the Father has life in himself, so he has granted the Son also to have life *in himself*" (John 5:26, emphasis added; Acacius, *Frg. c. Marc.*).

Despite affirming the likeness of the Father and the Son, the bottom line was that using the term *homoios* bolstered subordinationism. It was a further step away from the Nicene position. However, Acacius cautiously refrained from saying that the *homoios* Son was created "out of nonbeing" (*ex ouk ontōn*). Homoeans believed that the Son was created from the Father's will rather than from the Father's nature (Athanasius, *Syn.* 30).

Curiously, despite the fact that Homoeans constituted the more radical wing of anti-Nicenes together with Heteroousians (Sozomen, *Hist. eccl.* 4.29), no polemical treatises against Acacius are known. In addition, it might be difficult to see the anti-Heteroousian bias of at least some of the Homoeans from Chart Two, because the boxes are too close to indicate the degree of disagreement between these two groups.

Latin Homoeans

Latin Homoeans (second column from the right on Chart Three) confessed their faith with the Creed of Niké (Theodoret, *Hist. eccl.* 2.16). This key statement of Latin Homoeans, together with the edited Dated Creed, received imperial ratification at the Council of Constantinople in AD 360. To say anything beyond the statement "the Son is like [*similem*] the Father" was to make a claim to know more than had been revealed. A pro-Nicene Hilary of Poitiers had already sarcastically called the Homoean declaration of AD 357 the "Declaration of Ignorance" (*Syn.* 10)! The Homoeans believed the Son to be the only-begotten God, as distinguished both from the unbegotten God and from the creation, made "out of nonbeing." The Son was like the Father, yet essentially different from the unbegotten Father. To reject any utterance closer to the Nicene Creed than the word "like," Palladius of Ratiaria, for instance, wondered why an ontologically and eternally equal Son was subject to the Father in all things (*Scholia Arriana* 337). Was the nominal distinction between Father and Son just a sham, without any implication to their ontological status? The very fact that the Son became incarnate and suffered proved for Homoeans the Son's inferiority to the Father, who did not become incarnate and suffer. The Holy Spirit in turn was considered even a lesser being than the Son, for the Spirit was made by the only-begotten Son. After all, the Son could not have been the *Only*-begotten if the Spirit were his equal. Since the Holy Spirit was not God, the Spirit was not supposed to be worshipped. "The Father is greater than his Son; the Son is incomparably greater and better than the Spirit," asserted a collection of Homoean stock phrases called the *Arian Sermon* (24).

The Homoeans had a considerable influence on ecclesiastical affairs before Ambrose was elected as a bishop of Milan. D. Williams (1995, 70) summarizes:

"Western Homoianism [Homoeanism] was hardly a lame duck even after the death of Constantius and the temporary loss of imperial patronage." Especially during the reign of Valentinian II and his mother Justina, the Latin Homoeans experienced a significant comeback (Rufinus, *Hist. eccl.* 11.15). Eventually, the sole rule of Theodosius ended their right to exist under the sun. In AD 386 the Creed of Ariminum was proclaimed invalid, and the Homoeans became illegal heretics (*Codex Theodosianus* XVI.i.4). Nevertheless, as late as AD 427 or 428, Augustine had a debate with an outstanding Homoean Maximinus, who traveled and preached, knowing all too well that the imperial law was not on his side (*Conlatio cum Maximino Arianorum episcopo* 15.1).

Now, seminarians scandalized by the difference of one iota (*homoousios/ homoiousios*) and by the mere omitting of the word *ousia* (using *homoios* instead of *homoiousios*) as extreme cases of theological hairsplitting should think again: words indeed mean something. We are not dealing with mere theological niceties but with the very concept of the Christian God. If the implications of the technical terms are pushed, the *homoousios* Son can save us, but the *homoiousious* and *homoios* Son cannot—if one accepts the soteriological convictions assumed here. Furthermore, to revive another Athanasian argument, to worship the *homoousios* Son is to worship God, but to worship the *homoiousios* or *homoios* Son is to worship something less than God. To be "like" God may mean "perfect equality"; but to be "like" God may also imply a fundamental difference: being "unlike" God. While the pro-Nicene Homoeousian theologians understood the word "like" in the sense of "ontologically equal," the anti-Nicene Homoeousians and Homoeans took it in the sense of "ontologically unequal." But to assert that the Son (and Spirit) were of "like essence" with the Father or just "like" the Father could lead to tritheism rather than to belief in one Triune God.

Aetius and Eunomius, Heteroousians or Anomoeans

In Chart Two, both Homoeans and Heteroousians are placed on the right. Apart from the contextual column for non-Christian polytheism, the far right column is for those who emphasized the essential difference of the Father versus Son and Spirit, and the subordination of Son and Spirit to the Father. However, such placement causes a further problem of distinguishing between the groups Homoeans and Heteroousians, which could not conceptualize the Son and the Spirit as being *homoousios* or *homoiousios* with the Father. For this purpose, we need to introduce the term *anomoios* (unlike).

The opponents of Heteroousians called them "Anomoeans" (unlikers). This name gives an impression that their main representatives, Aetius and Eunomius, denied any similarity between the Father and the Son. To a certain extent it was true that "unlikers" (Anomoeans) reacted primarily to "likers" (Homoeans), and also to those who emphasized that the Father and Son were of "like essence" (Homoeousians). But we should clarify that "unlike" is not necessarily the absolute opposite of "like." Likeness presupposes similarity in difference. Whatever is "like" is neither identical to nor completely "unlike" the thing with which it is compared. Otherwise any comparison would be pointless. Consequently, a historian Philostorgius informs us that his cofactionist Eunomius had "never been found to teach . . . that the Son is 'unlike' the Father" (Philostorgius, *Hist. eccl.* 4.1). Philostorgius's line of reasoning was that Eunomius only denied the Son's being "like in *essence*" (*homoios kat' ousian*; cf. Eunomius, *Apologia* 1.22; Epiphanius, *Pan.* 73.22.1). Affirming similarity in difference, Eunomius confessed that the Son "resembles his begetter with a most exact likeness in accordance with the meaning which is proper to himself . . . as image . . . of the Almighty" (*Expositio fidei* 3). An effect (the Son) was at least in some sense like its cause (the Father). If the Son were completely "unlike" the Father, he could not have been the soteriological mediator (1 Tim 2:5), and it would make no sense for Christians to worship him. Thus, despite the fact that Aetius and Eunomius were accused of promoting the term *anomoios*, they actually rejected the unqualified use of the word "unlike." But the qualified usage of the term *anomoios* meant that the Son was of "other nature" (*heteroousios*) than the Father. Hence, we call Aetius and Eunomius "Heteroousians." Heteroousians asserted explicitly what was implied in Homoean teaching: the Father and the Son were of different nature.

Heteroousians had still other names. The term "neo-Arian" is a modern invention of an Athanasian bias. What caused the identification of Aetius and Eunomius as "neo-Arian" was the polemical juxtaposing of Arianism (charted right) and modalism (charted left) as the two opposite heresies in the pro-Nicene literature. Contemporary scholars, in turn, have called Heteroousians "radical Arians," evidently following the lead of Gregory of Nyssa: "Aetius . . . became notorious for even going beyond Arius, . . . or rather he perceived the consequences of all that Arius had advanced" (*C. Eun.* 1.6). Rufinus, too, asserted that after Arius's death "Aetius propounded this [Arian doctrine], and after Aetius Eunomius developed the doctrine even more vigorously and extensively" (*Hist. eccl.* 10.26). On the other hand, the theology of Aetius and Eunomius was unacceptable for most Arians (Eusebians). As a result, it is questionable whether Heteroousianism can be considered an Arian "hiccup" after all.

The crucial theological move of Heteroousians was to identify God's *ousia* with "unbegottenness" (*agen[n]ēsia*; Aetius, *Syntagmation* 4, 11, 18, 37; Eunomius, *Apol.* 1.7, 22; cf. Gregory of Nyssa, *C. Eun.* 1.39, 41; 2.9; *Apostolic Constitutions* 8.5). They argued that God the Father alone was "unbegotten." God was without any prior cause, eternal, and immutable (Aetius, *Synt.* 27; cf. John 8:41; 20:17; Rom 15:6; Plotinus, *Enn.* VI.7.37, "But the First has not come to be and has nothing prior to it"). Because God as a simple, noncomposite being had no accidents, attribution of God had to concern God's essence. Thus the name "unbegotten" was not an accidental but an essential attribute. If the essence of God the Father was "unbegotten," it followed that the only-*begotten* Son could in no way be said to be *homoousios* with the Father. One and the same divine essence, simple and indivisible, could not be simultaneously *gennētos* and *agennētos* (Aetius, *Synt.* 5; Eunomius, *Apol.* 1.10, 14). That was absurd! Aetius began his treatise *Syntagmation* provocatively with the question "Whether the ingenerate Deity can make the generate ingenerate?"

Since the assertion that God's *ousia* equaled *agennēsia* was the fundamental conviction of Heteroousians, I reiterate and rephrase it. In arguing with pro-Nicenes, Heteroousians agreed that if something was generated from an essence, it had to share the essence of the generator. But what they could not agree with was that the generated Son shared the ingenerate essence of the Father. Heteroousians reasoned that if God was "unbegotten essence" (*ousia agennētos*; Eunomius, *Apol.* 1.7–8), and if begetting indeed meant sharing the essence (*ousia*), then any caused "product" of God's essence had also to be "unbegotten." But this was clearly not the case with the Son, for the Scriptures called the Son "only-begotten." Hence it was correct to assert that the *ousia* of the Son was unlike (*anomoios*) the *ousia* of God the Father. The Heteroousian logic was more-or-less faultless, *if* one accepted the premise "God's nature equals 'unbegottenness'" (cf. Gregory of Nazianzus, *Or.* 29.12).

It is important to realize that despite the interchangeable usage of the words "God" and "Father," Eunomius—whom Gregory of Nyssa called "our neologian" (*C. Eun.* 1.20)—at times distinguished between the words "God" and "Father." He contended that God, the Absolute Unbegotten Being, *became* the Father in the begetting of the Son. The word "Father" did not really designate the essence of God (Eunomius, *Apol.* 1.24). "God" meant the "unbegotten" divine essence, and the name "Father" "manifested the activity [*energeia*] of the one who begot [the Son]" (1.24; in using Vaggione's translation [1987], I have changed "action" to "activity"). Let us elaborate on this subtle point about *energeia*.

Heteroousians distinguished and in a sense severed God's essence (*ousia*) from God's productive activity (*energeia*). They opined that if *energeia* belonged to *ousia*, God's *energeia* had to be coeternal with the divine *ousia*. But this would make the whole creation as the effect of God's operation coeternal with God, and that in turn would be nothing but paganism. Therefore, God's activity (*energeia*) had to be different from God's essence (*ousia*) and had to be linked with God's will (*boulē*; Epiphanius, *Pan.* 73.13.1). God's *energeia* had a beginning, but God's *ousia* was eternal.

Since God's causal activity (*energeia*), including the begetting of the Son, had to have a beginning, the resulting effects of this activity also had to have a beginning. Proverbs 8:22, the most widely used anti-Nicene proof text, squared well with the idea that the effect (the Son) was contemporaneous with its cause (God's *energeia*) and that both had a beginning: "The LORD created me at the beginning of his work, the first of his acts of long ago." Eunomius felt himself to be on secure, scriptural grounds to infer, "We recognize that the divine essence [*ousia*] is without beginning, simple, and endless, but we also recognize that its activity [*energeia*] is neither without beginning nor without ending" (*Apol.* 1.23). It followed that God's productive capacity (*energeia*) was *not* God's essential attribute; it was *not* something that belonged to God's *ousia*. Rather and once again, it was an act of God's *will* (1.12; Aetius, *Synt.* 5, 7). Since to beget (as we know it) was to be submitted to a process (*pathos*), and since process implied mutability and temporality, an *agennētos*, immutable, simple, and eternal God could not have been the begetter of the Son in any other sense than being his "maker/creator" by his will (cf. Gregory of Nyssa, *C. Eun.* 9.3). "Anything which can be said to come into existence by the action of another . . . has itself to be placed among created things" (Eunomius, *Apol.* 1.7). A Eunomian confession put it quite clearly: The Unbegotten "did not make use of his own essence [*ousia*] in begetting, but of his will [*boulēsei*] only" (1.28). Hearing this, Gregory of Nazianzus complained that Heteroousians made "the will into a new kind of mother in place of the Father" (*Or.* 29.6).

What followed from Eunomius's reasoning? It followed that since God was essentially *agennētos* and the Son *gennētos*, and since God's essence had to be distinguished from God's volitional activity, then God and God's Son had to be ontologically different. They could not be *homoousios*! "The whole account of our doctrines is summed up as follows: There is the supreme and absolute essence [*ousia*] and there is the essence which exists, on the one hand, *because of* that one and, on the other hand, *after* that one though before all others" (Eunomius, *Apol.* 2.1, emphasis added). Eunomius was adamant: the Unbegotten God had no sharer in his Godhead (cf. John 17:3). "My glory I will not give to another" (Isa 42:8 LXX). Therefore, *heteroousios*! Those agreeing with such conclusion confessed their belief in one God who was "unbegotten" (*agennētos*), "uncreated" (*aktistos*), and "unmade" (*apoiētos*); and in the Son who was "begotten" (*gennētos*), "created" (*ktistos*), and "made" (*poiētos*; Eunonius, *Apol.* 1.28). On the basis of Rom 1:20, "His . . . divine nature . . . [has] been understood and seen through the things he has *made*," they further contended that the *made* (the created) Son had revealed the Father (cf. Acts 2:36). For Heteroousians, Rom 1:20 was a theological rather than an economical statement. It concerned ontology, not soteriology.

Yet, the fact that the Son was begotten, created, and made did not mean that he was on par with the rest of the creation. The Son was the "only-begotten" through whom everything that existed was created. The Son would not be the "*only*-begotten" if the creation were exactly like him. God "begot and created and made only the Son by his power and activity prior to all things" (Eunomius, *Apol.* 1.28). Furthermore, the Son was not created out of nonbeing as the rest of the creation was (1.15). Eunomius did not even hesitate to use the Alexandrian variant reading of John 1:18, "only-begotten *God*," in connection with the Son (*Apol.* 1.21). This means that any caricature of the Heteroousian position in which they are made to equate the Son with the creation without qualification is unjustified. Heteroousians did not repeat Arius's mistake of saying that the Son originated *ex ouk ontōn* (Arius, *Ep. Eus. Nic.* 1.5). The reason why they are placed nevertheless a bit right from Arius's box (top of Chart Two) is that they emphasized the Son's essential unlikeness (*anomoios*) to the Father. Further-more, when Arius considered God's essence to be ineffable (Arius, *Thalia*), Het-eroousians confessed no apophatic "ignorance" about the essence of God (Epiphanius, *Pan.* 76.4.2). *Agennēsia* was God's essence. True, Eusebius of Cae-sarea also spoke about God's "unbegotten nature" (*agennētos physis*), but the church historian also added the qualifying phrase "ineffable essence" (*anekphras-tos ousia*), which seemed a misguided move for Heteroousians (*Dem. ev.* 5.1).

Heteroousians considered the Holy Spirit to be inferior to both the Father and the Son. "It was through the Son that he made [*epoiēsen*] the Holy Spirit ... by means of the activity [*energeia*] and power [*dynamei*] of the Son" (Eunomius, *Apol.* 1.28). Gregory of Nyssa summarized the Heteroousian teaching: "The whole account of our doctrines is summed up thus: there is the Supreme and Absolute Being, . . . and another being existing by reason of the First, but after it though before all others, . . . and a third being not ranking with either of these" (*C. Eun.* 1.13; cf. 1.15).

Just like Origen, Heteroousians preferred the natural or correspondence theory of language to the conventional theory of language. They were "realists" who taught that every name was an exact description of the entity it denoted. (At least here they certainly cannot be pejoratively accused of being "mere Aris-totelians"!) Heteroousians were adamant in insisting that the names "Father," "Son," and "Spirit" designated different essences (Eunomius, *Apol.* 1.12). "Since the names are different, the essences are different as well" (1.18; cf. Origen, *Cels.* 1.24, 5.45). The word *agennētos* was not a mere conventional mental construct (*epinoia*), arbitrarily predicated to God; instead, it provided a "real" knowledge of the essence of God (Eunomius, *Apol.* 1.8). Such an understanding of language constituted the fundamental disagreement between Heteroousians and the Cappadocian fathers (see below).

The above-mentioned Synod of Alexandria (AD 362) guaranteed the vic-tory of the Athanasian pro-Nicene theology and the corresponding refutation of Heteroousians. The formal and ecumenical condemnation of all kinds of Ari-ans, including Heteroousians, had to wait until the Council of Constantinople in AD 381 and until the imperial order to burn Eunomius's works in AD 398.

On Chart Three

The Second Half of the Fourth Century

Introduction

There is some considerable overlap between Chart Two and Chart Three. Readers are asked to be vigilant in seeing that the separation of the Cappadocian fathers (Basil the Great, Gregory of Nazianzus, and Gregory of Nyssa), Ambrose, Augustine, and partially also Homoeans and Heteroousians from previous figures and trajectories in Chart Two can be misleading. However, it seemed right to sacrifice the precise chronological and theological overlap for the sake of clarifying issues. Charts One and Two graphically depict the discussion about the Father's begetting of the Son; then Chart Three adds a (relatively) new element: the discussion of the full divinity of the Holy Spirit. In the middle of the fourth century, "full" Trinitarianism replaced the virtual "Binitarianism" of the earlier period. "The perfect Trinity . . . [must] go beyond Dyad, . . . and we must define [God as] a Trinity for the sake of completeness" (Gregory of Nazianzus, *Or.* 23.7). This is the reason for a separate chart.

Readers also need to notice that in Chart Three a new set of titles is suggested: "Sameness," "Equal Divinity of the Father, Son, and Holy Spirit," and "Unequal Divinity of the Father, Son, and Holy Spirit."

The contextual margin columns referring to non-Christian monotheism (left) and polytheism (right) are eliminated in Chart Three. Although Jewish and pagan religions continued to exist, they had an increasingly marginal role in the religious life of the Roman Empire. By the end of the fourth century, the empire had become "Christian," and the Trinitarian theology of the Council of Constantinople had become the imperial orthodoxy. The pro-Nicene "middle-columners" prevailed both theologically and politically. "Heretics" gradually lost their rights, writings, churches, and bishops. Therefore, the bold vertical lines do not separate Christian theology from non-Christian theology, but Christian *orthodoxy* from Christian *heresy*.

The fact that the middle column between the bold lines is a bit left of the central axis is due to the importance of subordinationist theologies in the end of the fourth century. This positioning does not imply any yielding to modalism, however.

125

I have already introduced Heteroousians, who appear again in the right column. I have also retained the "late 'nameless' Sabellians" in the left column primarily for the purposes of reminding the reader that modalist interpretations of the Nicene Creed were continuously perceived as threats to orthodoxy. That is, antimodalism continued to shape much of the Trinitarian theology, especially the Trinitarian theology written in Greek. "Fourth-century Trinitarian orthodoxy was the net product of rejecting modalism's claim as the necessary cost for defeating subordinationism" (M. Barnes, in Ayres and Jones 1998, 62). This is what Chart Three tries to convey.

I did hesitate, however, to move the representative Latin theologians (Ambrose and Augustine) a little left of the Greek theologians (the Cappadocians), because it may revive an inadequate notion, inadequate at least for the late fourth century, that "East" was more subordinationist and "West" more modalist. "If Augustine was softer toward modalism than he was toward other non-Nicene formulations, it is simply that . . . [modalists] had largely disappeared by Augustine's day" (Benner, in *IJST*, 2007, 29). On the other hand, many Greek theologians continued to perceive modalism as "a clear and present danger." But what "East" and "West" respectively argued against is not my reason for moving the representative Latin theologians a little left of the Greek theologians. My reasons are the following:

1. In the fourth century the success of a certain Trinitarian trajectory depended partially on emperors. The Eastern Emperors Constantius II and Valens supported the Homoean cause (Epiphanius, *Pan.* 69.12.5–13.1), while the Western Emperor Valentinian tolerated the pro-Nicenes (Socrates, *Hist. eccl.* 4.1). Here might be a good reason for keeping the "Eastern" Trinitarian trajectory a bit more on the right side.
2. As will be clear from a discussion of Augustine, he considered it problematic to make even a notional distinction between God's nature and the three divine persons. Greek theologians, however, continued to emphasize at least the notional distinction between God's nature and the three divine persons, together with an explanation of what had to be attributed to the common nature and what to the particular persons.

To conclude this introduction, I ask readers to note that Ambrose is contemporary with the Cappadocians (in the 380s). The literary debate between Augustine and his Homoean opponent Maximinian took place in the next century, the fifth.

Pneumatology

The relatively new element in Chart Three is pneumatology (teaching on the Holy Spirit). The wider theological discussion about the ontological status of the Holy Spirit did not surface before the 360s. As Basil put it, "The debate on this subject had not yet been stirred" (*Ep.* 258.2). In AD 325 the Nicene fathers thought it unnecessary to elaborate on the Holy Spirit. The creed laconically confessed the Christian faith "in the Holy Spirit." Now, in the second half of the fourth century, it was not so much the *economical* role of the Spirit, but especially the *theological* status of the Spirit that became controversial. The focus was on the Spirit's place in the eternal Godhead. It is significant that (Christian) Pentecost as a feast day in its own right and with its own liturgy was unknown before the end of the fourth century.

The Holy Spirit was no doubt mentioned in the ancient *regula fidei*. Christians worshipped the Spirit along with the Father and Son, and ultimately the theologians had to figure out the implications of such liturgical practice. When Basil made his case for the divinity of the Holy Spirit, his starting point was precisely public worship: "Lately, while I pray with the people …" (*Spir.* 1.3). There clearly was a correlation between the unity of worship and unity of nature of those who were worshipped. Basil added, "The profession of faith corresponds to our doxology in that together with the Father and Son we extol the Holy Spirit, because we are convinced that it does not stand outside the divine nature" (*Ep.* 159.2). Furthermore, the liturgy of baptism was performed in the name of the Father, Son, and Holy Spirit. The same divine nature of the three persons was indicated by the word "name" into which one was baptized. Curiously, "name" was in the singular (*Ep.* 210.3; Matt 28:19)!

The ontological status of the Holy Spirit became controversial when the *homoousios* divinity of the Spirit was denied by the so-called "Pneumatomachians" ("Spirit-Fighters") or "Tropici" (those who interpret the scriptural references to the Spirit metaphorically), and by Homoeans and Heteroousians. Among the Pneumatomachians, one should distinguish between the pro- and anti-Nicene Pneumatomachians.

1. The pro-Nicene type of Pneumatomachianism emerged as a variation of Homoeousianism. Some Homoeousians considered the Spirit to be a creature (Epiphanius, *Pan.* 73.1.7; 74.1.1–74.14.9). They were known as Macedonians (Macedonius, a pro-Nicene bishop of Constantinople, who actually lived before the pneumatological controversy). Macedonians allegedly acknowledged the consubstantiality of the Son with the Father, but denied it to the Spirit (Rufinus, *Hist. eccl.* 10.26). (This is why Latin Homoeans, who did not accept the consubstantiality of the Son with the Father, are placed to the right of Pneumatomachians in Chart Three.) Macedonians were worried that to insist on the equal divinity of the Spirit with the Father and the Son would threaten the unique status of the Son as the Only-begotten. If the Holy Spirit were divine, the Father had either two sons (the Holy Spirit proceeds from the Father), or a "grandson" (the Holy Spirit proceeds from the Father and Son). There were also scriptural texts, such as 1 Tim 5:21 ("In the presence of God and of Christ Jesus and of the elect angels …"), that men-

tion the Father and the Son, but seem to count the Spirit among the angels. There was also a confessional statement in 1 Cor 8:6 that mentioned only the Father and the Son. (The minuscules adding a phrase about the Holy Spirit are of a much later provenance than the fourth century.)

2. The anti-Nicene type of Pneumatomachianism emerged as a variation of Heteroousiansism. It denied the consubstantiality of both the Son and the Holy Spirit with the Father (Rufinus, *Hist. eccl.* 10.26). Anti-Nicene "Spirit-Fighters" argued on the basis of Amos 4:13 (God *creates* the wind = spirit) that the Holy Spirit, too, was a creature and ontologically "unlike" the Father. (However, in Amos 4:13 LXX, there is no definite article before the word "spirit," and thus the reference is likely either to the human spirit or the wind.) Eunomius stated explicitly that the Spirit was "third in both dignity and order" and "third in nature as well" (*Apol.* 25). Did not the Son himself proclaim that the Spirit would be "another" (*allon*; John 14:16)? In addition, John 1:3–4 reads, "All things came into being through him, and without him not one thing came into being. What has come into being in him was life." On the basis of such punctuation, Pneumatomachians and Heteroousians interpreted that the Holy Spirit was created through the Son, and therefore the Spirit was not divine even to the extent that the Son was "divine" ("without him not one thing came into being"). Because of the existence of such an interpretative possibility, some orthodox theologians preferred a different punctuation: "without him not one thing came into being that has come into being" (so that the sentence refers only to the creation because it is qualified, and therefore the *uncreated* Holy Spirit was necessarily excluded from the phrase; e.g., Gregory of Nazianzus, *Or.* 31.12).

Equal Divinity of the Father, Son, and Holy Spirit

The Cappadocian Fathers

Although the Cappadocian fathers (a modern designation for Basil of Caesarea, Gregory of Nazianzus, and Gregory of Nyssa) were closely related, these theologians should not be carelessly conflated as if their Trinitarian doctrines were identical. For instance, Basil was initially a less enthusiastic pro-Nicene— even hesitating to use the allegedly modalistic terms *homoousios* and *prosōpon*— than the two Gregories. Yet, as I attempt to group similar theologies and theologians together, it might still be helpful to consider all three as a group in one "box" for several reasons:

1. Through their writings, the Cappadocians gave a definite and long-lasting shape to the classical pro-Nicene doctrine of the Trinity, as affirmed at the

Council of Constantinople. At the same time, it is somewhat problematic to determine their individual contributions to the creedal pronouncement of the Council of Constantinople: Basil was dead, Gregory Nazianzus resigned as the president of the council, and Gregory of Nyssa is said to have delivered merely a funeral oration at the council.

2. The Cappadocians defended the full divinity and the distinct *hypostasis* of the Holy Spirit. Much of the argumentation for a distinct and eternal *hypostasis* of the Son in the mid-fourth century set up the preconditions for the argumentation for the distinct and eternal *hypostasis* of the Holy Spirit. Yet before the Cappadocians some theologians—such as Cyril of Jerusalem, the authors of the *Letter of George*, Didymus the Blind, and Athanasius—made their cases for the full divinity of the Holy Spirit.

3. The Cappadocians sorted out the Greek vocabulary, the meanings of the words *ousia* and *hypostasis*, which enabled them to express both the unalterable unity of and the irreducible distinctness within the Godhead. A distinction between *ousia* and *hypostasis* also prevented their acceptance of the language and theology of the Marcellian miahypostatic tradition. They believed that the one divine *ousia* "is contemplated in three persons [*prosōpa*] or hypostases [*hypostaseis*]" (Gregory of Nyssa, *Ad Graecos*).

Since the Cappadocian fathers upheld a nonmodalist and non-Arian understanding of the Nicene Creed, they are sometimes called "neo-Nicenes." Gregory of Nazianzus indeed came to Constantinople, to an overwhelmingly Arian city, as a new preacher of the Nicene faith. The Cappadocians were "neo-Nicenes" in the sense that they did not allow any subordination between the three persons of the Trinity on the level of *ousia*. The only "subordination" allowed was the causal subordination on the level of *hypostaseis* (the traditional doctrine of the monarchy of the Father). In the 380s the Emperor Theodosius affirmed the Cappadocian "neo-Nicene" position as the imperial orthodoxy. This marked the decline for both Arianism and Heteroousianism.

Basil of Caesarea

Basil of Caesarea, the elder brother of Gregory of Nyssa, died shortly before the Council of Constantinople (AD 381). Nevertheless, he was one of the architects of the theology of this council, which searched for the balance between a modalist interpretation of Nicaea and of Arianism. Basil was frustrated that while the "Westerners" anathematized Arius, they continued to be in communion with Marcellus, who was a "heretic" of the opposite sort. Basil even wrote six letters to Athanasius, insisting that the West should condemn Marcellus (e.g., *Ep.* 69.2). Athanasius never responded. However, the prime targets of Basil were Heteroousians (cf. his treatise *Against Eunomius*) and Pneumatomachians.

At least in his later works, Basil was indeed a convinced "neo-Nicene." He moved away from a Homoeousian position and toward a pro-Nicene position during the years after 360 (cf. *Ep.* 9 and 125).

Basil argued for the epistemological usefulness of concepts or *epinoiai* in theology. Using *epinoiai* (abstracted linguistic concepts) to speak about God could be sufficiently adequate without being absolutely adequate or insufficiently adequate. On the basis of biblical texts, such as Rom 11:33, Basil insisted that God's essence (*ousia*) remained unknowable. Nevertheless, the Scriptures used various *epinoiai* as predicates without making the claim that God was linguistically captured or, on the other hand, that such discourse was empty of meaning. Furthermore, since the Christian God was a self-communicating God, Basil took God's activities (*energeiai*) as the basis for using kataphatic *epinoiai* in theological discourse (cf. Clement of Alexandria, *Strom.* VI.18). "His operations [*energeiai*] come down to us, but his substance [*ousia*] remains inaccessible," taught Basil (*Ep.* 234.1). Especially the mystery of the incarnation allowed Christians to discourse about the ineffable God. God had "made sense" in the incarnated Son (Matt 11:27; John 14:9). "I know what is knowable of God" (Basil, *Ep.* 235.2). In short, Basil's point in assessing the value of *epinoiai* in theological discourse was twofold:

1. To show that the Heteroousians' favorite predicate *agennēsia* (unbegottennness) was itself an *epinoia* and thus still just a linguistic predicate rather than an exact description of God's essence. *Epinoiai*, which were abstracted from sense experience, "did not engage *ousiai* anyway" (Rousseau 1994, 111).
2. To argue that whatever was said about the infinite God in human finite language came short of the reality it tried to describe, yet such an "incommeasurement" did not invalidate theological discourse as hopelessly nonsensical, inadequate, and meaningless.

Basil proceeded with his anti-Heteroousian argument by showing that "unbegottenness" was not God's essence (*ousia*) but the individual characteristic of the person (*hypostasis*) of the Father (*C. Eun.* 2.28). In other words—and students of Trinitarian theology, please pay attention!—Basil sorted out the confusing semantic ambiguity of a condemnation added to the Nicene Creed, which employed the phrase "*hypostasis* or *ousia*." Although Basil had earlier used these terms as synonyms, he later made a distinction between the words *hypostasis* and *ousia*. Such a distinction enabled Basil to be more precise in speaking about the sameness and difference in the Godhead. When Aristotle had reserved the designation "primary substance [*ousia*]" to particulars (*Categoriae* 2a11–18), a (neo)Platonist Basil wrote, "Substance [*ousia*] has the same relation to person [*hypostasis*] as the general has to the particular" (*Ep.* 214.4; 236.6). In other words, Basil limited the overlapping semantic realm of the terms *hyposta-*

sis and *ousia* so that these words acquired a more technical sense: *hypostasis* was narrowed down to mean "person" (*prosōpon*) or "subsistence" (*hyparxis* or *hypokeimenon*); and *ousia* came to mean "nature" (*physis*; 236.6; cf. Gregory of Nazianzus, *Or.* 21.6, 42.16).

The twofold polemical context of Basil's theologizing explains his semantic refinement. Earlier and against Heteroousians, Basil argued that the three divine *prosōpa* were of the same essence (*ousia* or *hypostasis*). Later and against Marcellus, Basil devised the distinction between *ousia* and *hypostasis*, because the designation "three *prosōpa*" alone proved ineffective against modalists (*Ep.* 214.3–4). As a result, Basil could assert that in the Godhead, there were three "persons" and one "nature [or essence or substance]" (*Ep.* 125.1). He even opined, somewhat unconvincingly, that, in condemning a position, the Nicene fathers would not have used two different words if these words had been completely synonymous (125.1).

This said, it is crucial to clarify that Basil was talking only about a *notional* distinction between God's *ousia* and *hypostaseis*. He considered it a mystery exactly how the three *hypostaseis* were one God, but at least this much seemed clear: to sever the *hypostaseis* in any way from their common *ousia* resulted in distorted theology. Yet, the notional distinction between *ousia* and *hypostasis* proved to be so helpful that, by the end of the fourth century, the Nicene doctrine of the Trinity was increasingly understood in terms of three persons and one nature. "It can even be said that Basil is ultimately responsible for the formula, one *ousia* three *hypostaseis*, although Basil never used the phrase as such" (Hildebrand 2007, 99).

Yet Basil's contribution to the classical doctrine of the Trinity was much more than giving a fine-tuning to a few terms. Behr (2004, 305) has warned, "It would be a mistake to equate Basil's 'Trinitarian theology' with the distinction between the essence and *hypostasis*."

After defining *hypostasis* as "person," Basil distinguished between the *personal* and *common* names of the Trinity. Apparently he still had to explain why the one Godhead had three different names. Basil contended that the personal names, such as "unbegotten" and "begotten," applied exclusively to the respective *hypostaseis* in the Trinity (*Ep.* 214.4). "Unbegottenness" was the Father's personal name or hypostatic property (*idiōma*), just as "begottenness" was the Son's personal name or hypostatic property (*Ep.* 236.6; *C. Eun.* 2.28). These personal names of the particular *hypostaseis* could not be attributed to the common divine essence (*ousia*). In a phrase "God the Father (or Son or Spirit)," the word "god" referred to the common divine nature, and the word "father" to the personal name of the *hypostasis* (*Ep.* 236.6; cf. Gregory of Nyssa, *Gr.*). On the other hand, the common names—such as "dignity of nature," "agreement of will," and "identity of action"—applied equally to all the three divine persons. Because of such distinction between personal and common names, Basil could argue that the only-begotten Son was not less divine simply because he was "begotten."

Perhaps because of Origen's negative attitude toward the term *homoousios*, and also because of the modalist abuse of it, *homoousios* was not Basil's preferred formula. When Basil used this term, he added a telling phrase: "according to the proper interpretation of [it]" (*Ep.* 9.3). By the "proper interpretation" he meant the use of a qualifying phrase "without any difference" of nature (9.3). He deliberated that the term implied a hypostatic difference, because "nothing can be of one substance with itself" (52.3). Only in such qualified sense "the word [*homoousios*] has an excellent and orthodox use, defining as it does both the proper character of the hypostases, and setting forth the invariability of the nature" (52.3). The "proper interpretation" also meant rejecting the notion that, after some kind of division, a segment of the divine *ousia* belonged to the *homoousios* Son. The Son's divinity was not a (material) part of the total divinity, and there was no divine "substance" before Father and Son (and Holy Spirit) that was then divided between the three persons (52.3).

In his treatise *On the Holy Spirit* (*De Spiritu Sancto*), Basil of Caesarea investigated what the Christian confessions said about the third person of the Trinity. He examined the prepositions used in various doxological formulas to demonstrate the divinity of the Spirit. Yet many, including Gregory of Nazianzus, complained that Basil never called the Holy Spirit explicitly "God." But in controversies, radical statements are easy targets for refutation, and they often cause accusations of introducing novelties. So instead of calling the Spirit "God" and *homoousios*, Basil wisely argued for the Spirit's equality of honor (*isotimia*) or cohonor (*homotimia*; cf. Origen, *Princ.* Pref. 4). He also stated that the Holy Spirit "partakes of the fullness of divinity [*theotēs*]" (*Spir.* 18.46; *Ep.* 90) and that the Holy Spirit had "his subsistence from God" (*ek theou tēn hyparxin echon*; *Ep.* 105).

The evidence for the full divinity of the Spirit was available for the one who observed what the Holy Spirit did (*Spir.* 9.22; 15.36; cf. Athanasius, *Ep. Serap.* 1.19–25). Above all, the Holy Spirit sanctified and deified. Clearly, a mere creature could neither sanctify nor deify the other creatures, and therefore the Spirit had to be placed on the side of the eternal Creator rather than on the side of the temporal creatures (Basil, *Ep.* 125.3). At the same time, Basil was not giving up the causal order of the divine *hypostaseis*. In a causal sense, and only in a causal sense, the Spirit was still said to be the "third" (*C. Eun.* 3.1).

Gregory of Nazianzus

Gregory of Nazianzus was a close friend of Basil. His five *Theological Orations* are arguably one of the best presentations of the classical pro-Nicene Trinitarian theology. He also contended that God's *ousia* was incomprehensible. "No one has yet discovered or ever will discover what God is in his nature and essence" (*Or.* 28.17). But there was an important difference between Gregory's apophatic position and that of the Neoplatonists. The latter argued for the absolute unknowability of the One. For instance, Plotinus maintained that as an object of human knowledge, the One "eludes our words and we have no knowledge or intuition of it" (*Enn.* V.3.14; VI.9.3; cf. Proclus, *Stoich. theol.* Prop. 123, "The One is completely unknowable"). Gregory also maintained that God's essence (*ousia*) was unknowable, while affirming the knowability of God's observable gracious activities (*energeiai*), which indeed were God.

Gregory's qualified apophatic approach makes good sense when we perceive it as a countermove to the Heteroousians' assertion that the word "unbegotten" effectively captured the essence of God. Gregory, perhaps somewhat distorting Eunomius's claim and thinking that the latter bragged of having a "complete" understanding of God's essence (cf. Epiphanius, *Pan.* 76.4.2), insisted that theology was not so much syllogistic reasoning operating with exhaustive definition-like propositions, as it was a poetic expression of the inexpressible mystery.

If one only observed the traditional images for speaking about the Father and the Son—and also the actual preference of images over terms and definitions—the point is quite clear: fire and heat, source and stream, root and fruit, light and radiance, honey and sweetness, intellect and word, flower and fragrance. The usefulness of such images was that they implied both causality between and the symbiotic inseparableness of the entities involved. For instance, heat *was* fire. Fire and heat belonged together; there was no heat without fire. Yet fire was distinct from heat as a cause was distinct from the effect. Furthermore, these images were beneficial from the epistemological point of view: heat made fire known, just like the Son made the Father known. However, the downside of the analogical imagery was the implied materiality, and perhaps also the suggestion of an emanation-like process. The images also involved merely two elements and were more suitable for illustrating the begetting of the Son from the Father than the coming forth of the Son and the Holy Spirit.

Speaking about God's *ousia*, Gregory admonished his readers to keep in mind that God was, in a sense, "beyond *ousia*" (*hyperousios*). The designation *agennēsia* captured God as inadequately as any other *epinoia*, for in the final analysis the Trinitarian God was "incomprehensible" (*akatalēptos*)—which was just another inadequate linguistic predication and *epinoia*! "I have failed to find anything in this world with which I might compare the divine nature. If a faint resemblance comes my way, the more significant aspect escapes me, leaving me and my illustrations here in this world" (*Or.* 31.31). To call God "father" or "unbegotten" or "I AM WHO I AM" (*ho ōn* in Exod 3:14 LXX) was fair enough, yet these titles were *conventional* designations and did not provide any kind of direct, final, and exhaustive insights into God's very being. Even though some technical terms, such as *hypostasis*, helped Gregory to explicate his Trinitarian beliefs, he added a dismissive comment immediately after using such technical terms: "whatever other term one might invent that is more precise than [this] (for what we are thinking and talking about defeats my power of speech!)" (*Or.* 21.10). "So, in the end, I resolved that it is best to say 'good-bye' to images and shadows, deceptive and utterly inadequate as they are to express the reality" (*Or.*

31.33). (Arius's apophaticism in *Thalia*—his insistence on the unknowability of the Father—was primarily a Christological issue. For him, the Son, as a *created divine being, was* ignorant of the essence of his Creator. Gregory's apophaticism, however, was not about the Son's knowledge of the Father, but about *human* knowledge of God.)

To refute the Heteroousian argument that God's essence was "unbegotten-ness," Gregory made some crucial distinctions:

1. Like Basil and Athanasius, Gregory distinguished between the meaning of the words *ousia* and *hypostasis*. *Ousia* and *hypostasis* corresponded respectively to what was common (*koinon*) and what was individual (*idion*) in the God-head (*Or.* 25.16; 31.9). What was common in the Godhead was the divine *ousia*; what was individual were the three *hypostaseis*.
2. The three consubstantial *hypostaseis* were distinguished by their individual characteristics coming from their modes of origination (*tropos hyparxeōs*; 31.9). The Father's individual characteristic (*idion*) was his unbegottenness (*agennētos*), the Son's *idion* was his generation (*gennētos*), and the Holy Spirit's *idion* was the Spirit's proceeding (*ekporeuomen*; 29.2).
3. What was individual could not be predicated to what was common in the Godhead. Here Gregory used an anthropological analogy: it was inadequate to attribute individual characteristics of a class's representative to the whole class. If a man was dead, it did not mean that the whole humankind was dead. Likewise, *agennēsia* could not be attributed to the Son and the Holy Spirit just because it was attributed to the Father (29.15). It proved to be of crucial importance to discern what applied to *ousia* and what applied to *hypostaseis*, even though the divine *hypostaseis* were one God.
4. Heteroousians should also not confuse predication denoting the *essence* (*ousia*) of things/persons and predication denoting the *relation* (*schesis*) between things/persons. *Schesis* is a really important notion, because, in addition to the modes of origination, the divine persons could also be differentiated accord-ing to their relation (*schesis*). For instance, the name "Father" was a "name of a relation [*onoma scheseōs*]" (29.16). The name "Father" showed how the first person of the Trinity was related to the second and the third persons. (It is indeed worth asking whether the contemporary well-intended substitute des-ignations—such as Mother, Lover, and Friend [McFague 1982]; or Spirit-Sophia, Jesus-Sophia, and Mother-Sophia [Johnson 1992]—express the same relations as do the words "Father," "Son," and "Spirit." I doubt that.)

Combining the relational names with the modes of origination of the Father, Son, and Spirit, Gregory was able to state the difference between the three divine persons without giving up their consubstantiality: the relational name "Father" designated the God without origin, the relational name "Son" designated the only-begotten God, and the relational name "Spirit of the

Father" designated the proceeding God. The Father alone was without origin, the Son alone was begotten, and the Spirit alone was proceeding, but all three were fully God.

What were the implications of stating that the Father alone was without origin (uncaused) and that the Son and the Spirit were originated (caused)? Did it not prove subordinationists to be right? Gregory conceded that there was indeed an asymmetry in the Trinity. Yet this asymmetry did not imply the ontological inferiority of the Son and the Spirit. Gregory said explicitly that the superiority of the Father "does not apply to the nature, but only to origination," and continued like Origen, into whose works he was deeply immersed, "For in the consubstantial persons there is nothing greater or less in point of substance" (*Or.* 40.43). All three persons were equally divine, but only the Father was without origin.

Likewise, Gregory argued that the eternal Son and Spirit could not be "later" than God the Father. "They [the Son and the Spirit] are from him, not *after* him" (*Or.* 29.3). "When I speak of 'origin,' do not insert there a notion of time" (21.7). The Son was begotten "in a nontemporal [*achronōs*] way" (29.3). After all, if everything was created through the Son, including time, how could "the Master of time" be subject to time?

In short, Gregory, as well as the other Cappadocian fathers, retained the Origenist causal subordination of the Son and the Holy Spirit to the Father. The Father alone was the first principle (*archē*), the only First Cause. "We admit that in respect of being the cause, the Father is greater than the Son" (*Or.* 29.15). But the doctrine of the monarchy of the Father did not mean, yet again, that the Son and the Holy Spirit were lesser Gods. "The three are the single God" (39.11). "Though there is numerical distinction, there is no division in the being" (29.2). The generation of the Son and the procession of the Holy Spirit were no involuntary emanations, neither were they mere voluntary and temporal acts that deprived the Son and the Holy Spirit from their eternal divine *ousia*. "There is one nature [*ousia*] for all three: God" (42.15).

Gregory coined various Trinitarian formulas (*Or.* 21.35; 28.31; 31.28; 33.16; 42.15–16), which were abbreviated to a famous phrase: *mia ousia, treis hypostaseis*. This formula became the ultimate orthodox summary-formula for the Trinity. Yet, as Lienhard observes (in Davis et al. 1999, 99), "The exact formula is ... more a piece of modern academic shorthand than a quotation from the writings of the Cappadocians." The best English translation of the phrase *mia ousia, treis hypostaseis* is "one nature, three persons." But the Greek phrase has arguably an almost untranslatable nuance that is not conveyed in the Latin-based English using the word "person" (*persona*). Gregory wrote, "The Italians [Latin speakers] mean the same; but, owing to scantiness of their vocabulary and its poverty of terms, they are unable to distinguish between *ousia* and *hypostasis*, and therefore introduce the term 'persons' [*prosōpa*], to avoid being understood as asserting three *ousiai*" (*Or.* 21.35). Augustine indeed echoed the sentiment:

"The Greeks intend to posit a difference, though I do not know what it is, between *ousia* and *hypostasis*." Thus the bishop of Hippo translated the Greek formula as "one essence, three substances" (*una essentia tres substantiae; Trin.* 5.8.10). Here *substantia* translates *hypostasis* and testifies to the existence of the very confusion Augustine tries to avoid!

Obviously, the narrowing of the meaning of the word *hypostasis* and the corresponding assertion that, in the Godhead, there were three *hypostaseis* provoked reaction, just as any terminological novelty in theology would! For a long time *hypostasis* had been a synonym for *ousia*. Therefore, not every fourth-century theologian was happy with the Cappadocians' semantic refinement. Many did not dare to say that God had three *hypostaseis*, because they heard meanings that they could not accept despite all explanations. Jerome, for instance, "exploded" in his letter to Pope Damasus over the fact that he was asked to acknowledge "a newfangled term 'three *hypostaseis*.'" "What apostles, pray tell me, authorized it?" (*Ep.* 15.3).

Gregory of Nazianzus was *the* fighter against the Pneumatomachians and for the full divinity of the Holy Spirit. He called the Spirit explicitly both *theos* and *homoousios* (*Or.* 31.10) and in so doing appealed to the ancient liturgical tradition and especially to the writings of Gregory Thaumaturgos, the apostle of Cappadocia. Gregory of Nazianzus pointed out that Christ himself called the Holy Spirit "*another* Advocate" (John 14:16), which implied that Christ had to be the first. The Holy Spirit was intrinsic to what the Triune God was. "Insofar as he [the Holy Spirit] proceeds from the Father, he is no creature; inasmuch as he is not begotten, he is no Son, and to the extent that procession is the mean between ingeneracy and generacy, he is God" (*Or.* 31.8).

In *Oratio* 31.28, Gregory emphasized the gradual and progressive nature of revelation. He showed that the Old Testament had only a preliminary understanding of the Son and no doctrine of the Holy Spirit. After all, the patriarchs were monotheists, not crypto-Trinitarians. The Trinitarian understanding of the one God was a strictly Christian, postresurrection perception of God, even if it took a considerable time to figure out what the Trinitarian orthodoxy was.

Gregory of Nyssa

Gregory of Nyssa was the younger brother of Basil and a promoter of the Nicene Trinitarian theology at the Council of Constantinople (AD 381). Taking over Basil's literary battle with Heteroousians, Gregory penned his treatises *Against Eunomius* about the time of this council. (In *NPNF*² 5, book 2 of *Against Eunomius* is actually Gregory's *Refutation of Eunomius's Confession* [*Refutatio confessionis Eunomii*]. The attached *Answer to Eunomius's Second Book* is the original book 2 of *Against Eunomius*. References in the following text correspond to the widely used *NPNF*.)

Gregory was among those who responded to Eunomius's claim of having a "real" knowledge of God's unbegotten essence. Gregory insisted that the divine *ousia* remained absolutely beyond human comprehension. "We have learned to honor in silence that which transcends speech and thought" (*C. Eun.* 3.5). Referring to Matt 28:19, "baptizing them in the name of the Father and of the Son and of the Holy Spirit," Gregory drew attention to the facts that the word "name" was in singular and that it was not stated what that name was. The name that could not be told referred to God's *ousia* (2.3; cf. Basil of Caesarea, *Ep.* 210.3). Correspondingly, Gregory contended that whatever words theologians used, the essence of God remained beyond description. "It is clear that by any of the terms we use the Divine nature itself is not signified, but some one of its surroundings is made known" (*Ad Ablabium*). This meant that human (theological) discourse was really not about God's essence but rather about God's energies (*energeiai*), about God's *ad extra* activities. In other words, God's "unnameable essence" was named by that which was nameable, by God's energies (*C. Eun.* 7.4).

According to Gregory, Heteroousians misunderstood and misused the names "Father" and "Son." These words did not designate essences; instead, they designated relation (*schesis*). "Who does not know that some nouns ... are used to express relation" (*C. Eun.* 1.38); and again, "The title of Father does not present to us the essence, but only indicates the relation to the Son" (2.3). The names "Father" and "Son" concerned the *how* rather than the *what* of the Godhead. They showed the mode of existence of the Father, Son, and Spirit. At the same time, Gregory did not assert that the names "Father," "Son," and "Holy Spirit" were designations of a mere relation. The reason was that being in relation presupposed entities that could be in relation. Gregory did not affirm the relationality of the divine persons at the expense of their being an essence—as seems to be the case in some contemporary theories of the Trinity (e.g., Moltmann and Zizioulas). These theories reduce God's *ousia* to relationality and thereby undo the distinction between *ousia* and *hypostasis*, forfeit the simplicity of God's nature, and come rather close to tritheism.

The names "Father" and "Son" are not only relational names; they are also *correlational* names. Father implies the existence of a Son and vice versa. Thus, God cannot be called "Father" unless God has a Son; and God cannot be called "Son" unless he has a Father. Heteroousians reportedly preferred the designation "supreme and absolute Being" to that of the "Father" in order to avoid the clear implication of the name "Father" (*C. Eun.* 1.14). In *To the Greeks* (*Ad Graecos*), Gregory contended that the three persons "differ from one another according to the very significance of their names."

Gregory also pointed out that the names "Father" and "Son" were predicated to God in a special sense. Unlike human fathers, God was eternal, indivisible, and immutable. The realization of this difference had several important implications:

1. Since God was eternal, there could not be any temporal gap between the Father and his Son. "The divine nature is one, . . . not admitting in itself priority and posteriority" (*C. Eun.* 5.1).
2. Since God's essence was indivisible or simple, there could not be any substantial difference between the three persons. "Simplicity in the case of the Trinity admits no degrees" (1.19).
3. Since God was immutable, God had to be eternally the consubstantial Father, Son, and Holy Spirit.

Next, to counter the Heteroousian argument that the Son was a creature because the Son was a caused being (begotten), Gregory pointed out the many senses of the word "origin" (*archē*). To have an origin could be compatible with either "unbegotten" or "uncreated." The term "unbegotten" meant "without cause," and it was attributable to the Father only. Yet, although the Son and the Spirit were caused (they had their origin in the Father and were not "unbegotten"), all three, the Father, Son, and Holy Spirit, were "uncreated" (*C. Eun.* 1.33). To put it succinctly, in the case of the Son, Gregory composed a saying: "He exists by generation indeed, but nevertheless he never begins to exist" (1.39). In the process of eternal begetting and proceeding, the divine nature was communicated to the originated (caused) Son and Spirit.

To bolster his anti-Heteroousian case further, Gregory reinforced the distinction between the formerly synonymous terms *hypostasis* and *ousia* (e.g., *C. Eun.* 1.35). As we have seen, to insist on the difference between *hypostasis* and *ousia* was a relatively novel thing to do, because evidently some theologians still spoke about God being one *hypostasis* and three *ousiai* (*Ad Pet.* 1 [no longer unanimously attributed to Basil as his *Ep.* 38]; cf. Eusebius of Caesarea, *C. Marc.* 1.4.39). Gregory justified his distinction by pointing out the difference between the nouns with more general and with more particular meanings. *Ousia* denoted the general and *hypostasis* the particular. The Son was God as far as his *ousia* was concerned, but the Son was a particular divine person as far his *hypostasis* was concerned (*Pet.* 3, 5). It is important to realize here that the distinction between *ousia* and *hypostasis* was not an either/or but a both/and distinction. God was both an *ousia* and three *hypostaseis*. On the score of the *ousia*, God was One; and in the recognizable characteristics of the *hypostaseis*, God was "distributed" into Father, Son, and Holy Spirit (*C. Eun.* 2.2).

While defending the consubstantiality of the three divine *hypostaseis*, Gregory had to guard against a modalist misunderstanding of things. "In the case of the Trinity it is essential to keep the [hypostatic] distinctions free from all confusion with the help of the particularizing characteristics" (*Pet.* 3). To avoid any negligence of the "particularizing characteristics," Gregory insisted on the proper use of the term person (*hypostasis*). The term "person" and the hypostatic names Father, Son, and Holy Spirit designated the distinct existence of and the difference between the three divine, consubstantial, and coeternal persons. Once again, all three persons had their divine essence in common, but all three persons were distinguished by their particular hypostatic characteristics, which indicated their mode of origination or the lack of origination (the Father was *agennētos*).

In connection with this, one needs to understand that the word "person" (*hypostasis, prosōpon*) should not be confused with the modern notion of "personality." For Gregory, person meant a "unique collection of properties" (Porphyry, *Isagoge* 7.20–26), which was defined through relations to other persons (to other "unique collection of properties"). The "unique collection of properties" is that by "which the person is constituted as distinct" (Turcescu 2005, 57). So, there were three sets of "collections of properties" in the Godhead, which consisted of unique combinations of "particular characteristics": the Father was fully divine, eternal, and *unbegotten*; the Son was fully divine, eternal, and *begotten*; and the Holy Spirit was fully divine, eternal, and *proceeding* (Gregory of Nyssa, *Pet.* 4). These three sets of "collections of properties" distinguished between the three divine persons and indicated the relations between them.

The result of Gregory's linguistic fine-tuning was that the term *hypostasis* became synonymous with the term *prosōpon*. The theological use of the term *prosōpon* accentuated the fact that the Father, Son, and Holy Spirit were relational beings. (The prefix *pros-* in the word *prosōpon* means "toward.") It followed that the communion between the three persons was not a mere cosharing of *ousia*, but a communion-relation (*koinōnia*, later to be called *perichōrēsis*) between three distinct persons (*Pet.* 4). The mutual fellowship turned the abstract interacting "collection of properties" into true communion of relating persons.

One more thing: the restricting of the semantic field of the term *hypostasis* does not mean that Gregory and his colleagues emphasized what was individual (*hypostasis*) over what was common (*ousia*) in the Godhead, or that they somehow cared less for God's unity and consubstantiality than for the individuality of the divine persons and their *perichōrēsis*. (These allegations were made already at Gregory's time.) The polemical context of Gregory's arguments was to refute Pneumatomachians and Heteroousians, both of which made the distinction of persons without affirming the unity of nature. Thus, Gregory's sorting out the proper use of *hypostasis* could in no way have been conducted at the expense of God's unity. In the end of his life, he indeed wrote a treatise titled *To Ablabius: On Not Three Gods*. A modern Orthodox theologian Lossky (1974, 81) has urged us to bear in mind that God's "one nature and three hypostases are presented simultaneously to our understanding, with neither being prior to the other."

Gregory employed some other arguments for proving the consubstantiality and coeternity of the Father, Son, and Holy Spirit. Since discussing the very essence (*ousia*) of God was not an option, Gregory focused on what could be perceived and discussed: God's activities (*energeiai*). He thus made his case for the consubstantiality and coeternity of the divine persons on the basis of God's energies. Here Gregory employed some technical terms: *dynamis* (power) and *energeia* (activity). Any nature *(ousia)* has its power *(dynamis)*. Any nature also has its characteristic activity *(energeia)*, which comes from its power *(Abl.)*. While Eunomius refused to associate God's (temporal) activity *(energeia)* with God's (eternal) nature and power, Gregory argued that both God's power and energy were inherent in God's nature. Precisely because of the Heteroousian denial of the link between God's power and energy, it was very important for Gregory to affirm it. God's power was God, and God's energies were God. The divine nature was neither severed from God's power and energies, nor was God ever powerless or inactive. Gregory affirmed the equation "one power and one Godhead" *(Ad Eustathium* [or Basil, *Ep.* 189]).

The Scriptures do call the Son "the power [*dynamis*] of God" (1 Cor 1:24). What implications does this statement have for the ontological status of the Son? Gregory reasoned that because God acted by his power, the Son was inevitably involved in all the doings of God *(C. Eun.* 6.3). Gregory had in mind the *ad extra* activities of *God* as distinguished from the activity of the *Father* in begetting the Son. He reasoned that if the power that produced certain activities was the same, then the nature that had that power was also the same. Gregory's "one-power" argument was opposed to the Arian "two-power" argument. He believed that, in God, there were not two ontologically different powers, but the Son *was* the *dynamis* of God.

There was no explicit scriptural statement about the Holy Spirit being the power of God. Thus, in order to demonstrate the coeternity and consubstantiality of the Spirit with the Father and Son, Gregory appealed to the concept of *energeia (C. Eun.* 2.15; *Abl.*; M. Barnes [2001]). While 1 Cor 12:6 speaks about *God* activating *(energeō)* the spiritual gifts, verse 11 says that "all these are activated by one and the same *Spirit.*" Gregory concluded, "From the identity of operations [*tōn energēmatōn*] it results assuredly that the Spirit is not alien from the nature of the Father and the Son" *(C. Eun.* 2.15). "God is one, because no difference either of nature [*physis*] or operation [*energeia*] is contemplated in the Godhead" *(Abl.)*. Once again, "The oneness of their nature needs be inferred from the identity of their operation" *(Eust.).* The argument was basically the following: There were certain characteristic *ad extra* activities *(energeiai)* of God (e.g., creation and re-creation) that manifested the essential sameness of the three persons. Only God could create out of nonbeing and save what was lost. Because God's activities were the results of God's power, and because God's power belonged to God's nature, the energies testified to the coeternity and consubstantiality of the Father, Son, and Holy Spirit. Put differently, Gregory was able to argue from the uniqueness of God's activities to the coeternity and consubstantiality of those who were the agents of these activities: the three divine persons. If the divine energies were one, so was the power behind the energies, and so was the indivisible nature that underlaid the one power. Thus, *homoousios!*

Yet, there seemed to be a good objection to such reasoning. The Scriptures mentioned certain acts *(erga)* as characteristic to one of the divine persons: it was the Father who created, the Son who incarnated, and the Spirit who sanctified.

(Explanation: a particular act [*ergon*] is done by a person. An act is an actualization of an activity [*energeia*], which this person has as a particular kind of being. For instance, humans have a capacity to cry [*energeia*], but when a particular human person cries, one performs an act of crying [*ergon*].) Strictly speaking, these are persons who act and not natures. The Father, the Son, and the Spirit are the subjects of their respective acts. If so, then do not the particular hypostatic acts of the Father, Son, and Spirit prove the difference between the divine persons? Does the recognition of the particular hypostatic acts ultimately lead to postulating three Gods? To answer by using our example (above), the human capacity (*energeia*) to cry may prove the humanness of all who cry, but it does not prove that all humans cry when Tom cries. John may laugh when Tom cries and yet be as human as Tom is. John and Tom are two particular human beings who act independently. Now, does it not follow that the distinct hypostatic acts of the Father, Son, and Spirit prove the existence of three independent Gods? "No it does not!" responded Gregory.

To affirm monotheism and the unique unity of the consubstantial divine persons as the Trinity, Gregory argued not only for the oneness of the divine energies (*eneregeiai*) of the Father, Son, and Holy Spirit, but also for the oneness of their divine acts (*erga*). The logic of the Scriptures demanded a conclusion that all three divine persons were acting simultaneously as one God. "Very truly, I tell you, the Son can do nothing on his own, but only what he sees the Father doing; for whatever the Father does, the Son does likewise" (John 5:19). "My Father is still working, and I also am working" (5:17). "The Father who dwells in me does his work" (14:10b). Gregory consented, "In the case of the divine nature, we do not learn that the Father does [*poiei*] anything by himself in which the Son does not work conjointly, or again that the Son has any special operation apart from the Holy Spirit" (*Abl.*). Gregory pointed out that the Scriptures employ rhetorical devices, such as synecdoche, which mention a part for the whole and vice versa (any combination of one divine person for three, and three for one). Thus, even though a particular act (*ergon*) was attributed to a particular divine person, all three must be understood to be involved in this same act.

The fact that the Father, Son, and Holy Spirit always acted as one God undercut the validity of an analogy of three human beings acting together. The difference between the divine and human actions was that while all divine (external) acts were common to the three divine persons, human acts were not common to all human beings. In a sense, we can say that while performing an act the divine persons do not cooperate; instead, they operate as one. By contrast, human persons may cooperate as many individuals in the same act, but this act is never the act of the whole humanity. To use Gregory's example, while human orators or shoemakers act independently from each other (their actions can be distinct), the three divine persons never act independently from each other. The acts of the Father, Son, and Holy Spirit are the single act of one God. Every act of the Trinity "originates from the Father, and proceeds through the Son, and is perfected in the Holy Spirit" (*Abl.*). Thus, the unique thing about the Triune

God is precisely the fact that the divine *ad extra* acts are always one. And because the divine acts are one, we believe in one God the Trinity rather than in three Gods (*Abl.*).

In *Against Macedonius* (*Adversus Macedonianus, De Spiritu Sancto*), Gregory tackled the Pneumatomachian understanding of the Holy Spirit as something that was ontologically less than the Father and the Son. "The destroyers of the Spirit's glory" (Pneumatomachians) insisted on the inferiority of the Spirit, because everything was created by the Father and "through the Son" (John 1:3). But Gregory was adamant: in the divine *ousia*, there simply could not be any degrees of divinity, because the divine nature was simple and indivisible. To postulate a designation "lesser God" was a contradiction of terms. Again, Gregory battled the misconception that a relational name implied a different nature. For him, to call the Son "only-begotten" served the purpose of neutralizing the mockery of Pneumatomachians, who suggested that the Holy Spirit had to be the brother of the Son, or Father's grandson, if the Spirit was equally divine.

Finally, when Gregory considered the eternal (theological) begetting of the Son and the proceeding of the Spirit, he did not have the *filioque* issue in mind, but rather their mode of origination and hypostatic distinction. His point was that "there is one and the same person, that of the Father, from whom the Son is begotten and the Holy Spirit proceeds" (*Gr.*). Assessing the mode of origination or the causal order in the Trinity, he wrote, "One is the cause, the other is from the cause; and in that which is from the cause, we recognize yet another distinction: one is immediately from the first one, the other is through him who is immediately from the first one" (*Abl.*). Yet, even though the Son had some role in the proceeding of the Spirit, "the proper cause of the Spirit is the Father" (*Abl.*).

The Council of Constantinople (AD 381)

What is commonly known as the Nicene Creed is actually (and confusingly) the Niceno-Constantinopolitan Creed. The Nicene Creed proper (AD 325) is known from a letter of Eusebius of Caesarea, which is the earliest extant text of it (Athanasius, *App. Decr.*). It is also known from the letters of Athanasius, followers of Marcellus of Ancyra, Basil of Caesarea, Cyril of Alexandria, and from the conciliar sources that are later than the Creed of Constantinople (e.g., the documents of the Council of Ephesus, AD 431).

Likewise, the original text of the Niceno-Constantinopolitan Creed, the *Exposition* (*Ekthesis*) of AD 381, is not extant. It is known through the documents of the second session of the Council of Chalcedon (AD 451), where it was called "the faith of the 150 fathers." Alternative versions of the Creed of Constantinople exist in a fifth-century anti-Chalcedonian florilegium and in the *Exposition of Faith* of the Council of Constantinople (AD 681). Often there was no single original text because various scribes made multiple copies simultaneously, and the wording of the texts therefore varied.

Despite the unavailability of the original documents of the two creeds, in time the Niceno-Constantinopolitan Creed has become an ecumenical symbol of Christian faith (the World Council of Churches, Faith and Order, accepted it as such at Lausanne, 1927). It has become an ecumenical symbol despite the fact that the West, which had none of its representatives present at Constantinople, embraced the creed only after Gregory the Great confessed that he "accepted and venerated" the councils of Nicaea, Constantinople, Ephesus, and Chalcedon (*Registrum epistolarum* 1.24).

To follow the conventional (pro-Nicene) modeling of the rejected extremes, the theological context of the Council of Constantinople can be reconstructed as a balancing act between the Marcellian "modalism" (charted left) and Pneumatomachian/Heteroousian subordinationism (charted right). The council was supposed to bolster and unify the pro-Nicene (middle) position, and so it did. One hundred fifty Eastern bishops "updated" the creed of AD 325 and explicated it in the light of recent controversies, in the good faith of just being truthful to the first ecumenical council. The Son was confessed to be "begotten not made" (*gennēthenta*), "consubstantial" (*homoousios*) with the Father, and "true God from true God" (*theon alēthinon ek theou alēthinou*). But the theologians at the Council of Constantinople also modified the text of the Nicene Creed and did so not merely by omitting its condemnations. While retaining the term *homoousios*, the "ecumenists" avoided the modalist implications of it by dropping the Nicene phrase "from the substance" (*ek tēs ousias*) of the Father. As they spoke about the begetting of the Son, they eliminated the phrase "from the substance," which explicated the word "Only-begotten" (*monogenēs*), and added another phrase, "begotten . . . before all ages" (*pro pantōn tōn aiōnōn*). As a result, the text no longer read "the Only-begotten, begotten from the Father, that is, from the substance of the Father" (Nicaea, AD 325), but rather "the only-begotten Son of God, begotten from the Father before all the ages" (Constantinople, AD 381). To this latter creed the bishops of Constantinople also added an anti-Marcellian phrase "whose kingdom will have no end" (*hou tēs basileias ouk estai telos*), which was not quite up-to-date with the changes in Marcellus's theology.

What is perhaps most significant for the history of the doctrine of the Trinity is that the council appended an extended section on the Holy Spirit. Rather than calling the Spirit an impersonal power, the creed emphasizes the *personal*, the hypostatic existence of the Spirit. It named the Spirit as the one who (not "it") speaks through the prophets. At least the Latin rendering of the creed employs the masculine relative pronoun *qui* (who). The Spirit is also said to be "coworshipped" (*symproskynoumenon*) and "coglorified" (*syndoxazomenon*) with the Father and Son. The prefix "co-" (*syn-*) obviously targeted Pneumatomachians and Heteroousians, who considered the Sprit to be an inferior being. The creed further identified the Spirit as "the one proceeding forth from the Father" (*to ek tou patros ekporeuomenon*). The phrase "and [from] the Son" (*filioque*) is not found in the authentic "canonized" text of the Niceno-Constantinopolitan Creed.

At the same time and to the great disappointment of Gregory of Nazianzus, the council never called the Spirit *homoousios*. The word was omitted in connection with the Holy Spirit, despite the fact that the Council of Alexandria in AD 362 had already acknowledged that "the Holy Spirit too should be believed to be of the same substance and divinity [*ut ejusdem substantiae ac deitatis*] as the Father and the Son" (Rufinus, *Hist. eccl.* 10.30). Furthermore, the Council of Constantinople never called the Holy Spirit "God" (*theos*), never mentioned the idea of "coinherence" (*perichōrēsis*), and never ascribed "equality of honor" (*homotimia*) to the Spirit. Homoeans, who preferred theological vagueness and ambivalence, were perhaps satisfied with the Spirit being simply "coworshipped" and "coglorified" after all. The stronger and more explicit statements about the equally divine Spirit by Athanasius and Gregory of Nazianzus were passed over by the creed with a diplomatic silence, arguably for the sake of a greater ecclesial peace. Nevertheless, in the contemporary confessing of the creed, the full divinity of the Spirit is assumed and expressed: "We believe . . . in the Spirit . . . proceeding forth from the Father, coworshipped and coglorified with the Father and the Son."

The church as a whole is a conservative entity, and therefore it usually takes a considerable time for the larger church to adopt the various refinements of its theologians. Since matters always become more complicated when the meaning of something is expressed, there remains the nagging issue of how something (e.g., the creed) is to be interpreted. Some fifty years after the Council of Constantinople, Cyril of Alexandria wrote to Nestorius about the Nicene faith:

> It is not enough . . . only to agree in confessing the Symbol of the faith previously set out . . . by that holy and great Synod formerly gathered in Nicaea, for you have not understood or interpreted it correctly. (*Epistula ad Nestorium* 3.2)

Thus, rather than closing the "Trinitarian phase" of the theological controversy and solving all Trinitarian issues once and for all, the Council of Constantinople established the pro-Nicene theology as an imperially endorsed orthodoxy. Luckily for pro-Nicenes, the Emperor Theodosius came to their aid. He made the Nicene faith a "divine religion" of his empire and condemned Photinians, Arians, and Eunomians (*C. Th.* 16.5.6). The *Theodosian Code*, a collection of imperial constitutions, says in 16.1.2:

> The rest [those who did not follow catholic Christianity], however, whom We adjudge demented and insane, shall sustain the infamy of heretical dogmas, their meeting places shall not receive the name of churches, and they

shall be smitten first by the divine vengeance and secondly by the retribution of our own initiative.

In the sixth century, Emperor Justinian issued new ecclesiastical legislation. Constitution 131 (AD 545) equated the decisions of the first four ecumenical councils with imperial legislation: "For we accept the dogmas of the above-mentioned four councils just like the Holy Scripture and we keep their rules like law." But this is already going way beyond our account.

In AD 382 the bishops of the Council of Constantinople issued a letter that addressed mainly the church-political concerns of Rome. This letter included a summary of the council's position on the Trinity, which was made "for the sake of evangelic [Nicene] faith" (Theodoret, *Hist. eccl.* 5.9). While the Nicene key word *homoousios* was not mentioned, the Father, Son, and Holy Spirit were confessed to be of "one Godhead [*theotētos*], power [*dynameōs*], and substance [*ousias*]" (5.9). The letter further clarified that the distinction between the divine persons as three *hypostaseis* and *prosōpa* was an antimodalist/anti-Marcellian move, and that asserting the unity of the divine nature was an anti-Arian/anti-Pneumatomachean move. "Thus, there is no room for the heresy of Sabellius by the confusion of the hypostases, i.e., the destruction of the personal properties; thus, the blasphemy of the Eunomians, of the Arians, and of the Pneumatomachians is nullified, which divides the nature, and the Godhead" (5.9). In AD 383, the emperor summoned all heretics to a "postcouncil," where the anti-Nicene movement met its demise (Socrates, *Hist. eccl.* 5.10).

To summarize, the underlying double concern of the Council of Constantinople was to affirm both God's unity and the hypostatic distinction between the divine persons. This concern was reflected even in the postcouncil imperial decree. It was ordered that everyone should follow the bishops "who affirm the concept of the Trinity by the assertion of three persons and the unity of the Divinity" (*C. Th.* 16.1.3). Yet despite all clarity in this matter, the years following the Council of Constantinople demonstrated the increasing fragmentation of the pro-Nicene theologians, as the shift of emphasis moved to the related question of Christology (to the question of the relation between the divine and human nature in the incarnated Son of God). Perhaps contrary to the expectations of many and despite the imperial promotion of the Niceno-Constantinopolitan Creed, there was a puzzling silence about the creed for nearly the next half century or more.

Ambrose of Milan

The Trinitarian controversy, or better, the series of somewhat disjointed debates, was primarily an "Eastern" affair conducted in Greek. It was only when

Pope Julius sent his letter to Greek bishops in AD 341 and Hilary of Poitiers introduced the Alexandrian/Cappadocian Trinitarian theology to Latins that the West took an active interest in the matter.

The Council of Aquileia (AD 381) testified to the continuing tension between the pro- and anti-Nicenes in the West. (In the West, Homoeans became illegal only in AD 386.) Just as the Council of Constantinople had no "Western" presence, the Council of Aquileia had no "Eastern" presence. Unlike at the Council of Constantinople, however, no creed was issued at Aquileia. The "motor" behind the council was Ambrose, a learned bishop of Milan.

After replacing a Homoean bishop Auxentius of Milan, Ambrose had to deal with mostly Homoean clergy in his city. By publishing his *On the Faith* (*De fide*), Ambrose launched a literary anti-Homoean campaign in AD 378. He forcefully argued that the inevitable implication of the Homoean position was tritheism. Dividing the divinity, postulating three ontologically different persons, and calling all of them "divine" was nothing but teaching three Gods. The only permissible distinction between the Father and the Son was the one made on the basis of their hypostatic mode of origination. "Between Father and Son is the plain distinction that comes of generation" (*Fid.* 1.2.16). The Father is "ungenerated," but the Son is "generated." At the same time, the "ungenerated" Father and the "generated" Son were of the same substance (*homoousios, consubstantialis*), because generation extended the substance of the generator to the one generated. Moreover, being of the same substance meant that there were two persons sharing the divine, nonmaterial substance, rather than something being identical with itself. "Rightly, then, do we call the Son *homoousios* with the Father, forasmuch as that term expresses both the distinction of persons [*personarum*] and the unity of nature [*naturae*]" (*Fid.* 3.15.126).

Ambrose's *On the Faith* was an exegetical refutation of Arianism and its "mutants" (e.g., the theology of a Homoean Palladius of Ratiaria). At times Ambrose seems to have intentionally lumped together Arians, Homoeans, and Heteroousians, although he was clearly aware of their differences. It proved to be a clever move, because even if Arianism had experienced some imperial support, Heteroousianism definitely had not. As D. Williams (1995) has demonstrated, the bishop of Milan repeated his intentional grouping at the Council of Aquileia (AD 381), where he single-handedly conducted the business.

In *On the Faith*, the bishop of Milan operated with two major premises: (1) God was eternal and (2) God was immutable. If God the Father was Father eternally, and if God the Father never changed from not being a Father to being a Father, then the Son had to be coeternal with the Father (*Fid.* 1.9.58–61). If the Son were considered a temporal creature, as Arians insisted, then these Arians "worshipped and served the thing created rather than the Creator" (Rom 1:23; *Fid.* 1.16.103). To straighten out his opponents' exegesis of Prov 8:22–25, from where the idea of the Son's createdness derived, Ambrose pointed out that it was the custom of the Scriptures "that things to come are spoken of as though they were already present or past" (*Fid.* 1.15.97); Ambrose quoted Isa 45:11 (LXX) as "God . . . who hath made the things that are to be." Therefore, the phrase "the LORD created me" announced the incarnation, the creating of the humanity of Christ from the Virgin Mary, rather than the eternal begetting of the Son from the Father. "His being made must be referred to his manhood" (*Fid.* 3.4.34).

In the West, the debate over the status of the Holy Spirit had been gathering momentum since the mid-360s. Ambrose had to defend himself against the Italian Homoeans, who reacted strongly to his treatise *On the Faith.* An imperial inquiry(!) into the matters of the Holy Spirit further caused Ambrose to write *On the Holy Spirit* (*De Spiritu sancto*) right at the time of the councils of Aquileia and Constantinople (AD 381). Ambrose explained his reasons: "The heretics are accustomed to saying that the Holy Spirit is to be numbered among things [created corporeal things] for this reason, because it is written of the Son of God, 'All things were made through him' (John 1:3)" (*Spir.* 1.2.27). Accordingly, much of the discussion in *On the Holy Spirit* is preoccupied with showing that the Spirit was neither created nor made.

Arguing for the equal divinity of the Spirit, Ambrose highlighted the common operation of the Father, Son, and Holy Spirit as that which testified to their substantial unity. "Surely there is one operation [*operatio*], and where there is one operation, certainly the power [*virtus*] cannot be divided, and substance [*substantia*] separated" (*Spir.* 1.12.131). (This is a Latin equivalent to the Greek sequence *ousia* [nature] → *dynamis* [power] → *energeia* [activity] in a reversed order.) To prove the full divinity of the Spirit, Ambrose investigated what the Scriptures said about the Spirit's doings. One gathers an impression that Ambrose's treatise is almost like a concordance, as he systematically proceeded through the Scriptures. The bishop of Milan focused especially on the Spirit's activity as a sanctifier, which proved that the Spirit was God (someone who sanctified rather than someone who needed sanctification). "Who, then, shall dare to say that the Holy Spirit is separated from God the Father and from Christ, when through him we merit to be according to the image and likeness of God?" (*Spir.* 1.6.80).

Just like the Cappadocians, Ambrose also pondered about the curious "name" in singular in the threefold baptismal formula of Matt 28:19. He linked it with Acts 4:12, "There is no other name . . . by which we must be saved," and argued that since the name of the Trinity was one, the Spirit had to be of the same substance with the Father and Son (*Spir.* 1.13.132–39). Another curious proof text for the divinity of the Spirit came from John 3:6. Ambrose pointed out that "the Lord himself also said in the Gospel, 'For the Spirit is God'" (*Spir.* 3.10.59). In Latin translation, some manuscripts included the phrase *quia Deus Spiritus est* (for the Spirit is God) in John 3:6, while other manuscripts read *quia Dei Spiritus est* (for the Spirit is of God). Though Ambrose was confident but mistaken that "the ancient Greek manuscripts did not contain the words 'nor the

Son'" in Mark 13:32, he did not rush to point out that the sentence "for the Spirit is God" was indeed missing from Greek manuscripts of John 3:6 (*Fid.* 5.16.192).

Precisely to emphasize the unity of the Christian God, Ambrose wrote that the Holy Spirit "proceeds from [*procedit a*] the Father and the Son" (*Spir.* 1.11.20). Before anyone hurriedly identifies it as a proto-*filioque* position, one has to remember that Latin authors used the same word (*procedere*) for both theological proceeding and economical sending. (Novatian even used the verb "to proceed" in connection with the Son [*Trin.* 15].) These were the Greeks who had a word for everything: *ekporeuō* designated theological proceeding and *proïēmi* economical sending.

Augustine of Hippo

In discussing the Trinity, Augustine's starting point was neither God's unity nor plurality; it was the Trinity. The Trinity was "the one true God" (John 17:3) in a very particular, uniplural sense. "This Trinity, although having the property and subsistence of singular persons, nevertheless on account of its individual and inseparable essence or nature . . . [is] not three Gods but one God" (*Sermo.* 71.18). "The Trinity itself is one God, with the same eternity and equality of deity remaining without change in three: Father, Son, and Holy Spirit" (*Expositio epistulae ad Galatas* 24.7). Augustine had a Scripture verse, 1 John 5:7, "These three are one," to support his claim that the one true God was the Trinity. However, this is in the part of the verse after "testify," which scholars call "the Johannine Comma"; it is missing in the earliest Greek manuscripts but appeared in the Latin text of the New Testament during the fourth century. Because of God's threefold oneness, Augustine was even unhappy in voicing the phrase "Father, Son, and Holy Spirit," because the words proceeded in a temporal sequence and could not be said simultaneously (*Trin.* 4.5.30). The rhetorical "haze" that Augustine often created in speaking about the Trinity (e.g., the first sentence in *Trin.* 6.2.9) proved his point.

For Augustine, it took about twenty years to write his megatreatise, which was later titled *On the Trinity* (*De Trinitate*). In *sermon* 169.1.1 he confessed, "They [the books *On the Trinity*] involve much work, and I think that they can be understood only by a few." Having thus discouraged all interpreters, Augustine also provoked the curiosity of many. Perhaps at least something in this Trinitarian theology can be understood.

Augustine's *On the Trinity* was not composed during any particular Trinitarian controversy. Nevertheless, Hall (1991, 20) observes that "at times he [Augustine] puts himself into a kind of conventional polemic stance." The larger theological context of Augustine's Trinitarian deliberations was indeed the debate between the Latin pro-Nicenes and Homoeans (whom Augustine called "Arians"). Late in his life, Augustine also became engaged in this controversy.

Even though both pro-Nicenes and Homoeans had authoritative councils to back them up, the controversy focused mostly on biblical exegesis. In the person of Maximinus, Augustine faced a hard-core biblicist who flooded the debate with scriptural proof texts. Evidently a little irritated by the sheer volume of Maximinus's Bible citing, the bishop responded, "If you want to set aside the point of dispute between us and recite the whole gospel, ... how much time will we need?" (*c. Max.* 7). Teske (1995, 183) has acknowledged the sad fact that both pro-Nicenes and Homoeans were

> so firmly committed to their ... theological positions, each bolstered by batteries of proof texts from the Scripture, that neither quite hears the other or takes into account the possibility that the other has some legitimate theological concerns.

Augustine disagreed with the Homoean exegesis of John 14:28 and 1 Cor 15:28 (e.g., *De diversis quaestionibus octoginta tribus* 69; *In Johannis evangelium tractatus* 26.19.2; *Trin.* 1.3.18). In a typically pro-Nicene manner, he pointed out that these texts, which were suggesting subordination, were not applicable to the Son's *preexistence*. Rather, these were applicable to the Son's *incarnation*. "In the form of God the Son is equal to the Father. . . . In the form of a servant, however, he is less than the Father" (*Trin.* 1.4.22; cf. Phil 2:6–8). The "form of God" referred to the Son's eternal preexistence, and "the form of a servant" to the Son's incarnation. "Stay within this rule," the elderly bishop admonished his opponent. "Whenever you read in the authoritative words of God a passage in which it seems that the Son is shown to be less than the Father, interpret it as spoken in the form of the servant, in which the Son is truly less than the Father" (*c. Max.* 2.14.8).

Augustine, the bishop of Hippo, was a man of words, and thus expressions concerned him. He had written earlier, in *Doc. chr.* 1.5.11, that God was a single substance: "There is the Father and the Son and the Holy Spirit—each one of these is God, and all of them together are one God; each of these is full substance [*substantia*] and all together are one substance." But eventually Augustine came to dislike the word *substantia*. Although he employed the phrase "substance or essence" several times, he had particular philosophical reasons for preferring the word *essentia* to *substantia* as he was speaking about the divine nature (*c. s. Ar.* 36; *Ep.* 120.17). The word "being" (*essentia*) was from the verb "to be" (*esse*). God's nature was "to be." God was the *Being* rather than a substance that could exist or cease to exist (*Trin.* 5.1.3). Hilary of Poitiers had written in his *On the Trinity* 1.5, "There is nothing more characteristic of God than to be," and both Marius Victorinus and Augustine agreed.

There was another complication with the term *substantia*. Since God was simple, and since being simple meant being incapable of having accidental qualities, God was identical with God's attributes. This means that God's "quality and substance are one and the same" (*ctv. Det.* 11.10). God did not *have* being: God *was* being. God did not *have* love: God *was* love. If God were substance, "standing-under" (*sub* + *statuere*) qualities, God would not be simple, and the divinity would be prior to the divine persons. But the divine substance did not exist apart from or prior to the three divine persons.

What added to the terminological confusion was the fact that the Latin word *substantia* could function as a synonym to *ousia* or *hypostasis*. The unfortunate "God is one *substantia* (*ousia*) and three *substantiae* (*hypostaseis*)" was right linguistically, although absurd theologically and philosophically.

In addition, Augustine discerned some unwanted implications of another Trinitarian term: *persona*. He had defined the word *persona* as "the revealing form of a thing" (*De agone Christiano* 20.22). Yet again, the persons of the Father, Son, and Holy Spirit were neither something sensible nor the "forms" of an underlying (spiritual) "stuff." That would be modalism! Yet to speak about what was distinct in God, the Latin word *persona* might have been the best of bad options. For Augustine, even "three somethings" (*tria quaedam*) seemed better than "three persons" (*Trin.* 7.4.9). To say that God was three persons was just a linguistic crutch for expressing the diversity within the Trinity.

Perhaps knowing something about the Greek stock phrase *mia ousia/treis hypostaseis*, Augustine was nevertheless rather frustrated with such formulations. According to him, no one should have a false impression that God was finally captured by such precise words. Theological definitions were to be tolerated in order "that we may somehow express what we are completely unable to express," or "by the sheer necessity of saying something" (*Trin.* 7.3.7–8). Ayres (in JECS 2000, 67) has summarized Augustine's verdict on theological definitions: "All we have done is to show how our language of God may be given some coherent structure without slipping from the bedrock of right belief."

Because of his controversy with Homoeans, particularly with Maximinus, Augustine defended the coessentiality of the Father and the Son. The Son, who was begotten from the Father, had to be of the same essence with the Father, because "if the Son is of another essence than the Father, the Father had begotten a monster" (*Jo. ev. tr.* 89.3). A God unable to beget a coessential Son was neither omnipotent nor good. Such a God was even less than humans and animals, who always produced offspring of their kind (*c. Max.* 2.6). The bishop of Hippo demonstrated that by positing an essential difference between the unbegotten and the only-begotten God, Homoeans were actually worshipping two Gods (*c. s. Ar.* 1.1). "Shout as much as you want that the Father is greater and the Son lesser. I answer you that the greater and lesser are two" (*c. Max.* 2.23.1).

To substantiate his case for the coessentiality of the Father, Son, and Holy Spirit, Augustine turned to the argument of unity of activity or operation (*operatio*). Hilary and Ambrose had already emphasized that the Son did the same things as the Father (Hilary, *Trin.* 6.27; Ambrose, *Spir.* 1.12.131). Following the suit, Augustine contended with an increasing intensity that the activities of the divine persons (the activities "external" to the Godhead) were inseparable (*Trin.* 1.2.7). In the case of the Trinity, there is "the distinction of persons and the inseparableness of operation"(*Serms.* 52.14). Augustine reasoned that *some* activities were typical to certain natures, and therefore only these activities testified to the ontological sameness of the agents. The activities of the Father, Son, and Holy Spirit were the activities of *God* (e.g., creation, redemption, sanctification), and consequently, because these are the divine activities, only the divine persons could do them (cf. John 6:29). "No man could come to Him [God] unless it were given him by the Father, and consequently also by the Son Himself and by the Holy Spirit" (*Ep.* 194).

Affirming the unity of the divine activity was Augustine's Trinitarian "mantra." The unity of the divine activity was the first argument Augustine used in debating a Homoean Maximinus, who considered the respective activities of the Father, Son, and Holy Spirit to prove their different ontological status (*c. Max.* 5). It was relatively easy to gather the impression from the Scriptures that the acts of the three divine persons were distinct and separate. Was it not that the Son incarnated, died, and resurrected, and the Father and the Spirit did not? Was it not that the Father spoke as a voice, the Son stood in the river as a man, and the Holy Spirit appeared as a dove (*Jo. ev. tr.* 6.5; *Serms.* 169.2.5)? Undeniably, there seemed to be certain acts that were unique to the particular divine persons. "Many things are said separately in the Scriptures of the individual persons in order to present the Trinity. . . . [These persons] are also revealed individually and in sequence" (*Serms.* 169.2.5).

Augustine knew that the subject of a particular act was either the *person* of the Father, the *person* of the Son, or the *person* of the Holy Spirit. It was not their (common) divine nature that acted, but the three divine persons. However, the fact that a particular person performed an act did not mean that the involvement of the other coessential divine persons was thereby excluded (cf. John 5:19). Father, Son, and Spirit were active in the same *ad extra* acts, in the acts of economy. "The whole Trinity produced that flesh belonging to the Son alone as well as that voice which was the Father's alone and that form in which Holy Spirit alone appeared" (*c. s. Ar.* 15). In the same text, Augustine put it even more categorically, "The works of all are done by all, and the works of each one are done by all." The bishop of Hippo preached about the inseparable operation of the divine persons with almost redundant clarity:

> So that when the operation of the Father is spoken of, it is understood that he does not exercise it without the Son and the Holy Spirit; and when the operation of the Son is spoken of, it is not without the Father and the Holy Spirit; and when the operation of the Holy Spirit is spoken of, it is not without the Father and the Son. . . . It is the Trinity that performs the works of

each of the persons in the Trinity, two of them cooperating in the work of the other. (*Serms.* 71.26–27; cf. *Jo. ev. tr.* 5; *Serms.* 52.4–14; *Trin.* 2.5.8–9)

Thus, in a unique way, Father, Son, and Spirit were all inseparably active in their respective and particular hypostatic acts. The one divine act was done through the act of a particular divine person. The incarnation of the Son was the Father's doing with the cooperation with the Holy Spirit. "The Father, the Son, and the Spirit of both, work all things together, equally and harmoniously" (*Trin.* 13.11.15). Commenting on John 14:10, "But the Father who dwells in me does his works," Augustine observed. "The works [*operum*] have their origin in the one from whom the coworking persons have their very existence" (*Serms.* 71.26). And again, "The union of the persons in the Trinity is ... believed ... to be so inseparable, that whatever is done by the Trinity must be regarded as being done by the Father, and by the Son, and by the Holy Spirit" (*Ep.* 11.2). Because of such simultaneous involvement in an act performed by one of the divine persons, Father, Son, and Holy Spirit were not three gods but one Triune God (cf. Gregory of Nyssa, *Abl.*).

Next, Augustine was one of those who distinguished the Father, Son, and Holy Spirit on the basis of their *relations* with each other. These relations were both eternal and essential (as opposed to accidental) for what God was, the Trinity. How much Augustine had learned from the Cappadocians is difficult to assess (see *Trin.* 3.1), but the point is, no doubt, the same. Unbegottenness, begottenness, and procession were relative predications and not essential predications (names of the corresponding essences; *Trin.* 5.1.4–6). Those who confused relational predicates with essential predicates (e.g., Heteroousians) were just "marvelously blind" (*Trin.* 5.1.7).

However, there was a further problem in speaking about the relations between the divine persons and, at the same time, calling the Father "unbegotten." Was it not that "unbegottenness" designated a lack of relation? Arians were adamant that it definitely did. They argued that the word "unbegottenness" was employed in reference to God's essence before God became the Father (before the Father-Son relationship existed). In one sense, Augustine agreed: "When the Father is called unbegotten, it is not said what he is, but what he is not" (*Trin.* 5.1.7). But in this sentence the word "Father" stood for a divine *persona* rather than for the divine *essentia*. So, Augustine immediately added that the Father-Son relation was indeed eternal, and that unbegottenness was the personal property of the Father and not something that undermined the existence of the relation between the unbegotten Father and the only-begotten Son.

Augustine also warned against reducing Father, Son, and Holy Spirit to relations and against forgetting that a relation presupposed essences. "Every being that is called something by way of relationship is also something besides the relationship" (*Trin.* 7.1.2). Father, Son, and Holy Spirit were God and they were related as God the Father, God the Son, and God the Holy Spirit. In short, one had to speak about the relations within the context of the divine coessentiality and simplicity. Relational ontology did not cancel out the metaphysics of substance. Unfortunately, there was no one generic word, not even the word *persona*, that would have adequately captured the different relations within the one divine *essentia*.

Augustine is famous for his Trinitarian analogies. He turned to those because analogies were "more familiar for our mind in its weakness to examine" than the more profound topics (*Trin.* 9.1.2). Augustine received some inspiration from Marius Victorinus (e.g., the human soul as the analogy of the Trinity, and the Spirit as the bond between the Father and the Son). The best-known analogies are the anthropological ones: lover, the beloved, and love; existence, knowledge, and will; memory, understanding, will. The fact that humans were created according to the divine image gave certain legitimacy to his looking for significant similarities between the human (rational) mind and God. To these anthropological analogies, Augustine added some metaphysical ones, such as pointing out that every existing thing had its being, form, and quality: "whether a thing is, what it is, what kind it is" (*Ep.* 11.4). These three aspects of a given entity tolerated individual consideration but not separation; they were notionally distinct and yet indivisible. This was precisely what Augustine was looking for, something threefold in the created world that was "separately exhibited [but] whose operation is yet inseparable" (*Serms.* 52.17, 23).

The analogies that Augustine used were not straightforward correspondences, however. They were creative approximations. They were subtle and much more complicated cases than saying that Father equaled memory, the Son equaled understanding, and the Spirit equaled will. "I do not say memory is the Father, understanding is the Son, will is the Spirit" (*Serms.* 52.23). All three divine persons could be said to have memory, understanding, and will. As Augustine toyed with such comparisons, he was keenly aware of the differences in similarity. In *Confessions* 13.7.8 Augustine reminded his readers that analogical language contained "a resemblance, but also a difference." For instance, memory, understanding, and will were *in* the human being, but the three persons *were* God (*Serms.* 169.2.6). Thus, assessing various analogies, the bishop of Hippo had no illusion that he had found a perfect correspondence to the infinite Trinity in the finite world. "These three [memory, understanding, and will] should not . . . be thought to be comparable with the Trinity so as to match it in every respect" (*Serms.* 169.2.6). "It is ridiculous to think this illustration offers a real parallel" (*Conf.* 10.14.21). There was no absolute correspondence between the created realities and the uncreated Trinity. With his analogies Augustine merely tried to convey the idea of an inseparable operation of distinct entities.

Just like Hilary of Poitiers (e.g., *Trin.* 2.1), Augustine often called the Holy Spirit a "gift" (*donum*; e.g., *Trin.* 15.5.29). It was a biblical designation (e.g., Acts 8:20) that marked the hypostatic activity of the Spirit to bring humans into the union with God. Augustine preferred the name "gift" for another reason: it implied a relationship, a relationship between a giver, a receiver, and the gift given. The Spirit was a very particular kind of gift, for it was of the same nature as the gift-giver, the Father (and the Son). Augustine even asserted that the Holy Spirit was the very divinity (*deitas*) of the Father and the Son (*De fide et symbolo* 9.19–20). This perplexing statement was based on a textual variant of John 3:6, which Ambrose had also employed. In addition, the bishop of Hippo called the Holy Spirit the love between the lover (Father) and the loved (Son). Again, this analogy brought out the mutual relationship between the three divine persons. In the case of self-love of the Father and the Son, the Trinity would "collapse into a binity" (Ormerod 2005, 67); but in the case of mutual love, the Trinity exists as lover, love, and beloved.

A note on art: The idea that the Holy Spirit was a (mere) bond of love between Father and Son has an interesting consequence in Western medieval art. When the Father and the Son were depicted in the form of humans, the Spirit was placed between them in the form of a dove, as the bond between two persons. In Eastern iconography, for comparison, all three divine persons, including the Spirit, were drawn as angelic beings.

Augustine is also associated with the doctrine of *filioque*, which asserts that the Spirit proceeds from the Father *and the Son*. The bishop of Hippo clarified that the Spirit proceeded from the Father, principally so (*Trin.* 15.5.29), but also from the Son (*Trin.* 4.5.29). Such logic was implied in the notions of the divine simplicity, the common divine *ousia*, and the unity of operation. The Father was the (first) principle without being caused, and the Son was the caused principle of the first principle (*civ. Dei.* 11.10; *c. Max.* 2.14.1; a Latin rendering of John 8:25 also called the Son *principium* [origin]; *Trin.* 5.3.14). Thus, one could also say that the Holy Spirit was from the Son as from a secondary principle, for the Son was indeed the Father's Son, coeternal and coessential. The Son's mediation of the Spirit seemed to be a legitimate idea, as long as it did not imply the inferiority of the Spirit. (The fact that the Holy Spirit descended from the Father in the form of a dove upon the Son who was baptized [Matt 3:16] did not necessarily invalidate the concept of *filioque*, because it was Christ *as a human being* who received the Holy Spirit in baptism.)

In connection with the *filioque*, the reader should notice how Augustine distinguished between two linguistic operations: proper (or individual) supposition and improper (or common) supposition. The Father was God in the proper sense of the word, the Son and the Spirit were truly God, but in an "improper," that is, derived sense of the word (*Trin.* 5.3.12). While all three were rightly called "God," the common designation did not eradicate the fact that the Father alone was the causal principle within the Trinity. The Spirit was proceeding, in eternity and in time, both from the Father and also from the (caused/begotten) Son, to whom the Spirit was eternally given by the Father. The Father remained the "first cause" within the Trinity (*Trin.* 4.5.32; 15.6.47–48; cf. Gregory of Nyssa, *Abl.*). Augustine did not give up the doctrine of the "monarchy of the Father," though he did not use this expression. "We do, after all, call the Son God from God, but the Father we simply call God, not from God" (*Trin.* 2.1.2). In *sermon* 71.26, Augustine explained that the Father was the "first principle" of the works of the Trinity and also the "first principle . . . from whom is the existence of the persons who cooperate [with him] in working: for . . . the Son is born of him and the Spirit proceeds from him." (Unlike Augustine and because of egalitarian concerns, some contemporary Trinitarian theologians have refused to accept any hierarchy and patriarchy in God.)

At the same time, Augustine seems not to have distinguished clearly and consistently between the theological "proceeding" and economical "sending" of the Spirit (e.g., *Trin.* 15.6.45), although he was undoubtedly aware of the usage of verbs in John 15:26. (In the fourth century, theology and economy were not yet an established and clearly distinguished pair of technical terms.) The bishop alternated between saying that the Holy Spirit proceeded from the Father and saying that the Holy Spirit proceeded from the Father and the Son (*filioque*). The important thing, however, was that being sent did not mean that the Spirit was ontologically less than the Father and the Son, but rather that the Father was the first principle and the ultimate cause "within" the Trinity (*Trin.* 4.5.29, 32). The only-begotten Son was *not* the proper cause of the Holy Spirit; the Father was.

As far as the (Greek) argument of the Spirit's proceeding from the Father's *hypostasis* goes, Augustine understood the Father's being (*essentia*) and his being a person (*persona*) as basically the same (*Trin.* 7.3.11). Augustine contended that perceiving the divine *essentia* erroneously as something that is "under" or "behind" the divine *personae* had led to an inadequate separation of nature and persons. To be a person is to have a nature. Since Augustine refused to postulate a divine essence prior to and in addition to the three persons, the proceeding of the Spirit exclusively (1) from the divine essence or (2) from the person of the Father was out of question. The essential designation "God" was as eternal as was the personal designation "Father." One was unthinkable without the other. God was one essence *and* three persons. "The essence itself is not other than the Trinity" (*Ep.* 120.17).

Risking repetitiveness, let us make this point once again: both the Son's and the Spirit's essence and persons were eternally caused by the Father's essence and person. To speak of any of the divine persons was, at the same time, to speak of the divine essence. So, for Augustine, to assert that the Spirit was proceeding from the Father's *hypostasis* would neglect the fact that there was no *hypostasis* of the Father apart from the divine essence.

Here, in such a thought process, might be the reason why Augustine considered it justified to assert that the Holy Spirit proceeded from the Father *and the Son* (*filioque*). It helped him to affirm the necessary connection between God's essence and persons and, at the same time, to distinguish the Holy Spirit from the Son. If the relation of the Father to the Spirit were exclusive of the Son, the mutuality of their relationship and coessentiality would be violated. (It remains to be said that the Council of Toledo [AD 589] introduced the practice of confessing the Niceno-Constantinopolitan Creed with the inserted *filioque* at the Eucharist and thus caused the controversy with the Eastern Church.)

As a final point, there is something else that a seminarian has to consider with full seriousness. Augustine was not writing a merely speculative treatise when he composed his *On the Trinity*. Although the work contained much that was theoretical, the overall goal of his magisterial tome was *spiritual*: conforming to the image of the Triune God. One's mind had to ascend from (material) analogies to the knowledge of God, which was achieved through Christ, who revealed the Trinitarian God. Yet, in order to do just that, one "must purify [one's] mind with faith, by abstaining more and more from sin, and by doing good, and by praying with the sighs of holy desire that God will help [oneself] to make progress in understanding and loving" (*Trin.* 4.5.31). After reading Augustine's *On the Trinity* for the first time, I made myself a poster with the concluding words of his treatise: "May I remember you, understand you, and love you. Increase these gifts in me, until You have reformed me completely" (*Trin.* 15.6.51). The bishop of Hippo was among those who understood that knowing Trinitarian theology was not yet and not necessarily knowing God. Speaking *about* God had to be supplemented by speaking *to* God. To paraphrase von Balthasar, what Christians need is a "kneeling Trinitarian theology."

Accordingly, I would like to conclude with a prayer written by Marius Victorinus, which turns from the doctrine of the Trinity to the Trinity itself:

> Now, save us, O Father, pardon our sins. And indeed it is a sin to say of God what he is and how he is and with a human voice to will to express divine realities instead of adoring them. But since you have given us the Spirit, O holy all-powerful Father, we both have and express a partial knowledge of you. But when we have a total ignorance of you, we have knowledge of you. And again through faith we have a perfect knowledge of you when in every word and always we proclaim you to be God the Father, and the Son Jesus Christ, and the Holy Spirit. (*Cand.* 5.3)

Conclusion

Throughout Part 2, I have highlighted the technical discussion of the doctrine of the Trinity. No doubt the language of the Trinitarian discourse needs to be learned, especially by seminarians. However, I emphasize once again that such technical language can be found primarily in apologetic and polemic literature. Generally speaking, while discoursing about God, the early theologians often preferred poetic/liturgical expressions over the technical vocabulary of essence, person, and relation. It is quite significant that when trying to "name" his God, Augustine did not use the formula *una substantia in tribus cohaerentibus*, but he wrote the following:

> What are you, then, my God? Highest, best, most powerful, most all-powerful; most merciful and most just; most hidden and most present; most

beautiful and most strong, standing firm and elusive, unchangeable and all-changing; never new, never old; ever working, ever at rest; gathering in, yet lacking nothing; supporting, filling, and sheltering; creating, nourishing, and ripening; seeking, yet having all things. (*Conf.* 1.4.4)

This summary account, which is meant for learning the basics of the classical Trinitarian theology, comes to a close. Luckily, I can stop with the fourth century (plus early fifth-century Augustine), because this is a book about the formative period of Trinitarian orthodoxy. After the fourth century, the Trinitarian issue of the generation of the Son slowly yielded to the related Christological question of the coexistence of the divine and human nature in the incarnated Son. At the same time, the debates in the fifth and following centuries presupposed and interpreted the classical Trinitarian doctrine as they investigated the implications of the established Trinitarian beliefs for all other theological issues. Although providing no *causa finita est*, especially not for the West, and although "discovered" only in the fifth century, the late fourth-century Council of Constantinople nevertheless vindicated the Trinitarian doctrine of the Council of Nicaea by offering a nonmodalist and non-Arian interpretation of it. Eventually the Trinitarian faith of the Niceno-Constantinopolitan fathers received an official endorsement as ecumenical orthodoxy.

PART THREE

Third and Fourth Times Around

Explanation

Part 3 is a reference tool, a guide list for students who enjoy tackling primary sources on the classical doctrine of the Trinity. Since finding these texts either in English or in Greek and Latin can be a considerable hassle, such a guide hopefully saves some time and effort. The goal is for us to read these texts, and therefore a little extra help in locating the texts may prevent busy students from quitting too early.

The given guide list consists of works mentioned in Part 2. It means that these works are intended as recommended readings on the classical doctrine of the Trinity. Obviously, a more thorough reading of all the listed texts and more will remain a project to be completed after graduate theological education. But the purpose of providing an extended list is to suggest where one should begin when studying the Trinitarian theology of a particular author.

In composing this guide list, my primary criterion has been utility. I have tried to list sources that students are likely to be able to locate in their seminary or university libraries or on the Internet. This list is not exhaustive, but I have provided several alternative references for a particular text in the hope that at least one of these is readily available.

The guide list consists of four columns:

1. *The name of an author.*
2. *The title of a treatise.* The title is given in both English and Greek or Latin. To recognize a cited treatise in the commentary in Part 2, an abbreviation of the title is also provided. For instance, Athanasius, *Orations against the Arians* (*Orationes contra Arianos*); *C. Ar.*
3. *English translation(s) of primary texts (or sections of them).* Because the more contemporary editions are also the more accessible ones, as a rule translations older than the twentieth century are not listed. The late nineteenth-century series *ANF* and *NPNF*[1] and *NPNF*[2] (see below) are exceptions, because these have been recently reprinted and are probably the most widely used series of English translations of patristic texts. See http://www.ccel.org/fathers2/.
4. *Primary texts in Greek and Latin.* Rather than distinguishing between the nineteenth-century Migne's *Patrologiae cursus completus* (PG and PL) and modern critical editions, I have included both, again because PG (*Patrolo-*

gia graeca) and PL (*Patrologia latina*) are part of the collections of most libraries.

The guide list has a few special features:

1. A list of abbreviations before the chart provides a code for deciphering the references. For instance, an abbreviation FC stands for the series The Fathers of the Church (Washington, DC: Catholic University Press, 1947–).
2. Sometimes the relevant texts are found within other patristic works (e.g., Aetius's writings in Epiphanius's work). When this is the case, a directing symbol of an arrow (→) is used. For instance, to find the text of Aetius's *Syntagmation*, one possibility is to read Epiphanius's *Panarion* (→ Epiphanius, *Pan.* 76.12.1–37). The Greek text and English translations of Epiphanius's *Panarion* are mentioned in the abbreviation list.
3. Sometimes the texts sought after are attributed to other authors (e.g., Gregory of Nyssa's *To Peter* is known as Basil's *Letter* 38). In these cases a two-directional arrow is used (↔). For instance, perhaps the quickest way of finding Gregory's *To Peter* is to look up Basil's *Ep.* 38 (↔ Basil, *Ep.* 38, in *NPNF²* 8 and in FC 13).
4. Three entries have generic names: Gnostics, Monarchians, and Pneumatomachians (or Macedonians). The reason for generic names is that individual Gnostic, Monarchian, and Pneumatomachian authors and texts are not discussed in Part 2. The approximate equal sign (≈) indicates where in the patristic texts one can find information about the particular authors and their theology. Using this sign also serves the purpose of making a distinction between (1) texts and (2) the description of the authors or the authors' theology. For instance, Hippolytus's *Refutation of All Heresies* does not provide the full texts of Gnostic theologians, but it does provide information about several Gnostics and also quotes some of their writings. Thus, ≈ Hippolytus, *Haer.* 6.2–15 (Simon Magnus); 6.16, 24–32 (Valentius); 7.2, 8–15 (Basilides); 8.1–4 (Docetics) in *ANF* 5. In addition, collections of Gnostic texts are mentioned to facilitate the finding of primary texts in English, Greek, and Coptic.

There are also several free and trustworthy websites of English translations of relevant texts on the doctrine of the Trinity. Many of them provide alphabetical lists of authors and their writings and are thus convenient means for finding the texts:

http://wesley.nnu.edu/biblical_studies/noncanon/fathers.htm
http://ccel.org/fathers2/
http://www.earlychristianwritings.com/
http://www.fordham.edu/halsall/sbook2.html#fathers2

http://www.monachos.net/patristics/sources.shtml
http://www.myriobiblos.gr/library%20home_en.htm
http://www.newadvent.org/fathers/
http://www.synaxis.org/ecf/ecf.html
http://www.tertullian.org/fathers/
http://www.voskrese.info/spl/index.html
http://www2.evansville.edu/ecoleweb/

Web sites for various Greek and Latin texts and databases are not included. Most of them require a fee or (institutional) membership.

Abbreviations for Scholarly Sources

ACW	Ancient Christian Writers. New York: Newman, 1946
Alberigo	*Conciliorum Oecumenicorum Decreta.* Edited by J. Alberigo et al. Freiburg: Herder, 1962
ANF	*Ante-Nicene Christian Library.* Edited by A. Roberts and James Donaldson. Rev. ed. Edited by A. C. Coxe. Edinburgh: T&T Clark, 1867–72, Reprint as *Ante Nicene Fathers.* Peabody, MA: Hendrickson, 1994
APB	*Acta patristica et byzantina*
AugStud	*Augustinian Studies*
Behr	J. Behr. *Formation of Christian Theology.* Vol. 2, *The Nicene Faith.* Parts 1 and 2. Crestwood, NY: St. Vladimir's Seminary Press, 2004
Bindley	*The Oecumenical Documents of the Faith.* Edited by T. H. Bindley. 4th rev. ed. Edited by F. W. Green. London: Methuen, 1950
Bowden	*Encyclopedia of Christianity.* Edited by J. Bowden. Oxford: Oxford University Press, 2005
Boyle	I. Boyle. "Historical View of the Council of Nice [*sic*] with a Translation of Documents." In Appendix to *Eusebius' Ecclesiastical History.* Grand Rapids: Baker Books, 1990
CCSL	Corpus Christianorum. Series Latina. Turnhout: Brepols, 1953–
ChrCh	*Christian Church*
CP	Corona Patrum. Ed. M. Pellegrino et al. Turin: Società Editrice Internazionale, 1975–
CPS	Corona Patrum Salesiana. Turin: Società Editrice Internazionale, 1935–
CPT	Cambridge Patristic Texts. Cambridge: Cambridge University Press, 1899–1926
CSEL	Corpus scriptorum ecclesiasticorum latinorum. Vienna: Geroldi, 1866–
Denzinger	*Enchiridion symbolorum definitionum et declarationum de rebus fidei et morum.* Edited by H. Denzinger. Revised by P. Hünermann. 40th ed. Freiburg: Herder, 2005

Dossetti	G. L. Dossetti. *Il simbolo di Nicea e di Constantinopli*. Testi e ricerche di scienze religiose 2. Rome: Herder, 1967
Epiphanius	Epiphanius of Salamis. *Panarion haeresium*. Book 3:65–80. GCS Epiphanius 3 (1933, 1985). PG 42. English translations: *The "Panarion" of Epiphanius of Salamis: Books 2 and 3*. Translated by F. Williams. Nag Hammadi and Manichean Studies 36. Leiden: Brill, 1994. *The "Panarion" of Epiphanius of Salamis: Selected Passages*. Translated by P. R. Amidon. Oxford: Oxford University Press, 1990
FC	Fathers of the Church. Washington, DC: Catholic University Press, 1947–
FCh	Fontes Christiani. Freiburg: Herder, 1990–
FP	Florilegium Patristicum. Edited by D. Geyer and J. Zellinger. Bonn: Peter Hanstein, 1906–
GCS	Die griechischen christlichen Schriftsteller der ersten [drei] Jahrhunderte. Berlin: Akademie Verlag, 1897–
GNO	Gregorii Nysseni Opera. Edited by W. Jaeger. Leiden: Brill, 1960–
GOTR	*Greek Orthodox Theological Review*
Hanson	R. C. P. Hanson. *The Search for the Christian Doctrine of God: The Arian Controversy*. Edinburgh: T&T Clark, 1988
Hardy and Richardson	*Christology of the Later Fathers*. Edited by E. R. Hardy and C. C. Richardson. Library of Christian Classics. Philadelphia: Westminster, 1954. Reprint, Louisville: Westminster John Knox, 2006
Harrison	The Early Church Fathers. Edited by C. Harrison. London: Routledge, 1996–
IJST	*International Journal of Systematic Theology*
JECS	*Journal of Early Christian Studies*
JTS	*Journal of Theological Studies*
Kelly	J. N. D. Kelly. *Early Christian Creeds*. 3rd ed. Essex: Longman, 1972
LCC	Library of Christian Classics. Philadelphia: Westminster, 1953–66. Reprint, Louisville: Westminster John Knox, 2006
LCL	Loeb Classical Library. Cambridge, MA: Harvard University Press, 1912–
Mansi	G. D. Mansi. *Sacrorum conciliorum nova et amplissima collectio*. 54 vols. Florence: A. Zatta, 1759–98. Reprint, Paris: H. Welter, 1901–27. Reprint, Graz: Akademische Druck- und Verlagsanstalt, 1960–61
NBA	Nuova Biblioteca Agostiniana (Opere di sant'Agostino). 36 vols. Edited by P. A. Trapè. Rome: Città nuova, 1967–
NHC	Nag Hammadi Codices

Norris	R. A. Norris. *The Christological Controversy.* Edited by W. G. Rusch. Sources of Early Christian Thought. Philadelphia: Fortress, 1980
NPNF[1]	*A Select Library of the Nicene and Post-Nicene Fathers of the Christian Church.* Series 1. Oxford, 1887–1894. Reprint, Grand Rapids: Eerdmans, 1984–88
NPNF[2]	*A Select Library of the Nicene and Post-Nicene Fathers of the Christian Church.* Series 2. Oxford, 1890–1900. Reprint, Grand Rapids: Eerdmans, 1980–88
OECT	Oxford Early Christian Texts. Oxford: Oxford University Press, 1971–
OOSA	Opera omnia, Sancti Ambrosii Mediolanensis episcope (Tutte le opere di sant'Ambrogio). 6 vols. Ed. P. A. Ballerini and A. Nazari. Milan: E Typographia Sancti Joseph, 1875–83. Reprint, Rome: Città Nuova, 1977–2004
Opitz	*Athanasius Werke.* Vol. III, *Urkunden zur Geschichte des arianischen Streites, 319–328.* Edited by H.-G. Opitz. Berlin: De Gruyter, 1934–. *Urkunden* are republished in a different order in *Athanasius Werke* III.3, 2007
Paradosis	Paradosis. Fribourg, Switzerland: Éditions Universitaires, 1947–
PG	Patrologiae Cursus Completus: Series Graeca. Edited by J.-P. Migne. Paris, 1857–66
Pelikan and Hotchkiss	*Creeds and Confessions of Faith in the Christian Tradition.* Vol. 1, part 1, *Rules of Faith in the Early Church.* Edited by J. Pelikan and V. Hotchkiss. New Haven: Yale University Press, 2003
PL	Patrologiae Cursus Completus: Series Latina. Edited by J. P. Migne. Paris, 1844–64
PTS	Patristische Texte und Studien. Berlin: De Gruyter, 1963–
RBén	*Revue bénédictine*
Rusch	*The Trinitarian Controversy.* Edited by W. G. Rusch. Sources of Early Christian Thought. Philadelphia: Fortress, 1980.
SC	Sources chrétiennes. Paris: Cerf, 1941–
SJT	*Scottish Journal of Theology*
Socrates	Socrates. *Historia Ecclesiastica.* GCS, new series, 1 (1995). Books 1–5 in SC 306, 418, 493, 495 (1983–2005). PG 67. English translation, *NPNF*[2], vol. 2
Sozomen	Sozomen. *Historia Ecclesiastica.* GCS 50 (1960), new series 4 (1995). Books 1–4 in SC 306, 418 (1983–96). *Sozomenos, Historia Ecclesiastica = Kirchengeschichte,* 4 vols. Translated and edited by G. C. Hansen. In FCh 73.1–4 (2004). PG 67. English translations, *NPNF*[2], vol. 2. *The Ecclesiastical History of Sozomen: Comprising a History of the Church from A.D. 324 to A.D. 440.* Translated by E. Walford. London: Bohn, 1855.

	Reproduction, Ann Arbor, MI: University Microfilms International, 1978
SP	*Studia patristica: Papers Presented to the International Conference on Patristic Studies* (Oxford, England). Berlin: Akademie-Verlag, 1957–85; Leuven: Peeters, 1989–
Tanner	*Decrees of the Ecumenical Councils.* Vol. 1. Edited by N. P. Tanner. Washington, DC: Georgetown University Press, 1990
Theodoret	Theodoret of Cyr. *Historia Ecclesiastica.* GCS 19 (1911), 44 (1954), new series 5 (1998). Books 1–2 in SC 501 (2006). PG 82. English translation, *NPNF*[2], vol. 3
TS	*Theological Studies*
Vaggione	*Eunomius: The Extant Works.* Translated by R. P. Vaggione. OECT. Oxford: Clarendon, 1987
VC	*Vigiliae Christianae*
VCSup	*Supplements to Vigiliae Christianae: Texts and Studies of Early Christian Life and Language.* Edited by J. den Boeft et al. Leiden: Brill, 1987–
Williams	R. Williams. *Arius: Heresy and Tradition.* Rev. ed. Grand Rapids: Eerdmans, 2002
WSA	The Works of St. Augustine: A Translation for the 21st Century. Edited by J. E. Rotelle. New York: New City Press, 1990–
ZNW	*Zeitschrift für die neutestamentliche Wissenschaft und die Kunde der älteren Kirche*

Short sections of various relevant translated texts appear in the following anthologies:

Creeds, Councils and Controversies: Documents Illustrating the History of the Church, AD 337–461. Edited by J. Stevenson. Rev. ed. W. H. C. Frend. London: SPCK, 1989. Reprint, 2000.

Documents in Early Christian Thought. Edited by M. Wiles and M. Santer. Cambridge: Cambridge University Press, 1975. Reprint, 2004.

A New Eusebius: Documents Illustrating the History of the Church to AD 337. Edited by J. Stevenson. Rev. ed. W. H. C. Frend. London: SPCK, 1987. Reprint, 1999.

The Teachings of the Church Fathers. Edited by J. R. Willis. New York: Herder & Herder, 1966. Reprint, San Francisco: Ignatius, 2002.

Guide List to Ancient Works
on the Trinity

Name	Title	English Translation	Greek or Latin Text
Acacius of Caesarea	*Against Marcellus, fragments (Fragmenta contra Marcellum)*; *Frg. c. Marc.*	→ Epiphanius, *Pan.* 72.6.1–10.3 (*Against Marcellus,* fragments); → Epiphanius, *Pan.* 73.25.6–26.2 (a creed in the synodal letter of Seleucia); → Athanasius, *Syn.* 29 in *NPNF*[2] 4; → Socrates, *Hist. eccl.* 2.40 in *NPNF*[2] 2	
Aetius	*Syntagmation; Syn.*	→ Epiphanius, *Pan.* 76.12.1–12.37; T. A. Kopecek, *A History of Neo-Arianism*, vol. 1. Cambridge, MA: Philadelphia Patristic Foundation, 1979, 229–32, 266–68, 277–80, 291–94; L. Wickham, "The *Syntagmation* of Aetius the Anomoean." *JTS* 19, no. 2 (1968): 544–49	Wickham, "The *Syntagmation* of Aetius the Anomoean." *JTS* 19, no. 2 (1968): 540–44
Alexander of Alexandria	*Letter to Alexander of Thessalonica (or Byzantium or Constantinople)*; *Epistula ad Alexandrum* (*Ep. Alex.*)	*ANF* 6; Pelikan and Hotchkiss, 80–81 (fragment); Rusch, 33–44; → Theodoret, *Hist. eccl.* 1.3, in	Opitz, *Urk.* 14; Pelikan and Hotchkiss CD; PG 18

		NPNF[2] 3; Williams, 272–75 (fragment)	
	Letter to All Bishops ("one body") (*Henos sōmatos*); *Ep. om.*	*ANF* 6; Boyle, 31–35; → *Deposition of Arius* (*Depositio Arii*) in *NPNF*[2] 4; → Socrates, *Hist. eccl.* 1.6 in *NPNF*[2] 2	Opitz, *Urk.* 4b
Synod of Alexandria (362)	*Creed*	→ Athanasius, *Tom.* in *NPNF*[2] 4	Mansi, 3:345–56 (*Tomus ad Antiochenos*)
Ambrose of Milan	*On the Faith* (*De fide*); *Fid.*	*NPNF*[2] 10	*Ambrosius von Mailand, De fide* (*ad Gratianum*) = *Über den Glauben.* Trans. and ed. C. Markschies. FCh 47:1–3 (2005); CSEL 78 (1962); OOSA 15 (1984); PL 16
	On the Holy Spirit (*De Spiritu sancto*); *Spir.*	FC 44 (1963); *NPNF*[2] 10	CSEL 79 (1964); OOSA 16 (1979); PL 16
Synod of Antioch (340–341)	*Creed*	→ Athanasius, *Syn.* 23, in *NPNF*[2] 4; Hanson, 286–87; → Hilary of Poitiers, *Syn.* 29, in *NPNF*[2] 9; Kelly, 268–70; Pelikan and Hotchkiss, 89; → Socrates, *Hist. eccl.* 2.10 in *NPNF*[2] 2	*Athanasius Werke* III.3 (2007); Bindley, 62–63; Kelly, 268–70; Mansi, 2:1340–42; Pelikan and Hotchkiss CD
Arius	*Confession of Faith to Emperor Constantine*;	FC 69 (1978) (in *Letter of Candidus the Arian to Marius Victorinus the Rhetor*) 85–86;	Bindley, 55; Kelly, 189;

	Ep. Const.	Kelly, 189;	Opitz, *Urk.* 30;
		Pelikan and Hotchkiss, 78;	Pelikan and Hotchkiss CD
		Rusch, 61–62;	
		→ Socrates, *Hist. eccl.* 1.26, in *NPNF*[2] 2;	
		→ Sozomen, *Hist. eccl.* 2.27.6–10, in *NPNF*[2] 2;	
		Williams, 278–79	
	Letter to Eusebius of Nicomedia; *Ep. Eus. Nic.*	Boyle, 39–40;	Opitz, *Urk.* 1
		→ Epiphanius, *Pan.* 69.6.1–2;	
		Hardy and Richardson, 329–31;	
		Rusch, 29–30;	
		→ Theodoret, *Hist. eccl.* 1.4, in *NPNF*[2] 3	
	A Statement of Belief to Alexander (*Ekthesis pisteōs*); *Ep. Alex.*	→ Athanasius, *Syn.* 16, in *NPNF*[2] 4;	Opitz, *Urk.* 6;
		Behr, 136–37;	Pelikan and Hotchkiss CD
		→ Epiphanius, *Pan.* 69.7.2–8.3;	
		Hanson, 7–8;	
		Hardy and Richardson, 332–34;	
		Pelikan and Hotchkiss, 77–78;	
		Rusch, 31–32;	
		Williams, 270–72	
	Thalia	→ Athanasius, *C. Ar.* 1.5–6, 9, in *NPNF*[2] 4;	
		→ Athanasius, *Syn.* 15, in *NPNF*[2] 4;	
		Behr, 140–41	
Asterius	*Fragments*; *Frg.* (numbers given according to Vinzent [1993], see right column)	Hanson, 33–37 (fragments)	*Die Theologischen Fragmente, Asterius von Kappadokien.* Trans. and ed. M. Vinzent. VCSup 20. Leiden: Brill, 1993;

			G. Bardy, *Recherches sur saint Lucien d'Antioche et son école.* Paris: Beauchesne, 1936, 341–57
Athanasius of Alexandria	*Epistles to Serapion* (*Ad Serapionem*); *Ep. Serap.*	*Letters concerning the Holy Spirit.* Trans. C. R. B. Shapland. London: Epworth; New York: Philosophical Library, 1951; K. Anatolios, *Athanasius.* In Harrison, 2004, 212–23 (sections); *The Armenian Version of the Letters of Athanasius to Bishop Serapion concerning the Holy Spirit.* Ed. G. A. Egan. Studies and Documents 37. Salt Lake City: University of Utah Press, 1968 (includes texts in English and Armenian)	PG 26; SC 15 (1947)
	On the Councils of Arminium and Seleucia (*De synodis*); *Syn.*	*NPNF*[2] 4	*Athanasius Werke* II.1. Ed. H.-G. Opitz. Berlin: De Gruyter, 1935; PG 26
	On the Decrees of the Council of Nicaea (*De decretis*); *Decr.*	K. Anatolios, *Athanasius.* In Harrison, 2004, 176–211 (sections); *NPNF*[2] 4	*Athanasius Werke* II.1. Ed. H.-G. Opitz. Berlin: De Gruyter, 1935; PG 25
	Orations against the Arians (*Orationes contra Arianos*); *C. Ar.*	K. Anatolios, *Athanasius.* In Harrison, 2004, 87–175 (sections); Norris, 83–101 (book 3, sections); *NPNF*[2] 4; Rusch, 63–129 (book 1); *The Orations of S. Athanasius: Against the Arians.* The Ancient and Modern Library of Theological Literature. London: Griffith, Farran, 1889	*Athanasius Werke* I.1.2: *Die Dogmatischen Schriften.* Ed. M. Tetz. *Orationes I et II Contra Arianos.* Ed. K. Metzler and K. Savvidis. Berlin: De Gruyter, 1998; *Athanasius Werke* I.1.3: *Die Dogmatischen Schriften.* Ed. M. Tetz and D. Wyrwa. *Oratio III contra Arianos.* Ed. K. Metzler and K. Savvidis. Berlin: De Gruyter, 2000; *Athanasius: Die dritte Rede gegen die Arianer*, 3 vols. Trans. and ed. E. P. Meijering.

			Amsterdam: Gieben, 1996–98 (*Third Oration*); PG 26
	Tome or Synodical Letter to the People of Antioch (*Tomus ad Antiochenos*); *Tom.*	*NPNF*[2] 4	*Athanasius Werke* II.8: *Die "Apologien."* Eds. H. C. Brennecke, U. Heil, and A. von Stockhausen. Berlin: De Gruyter, 2006; PG 26
Augustine of Hippo	*Against an Arian Sermon* (*Contra sermonem Arianorum*); *c. s. Ar.*	WSA I.18 (1995)	CSEL 92 (2000); PL 42; Sant'Agostino, *Opere antiariane*. Trans. and ed. E. Peroli. NBA 12.2 (2000)
	Against Maximinus, an Arian (*Contra Maximinum Arianum*); *c. Max.*	WSA I.18 (1995)	PL 42; Sant'Agostino, *Opere antiariane*. Trans. and ed. E. Peroli. NBA 12.2 (2000)
	Letters 11 and 120; *Ep.*	FC 12 (1951) (*Ep.* 11); FC 18 (1953) (*Ep.* 120); *NPNF*[1] 1; WSA II.1 (2001) (*Ep.* 11); WSA II.2 (2003) (*Ep.* 120)	CCSL 31 (2004) (*Ep.* 11); CSEL 34.1 (1895) (*Ep.* 11); CSEL 34.2 (1898) (*Ep.* 120); *Lettere scelte, S. Aurelio Agostino.* Trans. and eds. G. Rinaldi and L. Carrozzi. CPS, Series Latina 9, Part 1 (1939) (*Ep.* 11); PL 33; S. Aurelii Augustini: Ad Consentium epistula. Ed. M. Schmaus. FP Fasc. 33 (1933) (*Ep.* 120); Sant'Agostino, *Le lettere.* Trans. and ed. T. Alimonti and L. Carrozzi. NBA 21.1 (1969)
	Sermon 52; *Serms.*	*NPNF*[1] 6 (as *Serm.* 2); WSA III.3 (1991)	PL 38; P. Verbraken, "*Le sermon LII de Saint Augustin sur la Trinité*," in

			RBén 74 (1964): 15–35; *Sant'Agostino, Discorsi.* Trans. and ed. L. Carrozzi. NBA 30.1 (1982)
	On the Trinity (*De Trinitate*); *Trin.*	*An Augustine Reader.* Ed. J. J. O'Meara. New York: Image Books, 1973 (books 2 and 7); *Augustine of Hippo: Selected Writings.* Trans. M. T. Clark. Classics of Western Spirituality. New York: Paulist Press, 1984 (books 8 and 14); *Augustine: On the Trinity, Books 8–15.* Trans. S. McKenna. Ed. G. B. Matthews. Cambridge Texts in the History of Philosophy. Cambridge: Cambridge University Press, 2002; *Basic Writings of Saint Augustine*, vol. 2. Ed. W. J. Oates. New York: Random House, 1948 (books 1, 2, 4, 6, 8, 9, 12, 15); FC 45 (1963; reprint, 1970); LCC 8 (1955; reprint, 2006) (books 8–15); *NPNF*[1] 3; WSA I.5 (1991)	*Augoustinou Peri Triados.* Ed. M. Papathomopoulos, I. Tsavarē, and G. Rigotti. Athens: Kentron Ekdoseōs Ergōn Hellēnōn Syngrapheōn, 1995; CCSL 50/50A (1968); *De Trinitate.* Trans. and ed. J. Kreuzer. Philosophische Bibliothek 523. Hamburg: Meiner, 2001 (books 8–11, 14–15, Appendix book 5); *La Trinité*, 2 vols. Trans. and ed. M. Mellet and T. Camelot. Bibliothèque augustinienne 15–16. Paris: Desclée de Brouwer, 1955; reprint, Études Augustiniennes, 1991–97; PL 42; *Sant'Agostino, La Trinità.* Trans. G. Beschin. NBA 4 (1973; 2nd ed., 1987)
Basil of Ancyra	*Epistle*; *Ep.* and *The Letter of George*; *Ep. Geo.*	→ Epiphanius, *Pan.* 73.2.1–11.11 (*Epistle*); → Epiphanius, *Pan.* 73.12.1–22.7 (*Letter of George*)	
Basil of Caesarea	*Against Eunomius* (*Contra Eunomium*); *C. Eun.*	(Vaggione, 1978 [quotations of Eunomius])	PG 29; SC 299, 305 (1982–83)
	Epistles 9, 52, 125, 236; *Ep.*	J. A. Stein, "An English Translation and Commentary to St. Basil's Letters CXVI to CXXVII." MA thesis. Catholic	*Basilio di Cesarea, Le Lettere = Epistulae.* Trans. and ed. M. F. Patrucco. CP 11.1 (1983) (*Ep.* 9);

		University of America, 1925 (with Greek passages) (*Ep.* 125);	LCL, 4 vols. (1926–34);
			Saint Basile, Lettres, 3 vols. Ed. Y. Courtonne. Collection des universités de France. Paris: Les Belles Lettres, 1957–66, 2003 (letters 9 and 52 in vol. 1; 125 in vol. 2; 236 in vol. 3)
		FC 13 (1951) (*Ep. 9, 52, 125*);	
		FC 28 (1955) (*Ep.* 236);	
		Saint Basil: The Letters. LCL. Vol. 1 (1926) (*Ep.* 9, 52); vol. 2 (1928) (*Ep.* 125); vol. 3 (1930) (*Ep.* 236);	
		*NPNF*² 8	
	On the Holy Spirit (*De Spiritu sancto*); *Spir.*	*NPNF*² 8; *On the Holy Spirit*. Trans. B. Jackson, rev. D. Anderson. Crestwood: St. Vladimir's Seminary Press, 1980	*Basilius von Cäsarea, De Spiritu Sancto = Über den Heiligen Geist*. Trans. and ed. H.-J. Sieben. FCh 12 (1993); PG 32; SC 17, 17 bis (1947, 1968, 2002)
Council of Constantinople (381)	*Creed*	Alberigo, 20; Bowden, 300; Hanson, 816; Kelly, 297–98; *NPNF*² 14; Pelikan and Hotchkiss, 163; Tanner, *25	Bindley, 64; Denzinger, n. 150; Dossetti, 234–51; Hanson, 877; Kelly, 297–98; Mansi, 3:565–66; Pelikan and Hotchkiss, 162; Tanner, 25
Cyril of Jerusalem	*Cachetical Lectures* 4, 10, and 11; *Catecheses Catech.*	FC 61 (1969) (*Catech.* 10, 11); LCC 4 (1955; reprint, 2006); E. Yarnold, *Cyril of Jerusalem.* In Harrison, 2000, 97–111 (*Catech.* 4), 119–39 (*Catech.* 10)	*Cyrilli Hierosolymarum archiepiscopi opera quae supersunt omnia*, vol. 1. Ed. W. C. Reischl and J. Rupp. München, 1848; reprint, Hildesheim: Olms, 1967; PG 33
Dionysius of Alexandria	*Letter, Ep. Alex.*	→ Athanasius, *Dion.* in *NPNF*² 4;	*The Letters and Other Remains of Dionysius of Alexandria.* Ed. C. L. Feltoe. CPT (1904);

		→ Athanasius, *Decr.* 25 in *NPNF*[2] 4; *St. Dionysius of Alexandria; Letters and Treatises.* Ed. C. L. Feltoe. Translations of Christian Literature, Series 1, Greek Texts. London, SPCK, 1918	PL 5
Dionysius of Rome	*Letter*	→ Athanasius, *Decr.* 26 in *NPNF*[2] 4; *ANF* 7	
Eunomius of Cyzicus	*Apology* (*Liber apologeticus*); *Apol.*	Vaggione, 35–75	→ Basil of Caesarea, *C. Eun.* (PG 30); Vaggione, 34–74
	Exposition of Faith (*Expositio fidei*); *Exp. fid.*	→ Gregory of Nyssa, *C. Eun.* 2.4–15 (*Refutation of Eunomius' Confession*) in *NPNF*[2] 5; Pelikan and Hotchkiss, 106–9; Vaggione, 150–59	Mansi, 3:645–50; Pelikan and Hotchkiss CD; Vaggione, 150–59
Eusebius of Caesarea	*Demonstration of the Gospel* (*Demonstratio evangelica*); *Dem. ev.*	*The Proof of the Gospel*, 2 vols. Trans. and ed. W. J. Ferrar. London: SPCK, 1920; reprint, Grand Rapids: Eerdmans, 1981; reprint, Wipf & Stock, 2001	GCS Eusebius 6 (1913); PG 22
	Profession of Faith at Nicaea (*Letter of Eusebius of Caesarea to his Congregation about the Council of Nicaea*); *Conf.*	→ Athanasius, *App. decr.* in *NPNF*[2] 4 (*Epistolae Eusebii*); Behr, 152–53; Boyle, 42–44; Hanson, 159; Kelly, 182 (the Creed of Caesarea); Pelikan and Hotchkiss, 83; Rusch, 57–60; → Socrates, *Hist. eccl.* 1.8 in *NPNF*[2] 2; Williams, 277	Bindley, 53; Kelly, 182; Opitz, *Urk.* 22; Pelikan and Hotchkiss CD

Gnostics		*The Coptic Gnostic Library: A Complete Edition of the Nag Hammadi Codices*, 5 vols. Ed. J. M. Robinson. Leiden: Brill, 2000;	*The Coptic Gnostic Library: A Complete Edition of the Nag Hammadi Codices*, 5 vols. Ed. J. M. Robinson. Leiden: Brill, 2000;
		≈ Epiphanius, *Pan.* 21.1.1–33.12.1 (Basilides, Valentius, etc.); 42.1.1–16.14 (Marcion, if grouped with Gnostics);	*The Facsimile Edition of the Nag Hammadi Codices*, 12 vols. Leiden: Brill, 1972–84;
		≈ Hippolytus, *Haer.* 6.2–15 (Simon Magnus); 6.16, 24–32 (Valentius); 7. 2, 8–15 (Basilides); 8.1–4 (Docetics) in *ANF* 5;	GCS, new series, 8 and 12 (2001–3);
			Testi gnostici in lingua greca e latina. Trans. and ed. M. Simonetti. Scrittori greci e latini. Milan: Fondazione Valla-Mondadori, 1993
		≈ Irenaeus, *Haer.* 1.1–11 (Valentius); 1.23 (Simon Magnus); 1.24 (Basilides) and their refutation in books 2–5 in *ANF* 1;	
		B. Layton, *The Gnostic Scriptures.* London: SCM Press; Garden City, N.Y.: Doubleday 1987; reprint, 1995;	
		The Nag Hammadi Library in English, 3rd ed. Ed. J. M. Robinson. San Francisco: HarperCollins, 1990;	
		≈ Tertullian, *Praescr.* 30, 33–34 (Valentius) in *ANF* 3;	
		≈ Tertullian, *Marc.* in *ANF* 3 (if Marcion grouped with Gnostics);	
		≈ Tertullian, *Val.* in *ANF* 3	
Gregory of Nazianzus	*Oration* 20; *Or.*	B. E. Daley, *Gregory of Nazianzus.* In Harrison, 2006, 98–105; FC 107 (2003)	SC 270 (1980); PG 35
	Theological Orations (27–31); *Or.*	F. W. Norris, *Faith Gives Fullness to Reasoning: The Five Theological Orations of Gregory Nazianzen.* VCSup 13. Leiden: Brill, 1991;	*The Five Theological Orations of Gregory of Nazianzus.* Ed. A. J. Mason. CPT. 1899; *Gregor von Nazianz: Die Fünf Theologischen Reden.* Trans.

		Hardy and Richardson, 128–214; *NPNF*[2] 7; *On God and Christ: The Five Theologcal Orations and Two Letters to Cledonius*. Trans. and ed. F. Williams and L. Wickham. Crestwood: St. Vladimir's Seminary Press, 2002; Rusch, 131–47 (*Or.* 29)	and ed. J. Barbel. Testimonia. Schriften der altchristlichen Zeit 3. Düsseldorf: Patmos, 1963; *Gregor von Nazianz, Orationes theologicae = Theologische Reden.* Trans. and ed. H.-J. Sieben. FCh 22. 1996; PG 36; SC 250 (1978)
Gregory of Nyssa	*To Ablabius: On Not Three Gods* (*Ad Ablabium: Quod non sint tres dei*); *Abl.*	Hardy and Richardson, 256–67; LCC 3 (1954; reprint 2006); *NPNF*[2] 5; Rusch, 149–61	GNO 3.1 (1958); PG 45
	Against Eunomius (*Contra Eunomium*); *C. Eun.*	*El "Contra Eunomium I" en la producción literaria de Gregorio de Nisa.* 6th International Colloquium on Gregory of Nyssa (Universidad de Navarra). Eds. L. F. Mateo-Seco and J. L. Bastero. Pamplona: University of Navarra, 1988; *Gregory of Nyssa: Contra Eunomium II: An English Version with Supporting Studies.* Proceedings of the 10th International Colloquium on Gregory of Nyssa (Olomouc, September 15–18, 2004). Ed. L. Karfiková et al. Boston: Brill, 2007; *NPNF*[2] 5 (*NPNF*[2] has substituted Gregory's *Against Eunomius*, book 2, with *Refutation of Eunomius' Confession*)	GNO 1.1–2 (1960); PG 45
	To Eustathius: On the Holy Trinity (*Ad Eustathium de sancta Trinitate*); *Eust.*	↔ Basil, *Ep.* 189 in *NPNF*[2] 8 and in FC 28; *NPNF*[2] 5	GNO 3.1 (1958); PG 46

	Against Macedonius (*Adversus Macedonianus, De Spiritu Sancto*); *Maced.*	*NPNF*[2] 5	GNO 3.1 (1958); PG 45
	To Peter: On the Difference between Ousia *and* Hypostasis (*Ad Petrum, De differentia essentiae et hypostaseos*); *Pet.*	↔ Basil, *Ep.* 38 in *NPNF*[2] 8 and in FC 13	PG 46
	To the Greeks: On Common Notions (*Ad Graecos ex communibus notionibus*); *Gr.*	D. F. Stramara, "Gregory of Nyssa, *Ad Graecos* . . .," *GOTR* 41.4 (1996), 381–91	GNO 3.1 (1958); PG 45
Hilary of Poitiers	*Against Valens and Ursacius* (*Liber adversus Valentem et Ursacium*); *C. Valens and Ursacius*	L. R. Wickham, *Hilary of Poitiers: Conflicts of Conscience and Law in the Fourth-Century Church: Against Valens and Ursacius.* Translated Texts for Historians 25. Liverpool: Liverpool University Press, 1997	CSEL 65 (1916); PL 10 (*Fragmenta*)
	On the Synods (*Epistula de synodis*); *Syn.*	*NPNF*[2] 9	PL 10
	On the Trinity (*De Trinitate*); *Trin.*	FC 25 (1954; reprint 2002); *NPNF*[2] 9	CCSL 62, 62A (1979–80); PL 10; SC 443, 448, 462 (1999–2001)
Irenaeus	*Against Heresies* (*Adversus haereses*); *Haer.*	ACW 55 (1992) (book 1); *ANF* 1; R. M. Grant, *Irenaeus of Lyons.* In Harrison, 1997 (sections); *The Treatise of Irenaeus of Lugdunum against the Heresies,*	*Irenäus von Lyon, Epideixis; Adversus haereses = Darlegung der apostolischen Verkündigung; Gegen die Häresien,* 5 vols. Trans. and ed. N. Brox. FCh 8.1–5. 1993–2001; "Irenaeus: *Adversus haereses* I; A New Edition of the Latin

		2 vols. Trans. F. R. M. Hitchcock. Early Church Classics. London: SPCK, 1916 (sections)	Text." J. S.A. Cunningham. Ph.D. diss., Princeton University, 1967; *Irenaeus of Lyons versus Contemporary Gnosticism: A Selection from Books I and II of Adversus haereses.* Ed. J. T. Nielsen. Textus minores 48. Leiden: Brill, 1977; PG 7; SC 34, 100, 152, 153, 210, 211, 263, 264, 293, 294 (1952–82)
Justin Martyr	*Dialogue with Trypho, a Jew* (*Dialogus cum Heraclide*); *Dial.*	ACW 56 (1997); *An Early Christian Philosopher; Justin Martyr's Dialogue with Trypho, Chapters One to Nine.* Trans. and ed. J. C. M. van Winden. Philosophia partum 1. Leiden: Brill, 1971; *ANF* 1; FC 6 (1948); *Justin Martyr: The Dialogue with Trypho.* Trans. A. L. Williams. Translations of Christian Literature, Series 1, Greek Texts. London: SPCK; New York: Macmillan, 1930; *Selections from Justin Martyr's Dialogue with Trypho, a Jew.* Trans. R. P. C. Hanson. World Christian Books 49. London: United Society for Christian Literature, 1963; New York: Association Press, 1964; *St. Justin Martyr: Dialogues with Trypho.* Trans. T. B. Falls (= FC 6), rev. T. P. Halton. Selections from the Fathers of the Church. Washington, DC: The Catholic University of America Press, 2003	*Dialogus cum Tryphone Iustini Martyris.* Trans. and ed. M. Marcovich. PTS 47 (1997); *Justin, Dialogue avec Tryphon,* 2 vols. Trans. and ed. G. Archambault. Textes et documents pour l'étude historique du christianisme 8–9. Paris: Picard, 1909; *Justin Martyr, Dialogue avec le Tryphon,* 2 vols. Trans. and ed. P. Bobichon. Paradosis 47 (2003); PG 6

	First Apology (*Apologia*); 1 *Apol.*	ACW 56 (1997); ANF 1; FC 6 (1948); The First Apology of Justin Martyr. Trans. J. Kaye. Edinburgh: John Grant, 1912	*Apologies, Justin.* Trans. and ed. L. Pautigny. Textes et documents pour l'étude historique du Christianisme 1. Paris: Picard, 1904; *The Apologies of Justin Martyr.* Ed. A. W. F. Blunt. CPT. 1911; *Apologie pour les chrétiens, Saint Justin.* Trans. and ed. C. Munier. Paradosis 39. 1995; *Apologie, S. Giustino Martire.* Ed. S. Frasca. CPS, Series graeca 3 (1938); *Apologies, Saint Justin.* Trans. and ed. A. Wartelle. Paris: Études Augustiniennes, 1987; *Die Apologien Justins des Märtyrers,* 4th rev. ed. (reprint of 1915 ed.). Ed. G. Krüger. Sammlung ausgewählter kirchen- und dogmengeschichtlicher Quellenschriften 1/1. Frankfurt a. M.: Minerva, 1968; *Giustino, Apologie.* Trans. and ed. G. Girgenti. Testi a fronte 25. Milano: Rusconi, 1995; *Iustini Martyris Apologiae pro Christianis.* Ed. M. Marcovich. PTS 38. 1994; PG 6; *S. Iustini, Apologiae duae.* Ed. G. Rauschen. FP Fasc. 2 (1911)
Marcellus of Ancyra	*Confession* (*Letter to Pope Julius* [*Epistula ad Iulium*]); *Conf.* and fragments; *Frg.* (numbers are given according to Vinzent	→ Epiphanius, *Pan.* 72.2.1–3.4 (confession); → Epiphanius, *Pan.* 72.6.1–10.3 (Acacius of Caesarea, *Against Marcellus,* fragments)	*Athanasius Werke* III.3 (2007); Bindley, 60–61; GCS Eusebius 4 (1906, 1972, 1991); *Markell von Ankyra: Die Fragmente, Der Brief an Julius*

	[1997]); *see right column*		*von Rom*, ed. M. Vinzent. VCSup 39. Leiden: Brill, 1997
Marius Victorinus	*Against Arians* (*Adversus Arium*); *adv. Ar.*	FC 69 (1981)	CSEL 83 (1971); *Marii Victorini Afri opera theologica.* Ed. A. Locher. Bibliotheca scriptorum Graecorum et Romanorum Teubneriana. Leipzig: Teubner, 1976; SC 68 (1960)
	Letter to Candidus; *Cand.*	FC 69 (1981)	CSEL 83 (1971); *Marii Victorini Afri opera theologica.* Ed. A. Locher. Bibliotheca scriptorum Graecorum et Romanorum Teubneriana. Leipzig: Teubner, 1976; SC 68 (1960)
	Hymns	FC 69 (1981)	CSEL 83 (1971); *Marii Victorini Afri opera theologica.* Ed. A. Locher. Bibliotheca scriptorum Graecorum et Romanorum Teubneriana. Leipzig: Teubner, 1976; SC 68 (1960)
Monarchians		≈ Epiphanius, *Pan.* 57.1.1–10.8 (Noetus), 62.1.1–8.5 (Sabellius), 65.1.1–9.4 (Paul of Samosata); ≈ Eusebius, *Hist. eccl.* 7.6 (Sabellius), 7.27, 30 (Paul of Samosata) in *NPNF*[2] 1; ≈ Hippolytus, *Haer.* 7.23 (Theodotus), 9.2–3 (Noetus), 10.23 (Noetus) in *ANF* 5; ≈ Hippolytus, *Noet.* in *ANF* 5; ≈ Tertullian, *Prax.* in *ANF* 3	
Council of Nicaea (325)	*Creed*	Alberigo, 4–5; → Athanasius, *App. Decr.* in	Bindley, 26; Denzinger, nn. 125–26; Dossetti, 225–41;

		NPNF[2] 4 as *Epistolae Eusebii*; → Basil, *Ep.* 125 in *NPNF*[2] 8 (without condemnations) and in FC 13; Behr, 155; Bowden, 300; Boyle, 44; Hanson, 163; Hardy and Richardson, 338; Kelly, 215–16; *NPNF*[2] 14; Pelikan and Hotchkiss, 159; → Socrates, *Hist. eccl.* 1.8 in *NPNF*[2] 2; Tanner, *5; → Theodoret, *Hist. eccl.* 1.11 in *NPNF*[2] 3; Williams, 278	Hanson, 876; Kelly, 215–16; Mansi, 2:665–68; Opitz, *Urk.* 24; Pelikan and Hotchkiss, 158; Tanner, 5
Novatian	*On the Trinity* (*De Trinitate*); *Trin.*	*ANF* 5; FC 67 (1974); R. J. DeSimone, *The Treatise of Novatian the Roman Presbyter on the Trinity: A Study of the Text and the Doctrine.* STD dissertation, The Pontifical Lateran University, Rome, 1970; *The Treatise of Novatian "On the Trinity."* Trans. H. Moore. Translations of Christian Literature, Series 2, Latin Texts. London: SPCK; New York: Macmillan, 1919	CCSL 4 (1972); *La Trinidad.* Trans. and ed. C. Granado. Fuentes patrísticas 8. Madrid: Ciudad Nueva Editorial, 1996; *Novatiani Romanae urbis presbyteri De Trinitate liber = Novatian's Treatise on the Trinity.* Ed. W. Y. Faussett. CPT (1909); *Novaziano, La Trinità.* Trans. and ed. V. Loi. CP 2 (1975); PL 3
Origen	*Commentary on the Gospel of John* (*Commentarii in*	FC 80 (1989), 89 (1993); J. W. Trigg, *Origen.* In Harrison, 1998, 103–49 (book 1)	GCS Origenes 4 (1903); PG 14;

	evangelium Joannis); *Comm. Jo.*		SC 120, 157, 222, 290, 385 (1966–92)
	Dialogue with Hercalides (*Dialogus cum Heraclide*); *Dial.*	ACW 54 (1992); LCC 2 (1954; reprint, 2006)	*Entretien d'Origène avec Héra-clide . . .* Trans. and ed. J. Scherer. Texts et documents 9. Cairo: Institut français d'archéologie orientale, 1949; GCS Origenes 5 (1913); SC 67 (1960, 2002)
	The First Principles (*De principiis*); *Princ.*	*ANF* 4; Norris, 73–81 (book 2, ch. 6); *On the First Principles*, trans. and ed. G. W. Butterworth. London : SPCK, 1936; Gloucester, MA: Peter Smith, 1957, 1973; New York, Harper & Row, 1966	GCS Origenes 5 (1913); *Origene, I principi*; *Contra Celsum e altri scritti filosofici.* Trans. and ed. M. Simonetti. Collana di classici della filosofia cristiana 7. Florence: Sansoni, 1975 (sections); *Origenes, Vier Bücher von den Prinzipien.* Trans. and ed. H. Gögermanns and H. Karpp. Texte zur Forschung 24. Darmstadt: Wissenschaftliche Buchgesellschaft, 1976; reprint, 1985; PG 11; SC 252, 253, 268, 269, 312 (1978–84)
Pneumato-machians or Macedonians		≈ Epiphanius, *Pan.* 74.1.1–14.9; ≈ Socrates, *Hist. eccl.* 2.45 in *NPNF*[2] 2; ≈ Sozomen, *Hist. eccl.* 4.27 in *NPNF*[2] 2; ≈ Theodoret, *Hist. eccl.* 2.5 in *NPNF*[2] 3	
(Western) Synod of Sardica (342/343)	*Creed* (the encyclical letter)	Hanson, 301–2; Pelikan and Hotchkiss, 91–93; S. G. Hall, "The Creed of Sardica," in *SP* 19 (1989): 173–84;	*Athanasius Werke* III.3 (2007); C. H. Turner, *Ecclesiae Ecclesia occidentalis monumenta iuris antiquissima* 1.3. Ed. C. H. Turner. Oxford: Clarendon, 1930, 651–53;

		→ Theodoret, *Hist. eccl.* 2.6 (Greek 2.8) in *NPNF²* 3	CSEL 65 (1916); F. Loofs, "Das Glaubens- bekenntnis der Homousianer von Sardica," in *Abhandlungen der Königlichen preussischen Akademie der Wissenschaften, Klasse* 1 (1909): 7–11; Mansi, 3:83–86; M. Tetz, "*Ante Omnia de sancta fide et de integritate veri- tatis*: Glaubensfragen auf der Synode von Serdica," *ZNW* 76 (1985): 252–54; Pelikan and Hotchkiss CD
Synod of Sirmium (359)	*Creed*	→ Athanasius, *Syn.* 8 in *NPNF²* 4; Hanson, 363–64; Kelly, 289–90; Pelikan and Hotchkiss, 98; → Socrates, *Hist. eccl.* 2.37 in *NPNF²* 2	Kelly, 289–90; Mansi, 3:264–66; Pelikan and Hotchkiss CD
Tertullian	*Against Praxeas* (*Adversus Praxean*); *Prax.*	*ANF* 3; Norris, 61–64 (ch. 27); *Tertulian* [sic]*: Against Praxeas.* Trans. A. Souter. Translations of Christian Literature, Series 2. London: SPCK, 1919; New York: Macmillan, 1919; (*Tertullian: Against Praxeas*) 1920; *Q. Septimii Florentis Tertulliani Adversus Praxean liber* = *Tertullian's Treatise Against Praxeas.* Trans. and ed. E. Evans. London: SPCK, 1948; reprint 1953	CCSL 2 (1954); CSEL 47.3 (1906); *Q. Septimii Florentis Tertulliani Adversus Praxean liber* = *Tertul- lian's Treatise Against Praxeas.* Trans. and ed. E. Evans. Lon- don: SPCK, 1948; reprint, 1953; *Q. S. F. Tertulliano, Adversus Praxean.* Trans. and ed. G. Scarpat. Biblioteca Loescheri- ana. Turin: Loescher, 1959; reprint, *Contro Prassea, Q. S. F. Tertulliano.* CP 12 (1985); PL 2; *Tertullian adversus Praxean.* Ed. E. Kroyman. Sammlung ausgewählter kirchen- und dogmengeschichtlicher

			Quellenschriften 2.8. Tübingen: Mohr, 1907; *Tertullian, Adversus Praxean* = *Gegen Praxeas*. Trans. and ed. H. J. Sieben. FCh 34 (2001)
Theophilus of Antioch	*To Autolychus* (*Ad Autolycum*); *Autol.*	*ANF* 2; *Theophilus of Antioch: Ad Autolycum*. Trans. and ed. R. M. Grant. OECT (1970)	PG 6; SC 20 (1948); *Tatiani Oratio ad Graecos*; *Theophili Antiocheni Ad Autolycum*. M. Marcovich. PTS 44 (1995); *Theophili episcopi Antiocheni Ad Autolycum libri tres*. Ed. J. C. T. Otto. Corpus apologetarum Christianorum saeculi secundi 8. Vienna: Manke, 1861; reprint, Wiesbaden: Sändig, 1969; *Theophilus of Antioch: Ad Autolycum*. Ed. R. M. Grant. OECT (1970)

Books for Further Study

Comprehensive General Studies

Ayres, L. 2004. *Nicaea and Its Legacy: An Approach to Fourth-Century Trinitarian Theology.* Oxford: Oxford University Press.

Barnes, M. R., and D. H. Williams, eds. 1993. *Arianism after Arius: Essays on the Development of the Fourth Century Trinitarian Conflicts.* Edinburgh: T&T Clark.

Behr, J. 2001. *The Way to Nicea.* Formation of Christian Theology, vol. 1. Crestwood, NY: St. Vladimir's Seminary Press.

———. 2004. *The Nicene Faith.* Part 1, *True God of True God.* Part 2, *One of the Holy Trinity.* Formation of Christian Theology, vol. 2. Crestwood, NY: St. Vladimir's Seminary Press.

Bobrinskoy, B. 1999. *Mystery of the Trinity: Trinitarian Experience and Vision in the Biblical and Patristic Tradition.* Trans. A. P. Gythiel. Crestwood, NY: St. Vladimir's Seminary Press.

Chadwick, H. 2001. *The Church in Ancient Society: From Galilee to Gregory the Great.* Oxford History of the Christian Church. Oxford: Oxford University Press.

Davis, S. T., D. Kendall, and G. O'Collins, eds. 1999. *The Trinity: An Interdisciplinary Symposium on the Trinity.* Oxford: Oxford University Press.

Ehrman, B. D. 1993. *The Orthodox Corruption of Scripture: The Effect of Early Christological Controversies on the Text of the New Testament.* Oxford: Oxford University Press.

Fortman, E. J. 1972. *The Triune God: A Historical Study of the Doctrine of the Trinity.* London: Hutchinson.

Gregg, R. C., ed. 1985. *Arianism: Historical and Theological Reassessments.* Philadelphia: The Philadelphia Patristic Foundation.

Gregg, R. C., and D. Groh. 1981. *Early Arianism—A View of Salvation.* Philadelphia: Fortress.

Grillmeier, A. 1975. *Christ in Christian Tradition.* Vol. 1, *From the Apostolic Age to Chalcedon (451).* Trans. J. Bowden. Atlanta: John Knox Press.

Hall, S. G. 1991. *Doctrine and Practice in the Early Church*. Grand Rapids, MI: Eerdmans.

Hanson, R. P. C. 1988. *The Search for the Christian Doctrine of God*. Edinburgh: T&T Clark.

Kelly, J. N. D. 1972. *Early Christian Creeds*. 3rd ed. London: Longman.

———. 1989. *Early Christian Doctrines*. 5th ed. London: A & C Black.

Margerie, B. De. 1982. *The Christian Trinity in History*. Trans. E. J. Fortman. Studies in Historical Theology 1. Still River, MA: St. Bede's Publications.

Marsh, T. 1994. *The Triune God: A Biblical, Historical, and Theological Study*. Mystic, CT: Twenty-Third Publications.

McGowan, A., B. Daley, and R. Norris, eds. (forthcoming). *God in Early Christian Thought*. Leiden: Brill.

Moltmann, J. 1990. *The Way of Jesus*. Translated by Margaret Kohl. London: SCM Press.

Ohlig, K.-H. 2002. *One or Three? From the Father of Jesus to the Trinity*. Trans. R. Henninge. Saarbrücker Theologische Forschungen 8. Bern: Peter Lang.

Ormerod, N. 2005. *The Trinity: Retrieving the Western Tradition*. Milwaukee: Marquette University Press.

Osborn, E. 1993. *The Emergence of Christian Theology*. Cambridge: Cambridge University Press.

Prestige, G. L. 1959. *God in Patristic Thought*. London: SPCK.

Rusch, W. G., ed. 1980. *The Trinitarian Controversy*. Sources of Early Christian Thought. Philadelphia: Fortress.

Stead, G. C. 1977. *Divine Substance*. Oxford: Oxford University Press.

———. 1994. *Philosophy in Christian Antiquity*. Cambridge: Cambridge University Press.

Studer, B. 1993. *Trinity and Incarnation: The Faith of the Early Church*. Trans. M. Westerhoff. Ed. A. Louth. Collegeville: Liturgical Press.

Watson, G. 1994. *Greek Philosophy and the Christian Notion of God*. Maynooth Bicentenary Series. Dublin: Columba.

Wiles, M. 1996. *Archetypal Heresy: Arianism through the Centuries*. Oxford: Oxford University Press.

Wilken, R. L. 2003. *The Spirit of Early Christian Thought: Seeking the Face of God*. New Haven: Yale University Press.

Young, F. M. 1991. *The Making of the Creeds*. London: SCM Press.

Comprehensive Particular Studies

Anatolios, K. 1998. *Athanasius: The Coherence of His Thought*. London: Routledge.

———. 2004. *Athanasius*. Routledge Early Church Monographs. London: Routledge.

Barnard, L. W. 1983. *The Council of Serdica, 343 A.D.* Sofia: Synodal Pub. House.

Barnes, M. R. 2001. *The Power of God: Δύναμις in Gregory of Nyssa's Trinitarian Theology.* Washington, DC: Catholic University of America Press.

Barnes, T. D. 1993. *Athanasius and Constantius: Theology and Politics in the Constantinian Empire.* Cambridge, MA: Harvard University Press.

Beeley, C. A. 2007 (forthcoming). *Gregory Nazianzus on the Trinity and the Knowledge of God: In Your Light We See Light.* Oxford: Oxford University Press.

Coakley, S., ed. 2003. *Re-Thinking Gregory of Nyssa.* Oxford: Blackwell.

Daley, B. E. 2006. *Gregory of Nazianzus.* The Early Church Fathers. London: Routledge.

DeSimone, R. 1970. *The Treatise of Novatian the Roman Presbyter on the Trinity: A Study of the Text and the Doctrine.* STD diss. The Pontifical Lateran University, Rome, 1970.

Douglass, S. 2005. *Theology of the Gap: Cappadocian Language Theory and the Trinitarian Controversy.* Bern: Peter Lang.

Ernest, J. D. 2004. *The Bible in Athanasius of Alexandria.* The Bible in Ancient Christianity 2. Leiden: Brill.

Gwynn, D. M. 2007. *The Eusebians: The Polemic of Athanasius of Alexandria and the Construction of the Arian Controversy.* Oxford: Oxford University Press.

Hildebrand, S. M. 2007. *The Trinitarian Theology of Basil of Caesarea: A Synthesis of Greek Thought and Biblical Truth.* Washington, DC: Catholic University of America Press.

Kannengiesser, C. 1991. *Arius and Athanasius: Two Alexandrian Theologians.* Brookfield, VT: Variorum / Grower.

Kopecek, T. A. 1979. *A History of Neo-Arianism.* 2 vols. Cambridge, MA: Philadelphia Patristic Foundation.

Lienhard, J. T. 1999. *Contra Marcellum: Marcellus of Ancyra and Fourth-Century Theology.* Washington, DC: Catholic University of America Press.

Lyman, J. R. 1993. *Christology and Cosmology: Models of Divine Activity in Origen, Eusebius, and Athanasius.* Oxford: Oxford University Press.

Meijering, E. P. 1982. *Hilary of Poitiers on the Trinity: "De Trinitate" 1, 1–19, 2, 3.* Philosophia partum 6. Leiden: Brill.

Parvis, S. 2006. *Marcellus of Ancyra and the Lost Years of the Arian Controversy, 325–345.* Oxford Early Christian Studies. Oxford: Oxford University Press.

Pettersen, A. 1995. *Athanasius.* Ridgefield, CT: Morehouse.

Rousseau, P. 1994. *Basil of Caesarea.* Berkeley: University of California Press. Reprint, 1998.

Trigg, J. W. 1998. *Origen.* Early Church Fathers. London: Routledge.

Turcescu, L. 2005. *Gregory of Nyssa and the Concept of Divine Persons.* Oxford: Oxford University Press.

Vaggione, R. P. 2000. *Eunomius of Cyzicus and the Nicene Revolution.* Oxford Early Christian Studies. Oxford: Oxford University Press.

Weinandy, T. G. 2007. *Athanasius: A Theological Introduction.* Aldershot, UK; Burlington, VT: Ashgate.

Widdicombe, P. 1994. *The Fatherhood of God from Origen to Athanasius.* Oxford: Clarendon.

Williams, D. H. 1995. *Ambrose of Milan and the End of the Nicene-Arian Conflicts.* Oxford: Clarendon.

Williams, R. 2002. *Arius: Heresy and Tradition.* Rev. ed. Grand Rapids: Eerdmans.

Other Works Cited

Ayres, L. 2000. "'Remember That You Are Catholic' (*Serms.* 52.2): Augustine on the Unity of the Triune God." *JECS* 8, 39–82.

———. 2004. "Articulating Identity." In Young, Ayres, and Louth, 414–63.

Barnes, M. R. 1995. "De Régnon Reconsidered." *AugStud* 26, 51–79.

———. 1998. "The Fourth Century as Trinitarian Canon." In *Christian Origins: Theology, Rhetoric, and Community.* Edited by L. Ayres and G. Jones. London: Routledge, 47–67.

Barr, J. 1961. *The Semantics of Biblical Language.* London: Oxford University Press.

Benner, D. C. 2007. "Augustine and Karl Rahner on the Relationship between the Immanent Trinity and the Economic Trinity." *IJST* 9:1, 24–38.

Böhm, T. 2004. "The Exegesis of Arius: Biblical Attitude and Systematic Formation." In C. Kannengiesser, *Handbook of Patristic Exegesis,* vol. 2. Leiden: Brill, 687–702.

Confessing the One Faith. 1991. *An Ecumenical Explication of the Apostolic Faith as It Is Confessed in the Nicene-Constantinopolitan Creed (381).* New rev. version. Geneva: WCC Publications.

Daly, R. J., ed. 1992. *Origeniana quinta: Papers of the 5th International Origen Congress, Boston College, 14–18 August 1989.* Bibliotheca ephemeridum theologicarum lovaniensium 105. Louvain: Peeters.

De Régnon, T. 1898. *Études de théologie positive sur la sainté Trinité.* Paris: Retaux.

Edwards, M. 2006. "The First Council of Nicaea." In Mitchell and Young, 552–67.

Evans, G. R., ed. 2004. *The First Christian Theologians: An Introduction to Theology in the Early Church.* The Great Theologians. London: Blackwell.

Farrelly, M. J. 2005. *The Trinity: Rediscovering the Central Christian Mystery.* Lanham, MD: Rowman & Littlefield.

Fitzgerald, A. D., ed. 1999. *Augustine through the Ages: An Encyclopedia.* Grand Rapids: Eerdmans.

Gericke, J. 2000. "Dimensions of the *Logos* from *Logos*-Philosophy to *Logos*-Theology." *Acta patristica et byzantina* 11, 93–116.

Harnack, A. von. 1997 [reprint]. *History of Dogma*, vol. 3. Translated by J. Milar. Eugene, OR: Wipf and Stock.

Heidegger, M. 1996. *Being and Time: A Translation of "Sein und Zeit"* [1953]. Translated by Joan Stambaugh. SUNY Series in Contemporary Continental Philosophy. Albany: State University of New York Press.

Hess, H. 1993. "The Place of Divination in Athanasian Soteriology." *SP* 26, 369–74.

Hunt, A. 2005. *Trinity: Nexus of the Mysteries of Christian Faith*. Maryknoll, NY: Orbis.

Johnson, E. A. 1992. *She Who Is: The Mystery of God in Feminist Discourse*. New York: Crossroad.

Kannengiesser, C. 1983. "Arius and the Arians." *TS* 44, 456–75.

La Due, W. J. 2003. *The Trinity Guide to the Trinity*. Harrisburg, PA: Trinity Press International.

Lienhard, J. T. 1999. "*Ousia* and *Hypostasis*: The Cappadocian Settlement and the Theology of 'One *Hypostasis*'." In Davies et al., 99–121.

Löhr, W. A. 1993. "A Sense of Tradition: The Homoiousian Church Party," in Barnes and Williams, 81.

Lorenzen, L. F. 1999. *The College Student's Introduction to the Trinity*. Collegeville, MN: Liturgical Press.

Lossky, V. 1974. *In the Image and Likeness of God*. Edited by J. H. Erickson and T. E. Bird. Crestwood, NY: St. Vladimir's Seminary.

Louth, A. 1989. "The Use of the Term *idios* in Alexandrian Theology from Alexander to Cyril." *SP* 26, 369–74.

Luther, Martin. 1868. *The Table-Talk*. Translated by W. Hazlitt. Philadelphia: Lutheran Board of Publication.

MacMullen, R. 2006. *Voting about God in Early Church Councils*. New Haven, CT: Yale University Press.

McCruden, K. B. 2002. "Monarchy and Economy in Tertullian's Adversus Praxeam." *SJT* 55/3, 325–37.

McFague, S. 1982. *Metaphorical Theology: Models of God in Religious Language*. Philadelphia: Fortress.

McGowan, A. 2006. "Tertullian and the 'Heretical' Origins of the 'Orthodox' Trinity." *JECS* 14/4, 437–57.

Moltmann, J. 1981. *The Trinity and the Kingdom*. Translated by M. Kohl. San Francisco: Harper & Row.

Nassif, B. 2005. "A Marriage Made in Byzantium." *ChrCh* 85, 34–35.

O'Collins, G. 1999. The Tripersonal God: Understanding and Interpreting the Trinity. New York: Paulist Press.

O'Meara, D. J. 1995. *Plotinus: An Introduction to the Enneads*. Oxford: Clarendon Press.

Olson, R. E., and C. A. Hall. 2002. *The Trinity*. Guides to Theology, edited by S. Bruyneel et al. Grand Rapids, MI: Eerdmans.

Rist, J. M. 2006. "Christian Theology and Secular Philosophy." In Evans, 105–14.

Runia, D. T. 2006. "Philo of Alexandria." In Evans, 77–84.

Stead, G. C. 1976. "Rhetorical Method in Athanasius." *Vigiliae Christianae* 30, 121–37.

Teske, R., ed. *Arianism and Other Heresies*. In WSA I.18. Hyde Park, NY: New City Press, 1995.

Tetz, M. 1988. "Ein enzyklisches Schreiben der Synode von Alexandrien." *ZNW* 79, 3–4, 261–81.

Von Balthasar, H. U., ed. 1984. *Origen: Spirit and Fire. A Thematic Anthology of His Writings*. Translated by R. J. Daly. Washington, DC: Catholic University of America Press.

Wiles, M. 1993. "Attitudes to Arius in the Arian Controversy." In Barnes and Williams, 31–43.

———. 1993. "A Textual Variant in the Creed of the Council of Nicaea." *SP* 29, 428–33.

Williams, R. 1993. "Baptism and the Arian Controversy." In Barnes and Williams, 149–80.

Wittgenstein, L. 1958. *Philosophical Investigations*. 3rd edition. Translated by G. E. M. Anscombe. Englewood Cliffs, NJ: Prentice Hall.

Young, F. M. 2006. "Monotheism and Christology. In *The Cambridge History of Christianity: Volume 1: Origins to Constantine*. Edited by M. M. Mitchell and F. M. Young. Cambridge: Cambridge University Press, 425–69.

Young, F. M., L. Ayres, and A. Louth. 2004. *The Cambridge History of Early Christian Literature*. New York: Cambridge University Press.

Zizioulas, D. 1985. *Being and Communion: Studies in Personhood and the Church*. Contemporary Greek Theologians 4. Crestwood, NY: St. Vladimir Seminary Press.

Made in the USA
Middletown, DE
01 October 2017